SEX DISCRIMINATION ACT 1975

by

MICHAEL J. BELOFF M.A. (Oxon.)

of Gray's Inn, Barrister, Atkin Scholar, sometime Demy of Magdalen College, Oxford, and Lecturer in Law of Trinity College, Oxford

with

HILARY MARGARET WILSON B.A. (Cantab.)

of Gray's Inn, Barrister

LONDON
BUTTERWORTHS
1976

Annotated Legislation Service Volume 237

ENGLAND
Butterworth & Co. (Publishers) Ltd.
London: 88 Kingsway, London WC2B 6AB

AUSTRALIA
Butterworths Pty. Ltd.
Sydney: 586 Pacific Highway, Chatswood, NSW 2067
Also at Melbourne, Brisbane, Adelaide and Perth

CANADA
Butterworth & Co. (Canada) Ltd.
Toronto: 2265 Midland Avenue, Scarborough M1P 4S1

NEW ZEALAND
Butterworths of New Zealand Ltd.
Wellington: 26–28 Waring Taylor Street, Wellington 1

SOUTH AFRICA
Butterworth & Co. (South Africa) (Pty.) Ltd.
Durban: 152–154 Gale Street, Durban

U.S.A.
Butterworth & Co. (Publishers) Inc.
Boston: 19 Cummings Park, Woburn, Mass. 01801

ISBN 0 406 54747 5

PREFACE

The Sex Discrimination Act 1975 is a milestone in the development of human rights in Great Britain. Major changes in the legal status of women have been wrought by Parliament over the last century. But, subject to specific exceptions, men, members of the socially dominant sex, retained the power to treat women differently for no other reason than that they were women in spheres where this difference had no practical significance whatsoever. It was this power that the Sex Discrimination Act, passed in International Women's Year, sought to take away, and, in taking away a male privilege, to confer a new female right.

The Sex Discrimination Act, although not unique in the international context, is, as the Rt. Hon. Roy Jenkins, M.P., the Secretary of State for the Home Department, said on the second reading of the Bill, "probably the most comprehensive . . . of its kind in the world . . . [It] makes sex discrimination unlawful in employment, training and related areas. . . . It also applies to the educational field, to licensing bodies, to partnerships and to the provision of the general run of goods, facilities and services to the public. It also covers discriminatory advertising, victimisation and pressure to discriminate . . . [It combines] the right of direct individual access to remedies with the creation of a powerful Equal Opportunities Commission to enforce the law in the public interest". There are many important fields where the Sex Discrimination Act does not seek to intervene, notably the fields of nationality, peerage, taxation, social security and national insurance law, but, with these exceptions, it outlaws discrimination on grounds of sex (and in the field of employment on the grounds of marital status) in those areas that are in the public sphere, and leaves untouched only the licence to discriminate in the private sphere. It is far bolder in its scope, and far more sophisticated in its techniques, than the Race Relations Act 1968, its spiritual ancestor, and has already, untested though it is, provided a model for the Race Relations Bill 1976, with which it is no doubt destined to fuse in some future incarnation.

But while the broad purpose of the Act is widely appreciated and welcomed, and while the publicity accorded to its effect is almost without precedent, its detailed provisions are not easy to understand, nor have they been readily understood. From the day of its commencement there has been a rash of cartoons in the popular press, figuring male bunnies, female boxers and persons imprisoned for uttering "sexist" remarks that illuminate general misconceptions about how the Act actually is intended to work in practice. And, to date, more serious analysis has been notable for its absence.

There are a variety of reasons for this unfortunate state of affairs whereby an Act, designed expressly to help John (and in particular Jane) Citizen, has emerged in linguistic clothing of such complexity as to daunt lawyers, let alone laymen. Firstly, the form of the Act was dictated at least in part by its subject matter. Racial differences (at any rate where the races cohabit in one territorial unit) may be no more than skin deep; but there are differences of substance between men and women. The Act had to derogate from its principles by the creation of numerous exceptions, and then prevent the exceptions from gutting the Act of force by creating in turn provisos to them. Secondly, the creators of the Act were both ambitious and cautious at the same time. They wanted to cover a wide area, but were unwilling to allow the courts the chance (which they had taken in the case of the Race Relations Act 1968) to construe it more like a tax statute than a charter of civil liberties. So they dotted every "i" and crossed every "t", and, by increasing the opportunities for error and ambiguity, increased the errors and ambiguity too. Further they provided not one but many procedures for enforcement. Thirdly, the draftsmen did not enjoy their happiest hour, and created by their awkward circumlocutions unnecessary obscurities which members of Parliament lacked either the will or the skill to eliminate.

My ambition therefore has been to write a commentary that would prove intelligible to the layman while assisting the practitioner. Early efforts to provide an account of the Act's provisions which, while reshaping its order, remained faithful to its text proved impossible when it was pointed out that my loyal paraphrase was as difficult to follow as the sections themselves. I have therefore recklessly "translated" the words of the statute, knowing that the authorised version is at least set out in the latter half of the work for those who wish to quarry it independently. I have made use of linking summaries, examples, real and hypothetical, charts and changes of typeface. Where others have trodden the same path, I have sought to give the reader the benefit of their thinking, giving, I hope, credit where credit is due and daring, I fear, to criticise where criticism seemed merited. Until such time as the courts and tribunals solve in a definitive manner the problems that the Act presents, I have sought to provide a tentative statement. If, in the course of my commentary, I depart from a neutral language and have characterised man as the oppressor and woman as the victim, I trust that I shall be forgiven for reflecting social reality if not legal theory. The Act in letter protects both sexes but in practice will assist one more than the other.

This book has many parents if but one author. My wife, Judith, encouraged me to continue at times when I would rather have stopped and made many a deft suggestion. My right-hand woman, Hilary Wilson, contributed enterprise, energy and a robust commonsense. Among my colleagues in chambers, Anthony Lester, Q.C., the Act's "onlie begetter", helped me to judge the Act's achievement in the light of its intention, and Dr. David Donaldson's comments were, as ever, in point. I am grateful to Dipak Nandy and Geoffrey Bindman for providing me with copies of the early Tribunal decisions. My publishers deserve a medal for patience. The faults in the text are, needless to say, my responsibility alone.

I dedicate this book to my children Rupert and Natasha in the knowledge that any discrimination that each may practise against the other, while being, of course, unacceptable, will not, at any rate, be illegal.

The law is stated as at 1st July, 1976.

MICHAEL J. BELOFF

The Temple,

1st July, 1976.

CONTENTS

ABBREVIATIONS

STATUTES

EPA   Equal Pay Act 1970

RRA   Race Relations Act 1968

RRB   Race Relations Bill 1976

SDA   Sex Discrimination Act 1975

TULRA   Trade Union and Labour Relations Act 1974

BOOKS AND ARTICLES

Bennion   F. A. R. Bennion, "Sex Discrimination and Equal Pay
                      Acts" (1976), 120 *Solicitors Journal* 2.

Bindman   G. Bindman, *The Sex Discrimination Bill and Race*,
                      London: Runnymede Trust, 1975.

G.   *Sex Discrimination: A Guide to the Equal Opportunities
                      Commission*, London: Home Office, 1976.

Hewitt   P. Hewitt, *Rights for Women*, London: NCCL, 1975.

Lester and Bindman   A. Lester and G. Bindman, *Race and Law*, London:
                      Penguin, 1972.

Plender   R. O. Plender, "The Sex Discrimination Bill" (1975),
                      New Community.

Rendel   M. Rendel, *What the Bill could do*, London: Runnymede
                      Trust, 1975.

Walker   D. J. Walker, *Sex Discrimination*, London: Shaw and
                      Sons Ltd., 1975.

SUMMARY OF THE ACT

Discrimination means less favourable treatment. A person discriminates against a woman if he treats her less favourably than he treats or would treat a man in similar circumstances, either directly on grounds of her sex, or indirectly by applying to her an unjustifiable requirement that he applies or would apply equally to a man but which operates against a person of her sex (SDA, s. 1). There is a looking-glass provision which prohibits similar discrimination against men (SDA, s. 2 (1)). (It remains lawful to favour a woman in connection with pregnancy or childbirth (SDA, s. 2 (2)).) It is also unlawful to discriminate on grounds of marital status either directly or indirectly in the field of employment only (SDA, s. 3) but there is no bar on discrimination against single persons. In addition, it is made unlawful to victimise someone for having taken some step under the SDA or EPA (SDA, s. 4).

THE FIELD OF EMPLOYMENT: GENERAL

It is unlawful for an employer to discriminate in recruitment (SDA, s. 6 (1)) or in treatment of employees (SDA, s. 6 (2)), which includes the way in which the employer affords access to opportunities for promotion, transfer, training and other benefits or dismisses employees. (But discrimination in treatment of employees which occurs when a woman is given less favourable contractual terms than a man in an identical job, or vice-versa, is dealt with under the EPA, not the SDA.) There are various exceptions. The most notable is that it is not unlawful to discriminate in recruitment or in affording opportunities for promotion, transfer or training, where being of a particular sex is a "genuine occupational qualification" for the job. This covers cases where employment of a person of a particular sex is necessary for reasons of decency or privacy, physiognomy or authenticity, the requirements of a social service or of welfare, the demands of national law or foreign custom, or where the job is one of two to be held by a married couple (SDA, s. 17). Another exception is where employment is for the purposes of a private household or for a business with no more than five employees (SDA, s. 6 (3)). And provision relating to death or retirement (as well as to pregnancy or childbirth: see above) is outside the scope of the SDA (SDA, s. 6 (5)). The SDA prohibits too discrimination against persons employed not by the principal employer himself but by another person who supplies them under a contract made with the principal—the genuine occupational qualification exception also applies (SDA, s. 9). The territorial ambit of this part of the SDA is basically restricted to Great Britain (SDA, s. 10).

THE FIELD OF EMPLOYMENT: PARTICULAR

The SDA prohibits discrimination by partnerships of six or more partners against persons seeking admission to the partnership or who are members of it (SDA, s. 11). It similarly covers trade unions, organisations of employers, and professional or trade bodies (SDA, s. 12); and "qualifying bodies" which have the power to confer authorisation or qualification for an engagement in a particular trade or profession (SDA, s. 13 (1)). Such bodies also have to take into account a record of discrimination in any case where character is relevant to the conferment of the authorisation or qualification (SDA, s. 13 (2)). Other bodies whose activities are affected by the SDA are vocational training bodies (SDA, s. 14); employment agencies—a word given wide definition (SDA, s. 15); the Manpower Services Commission and its agencies (SDA, s. 16). Employment in the police is included in the SDA (SDA, s. 17), but the police service is allowed to discriminate in relation to height, uniform or equipment, and in respect of pensions, special constables or police cadets (SDA, s. 17 (2)). The prison service, too, can discriminate as regards height requirements (SDA, s. 18 (1)). Men can now become Governors of women's prisons (SDA, s. 18 (2)). Employment in and authorisation and qualification for employment in organised religion is exempted from the SDA, where the doctrines of the religion or the susceptibilities of a large number of its adherents requires (SDA, s. 19). Men can now be employed as midwives; but can continue to be discriminated against as regards both their employment and their training (SDA, s. 20). Women can now be employed underground in mines, but not on jobs which would require them to spend a significant amount of their time below surface (SDA, s. 21 (1)).

EDUCATION

Educational establishments, in the private and public sectors, must not discriminate against persons seeking admission, or actual pupils (SDA, ss. 22, 24). Local education authorities must not discriminate in respect of any other of their functions (SDA, s. 23). And there is a general duty on bodies in the public sector not to discriminate (SDA, s. 25). In addition, the provisions dealing with goods, facilities and services also embrace education (SDA, s. 29), although there are procedural sections designed to limit their effect to institutions outside the normal educational system. There are exceptions for single-sex establishments (SDA, s. 26), but the SDA provides a scheme to facilitate lawfully the development of co-education (SDA, s. 27). Discrimination in courses in physical training and courses for teachers of physical training are also excepted (SDA, s. 28). The territorial ambit of this part of the SDA is also basically restricted to Great Britain (SDA, s. 36).

Summary of the Act

GOODS, FACILITIES AND SERVICES

It is unlawful for someone concerned with the provision to the public or a section of the public of goods, facilities or services to discriminate against a person seeking to use or obtain them (SDA, s. 29). There are examples specified (SDA, s. 29 (2)). The exceptions are when the goods, facilities or services are provided by political parties (SDA, s. 33); by non-profit-making non-statutory bodies (SDA, s. 34); at hospitals, prisons or other establishments for persons requiring special care, supervision or attention (SDA, s. 35 (1) (a)); at places used for purposes of organised religion where the doctrines of that religion or the susceptibilities of a large number of its followers require discrimination (SDA, s. 35 (1) (b)); or where the users of the facilities or services of one sex are likely to suffer serious embarrassment at the presence of members of the other sex, or they are likely to be undressed, or where there is physical contact between them (SDA, s. 35 (1) (c), (2)). The territorial ambit of this part of the SDA is also basically restricted to Great Britain (SDA, s. 36).

PREMISES

It is unlawful to discriminate in the disposal or management of premises, whether residential or not (SDA, s. 30 (1), (2)); but the discrimination in disposal does not apply to owner-occupier who does not use an estate agent or advertise the premises (SDA, s. 30 (3)). It is also unlawful for a landlord whose consent is required for assignment or sub-letting to discriminate (SDA, s. 31 (1)). There is an exception for those who provide or dispose of accommodation in "small premises" where the provider or disposer lives on the premises and where there is shared accommodation (SDA, s. 32); and for non-profit-making non-statutory bodies (SDA, s. 34). The territorial ambit of this part of the SDA is restricted to Great Britain (SDA, s. 30, 31).

OTHER UNLAWFUL ACTS

It is unlawful to operate a discriminatory practice, i.e. to apply discriminatory requirements over a period of time (SDA, s. 37). It is unlawful to publish discriminatory advertisements (SDA, s. 38); job descriptions with a sexual connotation, like waiter or waitress, must go (SDA, s. 38 (3)). It is unlawful to give instructions to discriminate (SDA, s. 39); to put pressure on someone to discriminate (SDA, s. 40); or to aid someone to discriminate (SDA, s. 42). Modified principles of vicarious liability apply under the SDA (SDA, s. 41).

GENERAL EXCEPTIONS

The SDA has a number of general exceptions, that apply to all its provisions. There are exceptions for charities conferring benefits on one sex only (SDA, s. 43); for participation in competitive sports (SDA, s. 44);

3

for insurance risks assessed by reference to actuarial or other data (SDA, s. 45); for acts involving the use of communal accommodation (SDA, s. 46); for acts done under the authority of statute or statutory order (SDA, s. 51); and for acts for safeguarding national security (SDA, s. 52). There are also exceptions permitting a form of positive discrimination by certain training bodies (SDA, s. 47) or employers (SDA, s. 48) where they aim to train employees of one sex to do work which none or few of them were doing before; and by trade unions, organisations of employers, or professional or trade bodies who wish to ensure representation of both sexes on their committees (SDA, s. 49).

THE EQUAL OPPORTUNITIES COMMISSION

The Commission (a body of not more than fifteen persons) is given the triple duty of working towards the elimination of discrimination; promoting equality of opportunity between men and women generally; and keeping under review the workings of the SDA and EPA (SDA, s. 53). It can to these ends undertake or assist research and education (SDA, s. 54); and it has a special duty to review discriminatory provisions in health and safety legislation (SDA, s. 55). It must also make annual reports (SDA, s. 56).

FORMAL INVESTIGATIONS

One of the Commission's two main—and novel—powers is the power to conduct formal investigations for any purpose connected with the carrying out of its duties (SDA, s. 57). In exercise of this power it need neither act on complaint nor have any reason to believe that an act of discrimination has been committed. But before it embarks upon such an investigation it must draw up terms of reference and give notice generally or to any persons named in the terms of reference (SDA, s. 58). In order to facilitate its investigation it is given powers to require any person by notice to furnish it with written or oral information or material documents (SDA, s. 59 (1)); but the powers may only be exercised on the authority of the Secretary of State where the terms of reference do not name persons who the Commission believes may have done or be doing acts of discrimination (SDA, s. 51 (2)). Nor can a person be compelled to furnish to the Commission that which he could not be compelled to furnish in civil proceedings (SDA, s. 59 (3)). If he is asked to attend at any place he must be paid his expenses (SDA, s. 59 (3)). If a person fails to comply with a notice requiring him to furnish information, etc., the Commission can apply to the county court for an order compelling him to do so (SDA, s. 59 (4)). Failure to comply with an order of the court is visited with a fine (SDA, s. 59 (4)); and destruction of a material document after receipt of a notice or the giving of false information is a criminal offence (SDA, s. 59 (5)). The Commission's power to disclose information given to it in the course of an investigation is limited in an effort to balance the demands of privacy and the public interest (SDA, s. 61). During or

4

also has various powers to assist an individual complainant in relation to her complaint by advising, assisting in a settlement, procuring legal representation, etc. The power is limited to cases involving some principle or of complexity or where there is other special reason for assistance (SDA, s. 75).

MISCELLANEOUS

The county court is given power to revise discriminatory contracts, which can in appropriate circumstances be in any event treated as void or unenforceable (SDA, s. 77). The Secretary of State is given power on the application of trustees to remove or modify discriminatory provisions in educational charities (SDA, s. 78). He is given power to amend certain provisions of the SDA itself (SDA, s. 80). There is a long interpretation provision (SDA, s. 82). Transitional commencement and provisions, amendments and appeals are dealt with in (SDA, s. 83). Financial provisions are dealt with in (SDA, s. 84). The SDA is applied to the Crown by SDA, s. 85. Title and extent are dealt with by SDA (SDA, s. 87). Schedule 1 contains amendments to the EPA and sets it out as amended; Schedule 2 deals with transitional exemption orders for educational admissions; Schedule 3 deals with the incorporation, status, etc. of the Commission; Schedule 4 deals with miscellaneous transitional provisions; Schedule 5 deals with minor and consequential amendments; Schedule 6 deals with further ancillary repeals.

CHAPTER ONE

DEFINITIONS OF DISCRIMINATION

INTRODUCTION

[1] The SDA applies to three kinds of discrimination. Discrimination means less favourable treatment. It applies to discrimination on grounds of sex against both men and women in the fields of employment, education, and the provision of goods, facilities, services and premises. Sex discrimination can be either direct or indirect. It is direct where a person intends to discriminate. It is indirect where, irrespective of his intention, a person applies to a woman, who is seeking a benefit from him, an unjustifiable condition, whose effect is to discriminate against her. It applies to discrimination on grounds of marital status against married persons *in the field of employment only*. Discrimination on grounds of marital status can also be direct or indirect. It does *not*, however, apply to discrimination against single persons. It applies to discrimination by way of victimisation against a person who has taken or who intends to take some step under the SDA or the EPA.

SEX DISCRIMINATION AGAINST WOMEN

[2] A person[1] discriminates against a woman[2] if, in specified situations:[3] (i) he treats her on the ground of her sex[4] less favourably than he treats or would treat a man[5] or, if he treats or would treat a man differently according to the man's marital status,[6] a man of the same marital status ("direct discrimination");[7] *or* (ii) he applies to a woman a requirement or condition which he applies or would apply equally to a man but is such that the proportion of women[8] who can comply with it[9] is considerably smaller than the proportion of men who can comply with it, *and* which he cannot show to be justifiable[10] irrespective of the sex of the person to whom it is applied, *and* which is to her detriment because she cannot comply with it ("indirect discrimination").[11]

Subject to general[12] and particular[13] exceptions the situations which are within the scope of the provisions of the SDA relating to sex discrimination against women are: (i) employment,[14] (ii) education,[15] (iii) the provisions of goods, facilities or services or the disposal of premises,[16] (iv) discriminatory advertisements.[17]

A comparison of the cases of a woman and a man for this purpose must be such that the relevant circumstances in the one case are the same as, or not materially different than, in the other.[18]

9

NOTES

1. Person includes any body of persons corporate or incorporate; Interpretation Act 1889, s. 19.

2. Woman includes "a female of any age" (SDA, s. 5 (2), and s. 82 (1) where, however, there is an obscure proviso, "Unless the context otherwise requires"). There is no precise legal definition of what constitutes a female: *Corbett* v. *Corbett*, [1971] Fam. 83.

3. See below, notes 14 to 17.

4. It is not discrimination simply to treat a woman less favourably than a man: the discrimination must be "on the ground of her sex". Motive to discriminate on ground of sex can be inferred from all relevant circumstances. See also "indirect discrimination", n. 11. Note that separate but equal treatment is not discriminatory under the SDA (*contra* RRA, s. 1(2).

5. SDA, s. 1 (1) (*a*). Man includes "a man of any age" (SDA, s. 5 (2), and s. 82 (1) where, however, there is an obscure proviso "Unless the context otherwise requires"). And see n. 2 above.

6. E.g., the state of being single, married, widowed or divorced.

7. SDA, s. 1 (2). The SDA does not prohibit discrimination against unmarried persons as such. The circular of the Newcastle Area Health Authority (Teaching) which provided "The following groups of staff must not, therefore, be discriminated against: men, women, married men, married women, married persons, single men, single women" went too far. *The Times*, 20th January, 1976. This provision provides that, e.g., where a person would treat an unmarried man less favourably than he would treat a married man, say, in the letting of accommodation or making a commercial loan, his treatment of an unmarried woman is to be compared with his treatment of an unmarried, not a married, man.

8. There is no guideline in the SDA as to the size of the groups from which the proportions of men and women are to be drawn for the purpose of this comparison. It may depend upon the circumstances of the particular case G.2.6; or it may refer to women and men at large: Walker, p. 4.

9. The test is whether women "cannot" comply with a condition, not whether they "cannot reasonably be expected" to comply with it (*contra:* Hewitt, p. 14; Births and Hewitt, "Equal Pay and Sex Discrimination" (1976), N.L.J. p. 307). To take an example from the parallel provisions relating to sex discrimination against men: The Grey Topper Club, Jacksdale, Nottingham, has ended its free nights out for women, but offered free entry to persons wearing skirts: *Daily Telegraph*, 19th January, 1976. Men can comply with this condition—indeed two Scotsmen promptly did, *ibid.* No indirect discrimination was therefore involved. And a requirement that all applicants for a managerial post within the company go on a three months' residential training course *could* be complied with by women with home responsibilities, albeit with difficulty.

10. The test is whether the condition is "justifiable", not whether it was justified. It can thus be justified after the event. The offer of concessionary fares to pensioners would discriminate against men, but might be justifiable on grounds of administrative convenience. A condition of employment for an airline pilot might demand so many days per year away from home. This might discriminate against women with children, but would be justifiable.

11. SDA, s. 1 (1) (*b*). This provision, it is submitted, applies to a situation where, say, an employer refused to employ secretaries below 6 ft. 3 ins. in height without the intention to discriminate, but with the obvious effect of so doing. Fewer women could comply with it than could men. Nor would the condition be justifiable. It would be otherwise, for example, if there were a measurable strength requirement for navvies. Rigid seniority rules (which militate against women who temporarily leave work to rear a family) might also be caught by this provision. See *Lading* v. *Headway Shopfitting, Ltd.*, I.T. 2096/76 and *Thom* v. *Meggitt Engineering, Ltd.*, I.T. 5032/76.

12. See "General Exceptions" in Chapter 3.

13. See "Particular Exceptions" in Chapters 4, 5 and 6 which relate to the particular fields of discrimination.

14. See Chapter 4; SDA, Pt. II.

15. See Chapter 5; SDA, Pt. III.

16. See Chapter 6; SDA, Pt. IV.

17. See Chapter 2, paras. [**10**]–[**12**]; SDA, s. 38.

18. SDA, s. 5 (3). This provision, which is infelicitiously phrased, appears to have been inserted *ex abundanti cautela*. Its effect is that a woman who claims that she has been discriminated against must compare her case with that of a man whose circumstances are the same or substantially similar. A woman without a university degree who is rejected for a teaching post must claim comparison with a non-graduate man: an actual man, if one has applied, a hypothetical man if one has not. The acid test is—would such a man have

been treated more favourably? But the requirement of the comparison of like with like is inherent in the case of direct discrimination. To prefer a man with a Nobel prize for a University Chair over a woman without one on that ground cannot be unlawful discrimination at all. Equally if a woman cannot comply with a condition for some reason not connected with her sex (e.g., because she is untrained), there is no scope for the operation of the indirect discrimination provision.

SEX DISCRIMINATION AGAINST MEN

[3] A person[1] discriminates against a man[2] if in specified situations:[3] (i) he treats him on the ground of his sex[4] less favourably than he treats or would treat a woman[5] or, if he treats or would treat a woman differently according to the woman's marital status,[6] a woman of the same marital status ("direct discrimination");[7] or (ii) he applies to a man a requirement or condition which he applies or would apply equally to a woman but is such that the proportion of men[8] who can comply with it[9] is considerably smaller than the proportion of women who can comply with it, *and* which he cannot show to be justifiable[10] irrespective of the sex of the person to whom it is applied, *and* which is to his detriment because he cannot comply with it ("indirect discrimination").[11]

Subject to general[12] and particular exceptions[13] the situations which are within the scope of the Act relating to sex discrimination against men are: (i) employment,[14] (ii) education,[15] (iii) the provision of goods, facilities or services or the disposal of premises,[16] (iv) discriminatory advertisements.[17] A comparison of the cases of a man and a woman for this purpose must be such that the relevant circumstances in the one case are the same as, or not materially different from, those in the other.[18]

NOTES

1. Person includes any body of persons corporate or unincorporate: Interpretation Act 1889, s. 19.
2. Man includes "a man of any age" (SDA, s. 5 (2), and s. 82 (1) where, however, there is an obscure proviso, "Unless the context otherwise requires"). There is no precise legal definition of what constitutes a man: *Corbett* v. *Corbett*, [1971] Fam. 83.
3. See below, notes 14–17.
4. See para. [2], n. 4.
5. SDA, s. 2 (1). Woman includes "a female of any age" (SDA, s. 5 (2), and s. 82 (1) where, however, there is an obscure proviso, "Unless the context otherwise requires").
6. See para. [2], n. 6.
7. See para. [2], n. 7.
8. See para. [2], n. 8.
9. See para. [2], n. 9.
10. See para. [2], n. 10.
11. SDA, s. 2 (1); see para. [2], n. 11.
12. See "General Exceptions" in Chapter 3.
13. See "Particular Exceptions" in Chapters 4–6, and para. [4], below.
14. See Chapter 4; SDA, Pt. II.
15. See Chapter 5; SDA, Pt. III.
16. See Chapter 6; SDA, Pt. III.
17. See Chapter 2; SDA, s. 38.
18. SDA, s. 5 (3); see para. [2], n. 18.

EXCEPTION: PREGNANCY OR CHILDBIRTH

[4] It is not sex discrimination against a man to afford a woman special treatment in connection with pregnancy or childbirth.[1]

NOTE

1. SDA, s. 2 (2). E.g. giving a female employee time off to have a child. And see Employment Protection Act 1975 for the right to paid maternity leave and the right to return to work with the same employer; see particularly ss. 35, 36 and 48 of that Act.

DISCRIMINATION AGAINST MARRIED PERSONS

[5] A person[1] discriminates against a married person of either sex if, in the field of employment:[2] (i) he treats that person on the grounds of marital status[3] less favourably than he treats or would treat an unmarried person of the same sex ("direct discrimination");[4] *or* (ii) he applies to that person a requirement or condition which he applies or would apply equally to an unmarried person, but it is such that the proportion of married persons[5] who can comply with it[6] is considerably smaller than the proportion of unmarried persons of the same sex who can comply with it *and* which he cannot show to be justifiable[7] irrespective of the marital status of the person to whom it is applied *and* which is to that person's detriment because he or she cannot comply with it ("indirect discrimination").[8]

There are general[9] and particular exceptions[10] applicable in the field of employment.

A comparison of the case of a married person and an unmarried person for this purpose must be such that the relevant circumstances in the one case are the same as, or not materially different than, in the other.[11]

NOTES

1. Person includes any body of persons corporate or unincorporate: Interpretation Act 1889, s. 19.

2. See Chapter 4; SDA, Pt. II. Walker, p. 6, considers that discrimination on grounds of marital sex is prohibited in every section covered by the SDA. This is obviously not so, although anomalies are thereby created; e.g., a married woman cannot be excluded from a course of vocational training on the ground of her married status but can be excluded from some other educative course.

3. It is not discrimination simply to treat a married person less favourably than an unmarried person; the discrimination must be on the ground of marital status. Motive to discriminate on the grounds of marital status can be inferred from all relevant circumstances. See *Mclean* v. *Paris Travel Service, Ltd.*, I.T. 4767/76/E. The victim must be married, not about to be married: see *Bick* v. *Royal West of England School for Deaf*, I.T. 11664/76.

4. SDA, s. 3 (1) (*a*).

5. There is no guideline in the SDA as to the size of the groups from which the proportions of married persons and unmarried persons are to be drawn for the purposes of this comparison. It may depend upon the circumstances of the particular case (G.2.6./2.11), or refer to married persons and unmarried persons at large (Walker, p. 4).

6. The test is whether a married person "cannot comply" with a condition, not whether he or she "cannot reasonably be expected to" comply with it. See para. [2], n. 9 above.

7. The test is whether the condition is "justifiable" not whether it was justified. It can thus be excused after the event.

8. SDA, s. 3 (1) (*b*).

9. See "General Exceptions", Chapter 3.

10. See "Particular Exceptions" in Chapters 4–6.

11. SDA, s. 5 (3). See the discussion, para. [2], n. 18. Note also that in any comparison of married or unmarried persons, the married and unmarried persons to be compared must be of the same sex. The unmarried person can be, if a man, a bachelor, a widower or divorced; if a woman, spinster, widow or divorcee.

DISCRIMINATION BY WAY OF VICTIMISATION

[6] A person[1] ("the discriminator") discriminates against another person ("the person victimised") if, in specified situations,[2] he treats the victim less favourably than in those circumstances he treats or would treat other persons, and does so by reason that the person victimised has either brought proceedings against the discriminator or any other person under the SDA or the EPA;[3] or given evidence or information in connection with proceedings brought by any person against the discriminator or any other person under the SDA or the EPA;[4] or otherwise done anything under or by reference to the SDA or EPA in relation to the discriminator or any other person;[5] or alleged that the discriminator or any other person has committed an act which (whether or not the allegation so states) would amount to a contravention of the SDA or give rise to a claim under the EPA[6] unless the allegation was false and not made in good faith;[7] or by reason that the discriminator knows the person victimised intends to do any of those things, or suspects the person victimised has done, or intends to do, any of them.[8] The situations are the same as those within the scope of the provisions of the SDA relating to sex discrimination against women and subject to the same general and particular exceptions.[9]

Note that the person victimised need not have acted against the discriminator but against another person. The SDA aims to prevent blacklisting or collusion.

NOTES

1. Person includes any body of persons corporate or unincorporate: Interpretation Act 1889. s. 19.

2. See text to note 9 below.

3. SDA, s. 4 (1) (*a*): i.e., proceedings taken under SDA, Pt. VII.

4. SDA, s. 4 (1) (*b*). Victimisation on this ground would be a contempt of court at common law but would not support an action for damages: *Chapman* v. *Honig*, [1963] 2 Q.B. 502.

5. SDA, s. 4 (1) (*c*); e.g., giving information to the Equal Opportunities Commission on the basis of which they carry out a formal investigation under SDA, s. 57. See *Gilbert* v. *Johnson's Shoes*, I.T. 3527/76/B.

6. SDA, s. 4 (1) (*d*).

7. SDA, s. 4 (2). This could apply to allegations made in the course of proceedings brought by the person victimised or to by a third party or to allegations made in the course of a formal investigation by the EOC or to allegations made informally: i.e. to SDA, s. 4 (1) (*b*), (*c*) or (*d*).

8. SDA, s. 4 (1).

9. See para. [2], notes 12–17 and text thereto.

CHAPTER TWO

DISCRIMINATORY PRACTICES AND ANCILLARY LIABILITY

INTRODUCTION

[7] The SDA supplements the provisions dealing with indirect discrimination, enforceable at the suit of individuals, with a provision dealing with discriminatory practices that do or might involve indirect discrimination, the relevant provision being enforceable at the suit of Commissioner only. It also supplements the provisions dealing with actual acts of discrimination with provisions dealing with acts, which, while not themselves constituting unlawful discrimination, are calculated to or could result in such unlawful acts, i.e., it concerns itself with accessories as well as with principals. The categories of secondary liability comprise: instructions to discriminate and pressure to discriminate, the relevant provisions being enforceable at the suit of the Commission only, and aiding unlawful acts and vicarious liability, the relevant provisions being enforceable at the suit of individuals.

DISCRIMINATORY PRACTICES

[8] It is unlawful for a person[1] *either* to apply a practice which calls or would call for the application of a requirement or condition which results in an act of indirect discrimination[2] (whether on grounds of sex or of marital status)[3] *or* to apply a practice which would be likely to result in such an act of indirect discrimination if the persons to whom it is applied were not all of one sex[4] *or* to operate practices or other arrangements which in any circumstances would call for the application by him of either kind of practice.[5]

NOTES

1. Person includes any body of persons corporate or unincorporate: Interpretation Act 1889, s. 19.

2. See para. [2], n. 11 and text thereto; SDA, ss. 1 (1) (*b*), 3 (1) (*b*).

3. SDA, s. 37 (1) (first limb). This provision is directed against a practice which embodies a condition or requirement which has to be complied with before some benefit can be obtained, and which would amount to indirect discrimination if it were applied to a person seeking the benefit.

4. SDA, s. 37 (1) (second limb). It may be that the offensive condition or requirement is so effective a deterrent that no woman applies, and therefore no woman is refused the benefit. This provision blocks that loophole, and makes such a practice unlawful nonetheless. Curiously, although this provision complements the provisions of the SDA dealing with indirect discrimination whether on grounds of sex or of marital status, it does not

appear to outlaw a discriminatory practice that is so effective a deterrent that no married person ever applies.

5. SDA, s. 37 (1), (2). Proceedings in respect of contravention of this section can be brought only by the Commission, i.e. by serving a non-discrimination notice (see Chapter 12, para. [**135**]), or, if that is ignored, by applying to court for an injunction (see Chapter 12, para. [**144**]). This section outlaws not merely actual discriminatory practices, but practices etc. which in any circumstances would (n.b., not "could") call for the application by someone of a discriminatory practice.

ADVERTISEMENTS

[**9**] It is unlawful to publish or cause to be published an advertisement[1] which indicates[2] or might reasonably be understood as indicating[3] an intention by a person to do any act[4] which is or might be unlawful by virtue of Part II[5] or Part III of the Act[6] (i.e. the sections relating to employment, education, goods, facilities, services and promises).[7]

NOTES

1. "Advertisement" includes every form of advertisement, whether to the public or not, and whether in a newspaper or other publication, by television or radio, by display of notices, signs, labels, showcards or goods, by distribution of samples, circulars, catalogues, price lists or other material, by exhibition of pictures, models or films, or in any other way, and references to the publishing of advertisements shall be construed accordingly: SDA, s. 82 (1).

The Commission is seeking to discourage advertisers from showing women at domestic tasks in the course, for example, of trying to sell people household items, although these stereotypes are not illegal. The periodical Publishers Association has warned its members that if advertisements are submitted showing women in old-fashioned roles they will ask for an assurance that the balance will be redressed in the course of a series. The Institute of Practitioners in advertising by contrast has issued guidelines stressing that in this area the Commission can recommend, but cannot enforce: *The Times*, 30th December, 1975. See also para. [**128**] on the duties of the Commission, which has published guidelines.

2. Use of a job description with a sexual annotation (such as "Waiter," "Sales-girl", "postman" or "stewardess") shall be taken to indicate an intention to discriminate, unless the advertisement contains an indication to the contrary: SDA, s. 38 (3).

3. It is submitted that the test is an objective one. The advertisement should be judged by the standards of the reasonable reader. An advertisement for "Gentleman's Relish" referred to the Commission would not be held to infringe the SDA. *The Times*, 26th January, 1976. For a criticism of the impact that these provisions may have on the English language see Howard "One Area where sexism is welcome", *The Times*, 31st January, 1976.

4. "Act" includes a deliberate omission: SDA, s. 82 (1).

5. See Chapter 4.

6. See Chapters 5 and 6.

7. SDA, s. 38 (1). See for further examples: Hewitt, pp. 22, 23. The Commission has unique powers to enforce this provision: s. 72. It is not unlawful to publish or cause to be published a discriminatory advertisement before 1st April, 1976 if it was prepared before 15th December, 1975: S.I. 1975 No. 2112.

Exception: Where the Act Would Not Be Unlawful

[**10**] It shall not be unlawful to publish an advertisement which indicates or might reasonably be understood as indicating such an intention if the intended act would not in fact be unlawful.[1]

NOTE

1. SDA, s. 38 (2). This renders superfluous the reference to an advertisement indicating an intention to do an act "which might be unlawful" in SDA, s. 38 (1). As advertisement for a "super girl" is lawful where the employer employs only four people: SDA, s. 6 (3) (*b*). So too is one for women's clothes entitled "pour la femme": SDA, s. 29 (3). Misconceived complaints about such advertisements in the issue of *The Times* of 14th January, 1976, appear to have been made to the EOC: *The Times*, 22nd January, 1976. Also lawful would be an advertisement phrased "Women wanted for cleaning" where the premises are small dwellings: SDA, s. 33.

Reliance on Statement of Third Party: Defence

[11] The publisher of an unlawful advertisement shall not be subject to any liability in respect of the publication if he proves that the advertisement was published in reliance on a statement[1] made to him by the person who caused it to be published to the effect that the publication would not be unlawful because of the exception.[2]

NOTES

1. The person making such a statement commits an offence if the statement was made knowingly or recklessly and becomes liable for a fine of up to £400: SDA, s. 38 (5).
2. SDA s. 38 (4).

INSTRUCTIONS TO DISCRIMINATE

[12] It is unlawful for a person[1] who has authority[2] over another person or in accordance with whose wishes that person is accustomed to act[3] to instruct him to do any act[4] which is unlawful by virtue of Part II[5] or Part III[6] of the SDA, or to procure or attempt to procure the doing by him of any such act.[7]

NOTES

1. Person includes any body of persons corporate or unincorporate: Interpretation Act 1889, s. 19.
2. SDA, s. 39 (*a*). Authority appears to mean actual authority as well as legal authority.
3. SDA, s. 39 (*b*).
4. "Act" includes a "deliberate omission" SDA, s. 82 (1).
5. Employment, see Chapter 4.
6. Education: see Chapter 5. The provision of goods, facilities, services or premises: see Chapter 6. But it is not unlawful to instruct someone to do an act which is unlawful by virtue of Part IV, e.g. publication of advertisements.
7. SDA, s. 39. The Commission has unique power to enforce this provision, see para. **[148]**.

PRESSURE TO DISCRIMINATE

[13] It is unlawful to induce[1] or attempt to induce a person to do any act[2] which contravenes Part II[3] or Part III[4] of the SDA by providing or offering to provide him with any benefit[5] or subjecting or threatening to subject him to any detriment.[6] The offer or threat may be made directly to the other person or, if not directly, in such a way that he is likely to hear of it.[7]

NOTES

1. Inducing connotes a positive act: *Stepney Case, Rushmere* v. *Isaacson*, (1892), 4 O'M. & H. 178.
2. "Act" includes a deliberate omission: SDA, s. 82 (1).
3. The employment field Chapter 4.
4. Education: Chapter 5. The provision of goods, facilities, services or premises: Chapter 6. But it is not unlawful to put pressure on someone to do an act which is unlawful by virtue of Part IV, e.g., publication of advertisements.
5. SDA, s. 40 (1) (*a*).
6. SDA, s. 40 (1) (*b*).
7. SDA, s. 40 (2). The Commission has unique power to enforce this provision, see para. **[149]**.

AIDING UNLAWFUL ACTS

[14] A person[1] who knowingly aids[2] another person to do an act[3] made unlawful by the SDA shall be treated for the purpose of the SDA as himself doing an unlawful act of like description.[4]

NOTES

1. Person includes any body of persons corporate or unincorporate: Interpretation Act 1889, s. 19.
2. "Aids": gestures or a wink intended to imply approval could be sufficient: *R.* v. *Coney*, 51 L.J.M.C. 78.
3. Act includes a "deliberate omission": SDA, s. 82 (1). Note that any act made unlawful by the SDA is relevant, cf: paras. **[12]** n.6 and **[13]** n.4.
4. SDA, s. 42 (1). An employee or agent for whose act the employer or principal is liable under the SDA (see para. **[16]**) or would be liable but for the statutory defence (see para **[17]**) is deemed to aid the doing of the act by the employer or principal: SDA, s. 42 (2).

Exception

[15] A person[1] who acts in reliance on a statement made to him by that other person that, by reason of any provision of the SDA,[2] the act which he aids would not be unlawful, where it is reasonable for him to rely upon such statement, is not treated as having knowingly aided that other person to do that act.[3]

NOTES

1. Person includes any body of persons corporate or unincorporate: Interpretation Act 1889, s. 19.
2. See the general exceptions (Chapter 3) or the particular exceptions, *passim*.
3. SDA, s. 42 (3). It is an offence punishable on summary conviction with a fine not exceeding £400 for a person acting unlawfully, knowingly or recklessly to make a materially false or misleading statement to a person aiding him as to the lawfulness of the conduct in which they are engaged: SDA, s. 42 (4).

LIABILITY OF EMPLOYERS AND PRINCIPALS

[16] Anything done by a person[1] in the course of his employment[2] shall be treated for the purposes of the SDA as done by his employer as well as by him, whether or not it was done with the employer's knowledge or approval.[3] Anything done by a person[1] as agent for another person with the authority (whether express or implied, and whether precedent or subsequent)[4] of that other person shall be treated for the purposes of the Act as done by that other person as well as by him.[5]

NOTES

1. Person includes any body of persons corporate or unincorporate: Interpretation Act 1889, s. 19.
2. An act is done in the course of the employees' employment if it is *either* a wrongful act authorised by the master *or* a wrongful and unauthorised mode of doing some act authorised by the master: *Poland* v. *John Parr and Sons*, [1927] 1 K.B. 236, C.A., at p. 240; *Ilkiw* v. *Samuels*, [1963] 1 W.L.R. 991, C.A., at pp. 997, 1002, and 1004. Even an express prohibition of the wrongful act is no defence if what was done was done for the purposes of the employer's business: *Rose* v. *Plenty*, [1976] 1 All E.R. 97.
3. SDA, s. 41 (1), see *Defence*, para. **[17]**.
4. But not, it appears, where the agent only has ostensible or apparent authority or authority of necessity. See further 1 Halsbury's Laws, 4th Edn. paras. 818–20, 824. Shop stewards may have implied authority by virtue of a Trade Union's constitution, rules

and practice, to act in the interests of the members they represent and in particular to defend and improve their rates of pay and working conditions, which they might do by negotiation or by industrial action at the relevant place of work, but they were not authorised to do any act outside union rules or policy: *Heatons Transport (St. Helens), Ltd.* v. *Transport and General Workers Union*, [1973] A.C. 78.

5. SDA, s. 42 (2). There is no defence to principals similar to that available to employers, see n. 3 above.

Defence: Reasonable Steps

[17] In civil proceedings, brought under s. 66 of the SDA, against any person in respect of an act alleged to have been done by an employee, it is a defence for that person to prove that he took such steps as were reasonably practicable to prevent the employee from doing in the course of his employment acts of that description.[1]

NOTE

1. SDA, s. 41 (3). The burden of proof is on the employer. In *The Race Relations Board* v. *Harris (Mail Order), Ltd.* 1971 (Rep. of R.R.B. 1973, p. 38) Judge Ruttle construed the equivalent provision of the Race Relations Act 1968. s. 13 (3), to mean that the employer "must take such steps as are reasonably practicable . . . in the context of the particular employer". In *R. R. B.* v. *Upper Globe Hotel Bradford* (Rep. of R.R.B., 1973, p. 44) Judge McKee held that the section "would only apply in circumstances where staff were told plainly that there should be no discrimination on grounds made unlawful by the Act".

DISCRIMINATORY TERMS IN CONTRACTS

[18] A term of a contract is void where its inclusion constitutes a breach of the SDA,[1] or where it is in furtherance of,[2] or provides for,[3] such a breach. But, where the victim of the discrimination is a party to the contract, the term is not void, but is unenforceable against that person.[4] Any person interested in a contract which contains a discriminatory term which is unenforceable may seek an order from a county or sheriff court modifying or removing that term.[5] The court shall not make such an order unless all persons affected have been given notice of the application (unless notice can be dispensed with under rules of court) and have been afforded an opportunity to make representations to the court.[6]

A term in a contract is unenforceable by the person in whose favour it would otherwise operate where it purports to exclude or limit any provision of the SDA (or EPA).[7] This does not apply, however, in respect of *either* an agreement settling a complaint made to an Industrial Tribunal under the SDA or the EPA where the agreement is made with the assistance of a conciliation officer[8] or to an agreement settling a claim in the county court.[9]

NOTES

1. SDA, s. 77 (1) (*a*). It is not clear whether the making of a contract (as opposed to the doing of an act in pursuance of a contract) is made unlawful by the SDA. Making a contract might be a discriminatory practice, see para. [8] above.

2. SDA, s. 77 (1) (*b*), e.g. a term of an agreement between an employer who refuses to employ women and his doorman whereby his doorman is obliged to turn away female applicants for jobs.

3. SDA, s. 77 (1) (*c*), e.g. a term of an agreement between an employment agency and an employer that the employment agency will not send women for interview.

4. SDA, s. 77 (2). But it is not unenforceable by the victim, which may be of benefit where the term is partly to his advantage: Walker, p. 78.

5. SDA, s. 77 (5). For procedure, see County Court Practice 1976.

6. SDA, s. 77 (5). The order may contain provision as respects any period before the making of the order e.g., as to compensation: SDA, s. 77 (6).

7. SDA, s. 77 (3).

8. SDA, s. 77 (4) (*a*); but not to a settlement agreement where the agreement is made *without* the assistance of a conciliation officer.

9. SDA, s. 77 (4) (*b*). The Guide states that a settlement agreement "cannot affect a person's right to complain about any other alleged contravention of the SDA or the EPA. For example, if a woman made a complaint that her employer had discriminated against her in his selection of employees for a training course, and if one of the terms of the contract (made with the assistance of a conciliation officer) settling the complaint was that the women agreed not to complain again about the employer's selection procedure, that term could not be enforced against her": G.6.15. It is submitted that this is not correct. Such a term would be part of "a contract settling a complaint", The term would "purport to exclude or limit" a provision of the SDA. *Prima facie* unlawful, by virtue of SDA, s. 77 (3), it would be made lawful by virtue of SDA, s. 77 (4).

CHAPTER THREE

GENERAL EXCEPTIONS

INTRODUCTION

[19] The SDA contains miscellaneous general exceptions, which apply, where appropriate, to all its provisions which would otherwise outlaw discrimination on whatever grounds. These exceptions are (i) where effect is given to a provision of a charitable instrument for conferring benefits on members of one sex only; (ii) where the act relates to participation as a competitor in a sport in which physical strength, stamina or physique are important; (iii) where there is discrimination in relation to certain types of insurance on the basis of reliable acturial or other data; (iv) where communal accommodation (i.e. shared sleeping accommodation for one sex only in residential premises) is necessarily involved; (v) where there is positive action by certain specified training bodies to limit training for particular work to persons of a particular sex when persons of that sex have in the past engaged in such work not much or not at all (or to encourage such members of that sex to take advantage of opportunities for doing that work); (vi) where an employer provides access to facilities for training for such members of that sex only, or to encourage such members of that sex to take advantage of opportunities for doing that work; (vii) where trade unions, employers' organisations and the like take positive action to ensure that members of both sexes are fully represented at various levels in the organisation; (viii) where the act was done under statutory authority or the authority of a statutory instrument; (ix) where the act was done for the purpose of safeguarding national security.

CHARITIES

[20] Nothing in the SDA shall *either* be construed as affecting a provision which is contained in a charitable instrument[1] for conferring benefits to persons of one sex only (disregarding any benefits to persons of the opposite sex which are exceptional or are relatively insignificant); *or* render unlawful an act which is contained in such a provision.[2]

NOTES

1. "Charitable instrument", for the purposes of England and Wales, means an enactment or other instrument passed or made for charitable purposes (i.e. purposes which are exclusively charitable according to the law of England and Wales (SDA, s. 43 (3) (b)) or an enactment or other instrument so far as it relates to charitable purposes (SDA, s. 43 (3) (a)). As to what are charitable purposes, see *Income Tax Special Purposes Commrs.* v. *Pemsel*, [1891] A.C. 531 at p. 538, H.L.; Halsbury's Laws, 4th Edn., Vol. 5, paras. 501–558.

("Charitable instruments" for the purpose of Scotland means an enactment or instrument passed or made by or on behalf of a body of persons or a trust established for charitable purposes only: SDA, s. 43 (4).)

2. SDA, s. 43; e.g., a trust for the assistance of young women having a first baby in a Salvation Army home (*Re Mitchell, Public Trustee* v. *Salvation Army*, [1963] N.Z.L.R. 934) would remain unlawful.

Special provision is made in the SDA to enable educational trusts whose benefits are confined to one sex only (e.g. The Rhodes Trust) to apply (if the trustees so wish) to the appropriate Secretary of State for a scheme to permit the trust to offer its benefits to both sexes: SDA. s. 78 (educational charities in England and Wales); SDA, s. 79 (educational endowments etc. to which Part VI of the Education (Scotland) Act 1972 applies). King's College, Cambridge are applying to vary the Durham bequest which has an anti-feminine clause: *The Times*, 29th June, 1976.

SPORT

[21] Nothing in the SDA shall, in relation to any sport, game or other activity of a competitive nature where the physical strength, stamina or physique of the average woman puts her at a disadvantage to the average man,[1] render unlawful any act relating to the participation of a person as a competitor in events involving that activity[2] which are confined to competitors of one sex.[3]

NOTES

1. E.g. Association Football or Tennis, but not Show Jumping or Chess.

2. It is submitted that it is unlawful to discriminate against, say a woman referee or trainer: see too *Nagle* v. *Fielden*, [1966] 2 Q.B. 633 for the common law position. There is an instructive comparison from the field of football. A man's team, Aristas, was fined £20 by the Middlesex League for playing Miss Donna Chapman against Lyners: *Evening Standard*, 6th February, 1976. But Miss Jenny Barclay was allowed to referee the Croydon Old Boys v. South Alchester Match in the Thornton and District League: *Sunday Times*, 8th February, 1976.

3. Despite Billy Jean King's victory over Bobby Riggs it is submitted that the Wimbledon Lawn Tennis Championships can still maintain separate Singles Competitions for men and women. The stewards of the Jockey Club have decreed that from 16th February, 1976 the Rules of Racing would be changed to allow women to ride against men, not only on the flat but also in hurdle races and steeplechases. They have also inquired of the EOC as to whether or not they should ban flat races restricted to ladies only: *Daily Telegraph*, 20th January, 1976. It is submitted that they would have had an argument based on this provision for maintaining the *status quo* notwithstanding the exploits of such horsewomen as Princess Anne. Lord Denning did not seem to envisage the possibility of female jockeys; *Nagle* v. *Fielden*, [1966] 2 Q.B. 633, at p. 647. Diana Thornein in the 4.15 at Stratford on 7th February, 1976 was the first woman to win a National Hunt race over men rivals: *The Times*, 9th February, 1976. See generally "Sport: women catching up with Men": *The Times*, 22nd March, 1976.

Note this provision exists only to prevent certain forms of discrimination against women, and not against men. The British Heart Foundation sought, however, to rely on it as justifying a women-only context where physique was under scrutiny: *The Guardian*, 10th February, 1976.

COMMUNAL ACCOMMODATION

Definition

[22] Communal accommodation is defined as residential accommodation which *either* includes dormitories or shared sleeping accommodation which, for reasons of decency or privacy, should be used by one sex only (notwithstanding that the residence may include either some sleeping accommodation which is shared by men and other sleeping accommodation which is shared by women, or some sleeping accommodation which

is not shared) *or* should be used by one sex only because of the nature of the sanitary facilities serving the accommodation.[1]

NOTE

1. SDA, s. 46. The communal accommodation exception is without prejudice to the generality of SDA, s. 35 (1) (*c*) which deals specifically with the provision of services and facilities in situations where decency requires discrimination: see para. [**84**] below; SDA, s. 46 (8).

Admission to Communal Accommodation

[**23**] Subject to a proviso[1] nothing in the SDA makes unlawful sex discrimination in the admission of persons to communal accommodation[2] provided that it is managed in such a way that men and women are treated as fairly and equitably as the exigencies of the situation permit.[3] In deciding whether it is so managed, account must be taken[4] of whether and how far it is reasonable to expect the accommodation to be altered or extended, or additional accommodation to be provided so as to cater more equally for the sexes, and, in addition the frequency of the demand or need for use of the accommodation by men as compared with women or vice-versa.[5]

NOTES

1. See para. [**24**] below.
2. See para. [**22**] above.
3. SDA, s. 46 (3).
4. Presumably among other relevant considerations.
5. SDA, s. 46 (4). There are, in this context, as appears, a range of matters on which a court or tribunal are going to have to make rulings, e.g. as to how far it is unreasonable for someone to alter his accommodation. How much time or money is he expected to spend?

Proviso

[**24**] The exception in relation to admission to communal accommodation[1] does not apply where the provision of admission falls within the scope of the employment provisions of the SDA[2] unless such arrangements as are reasonably practicable are made to compensate those members of the sex for whom such accommodation has been refused for any detriment caused by that refusal.[3]

NOTES

1. See para. [**22**] above.
2. See Chapter 4 below.
3. SDA, s. 46 (6).

Provision of Benefits etc. to Persons Using Communal Accommodation

[**25**] Where a benefit, facility or service can only properly or effectively be provided to persons using communal accommodation,[1] and it is not unlawful to refuse admission to such accommodation,[2] then subject to a proviso,[3] it is also not unlawful to discriminate in providing the benefit, service or facility to which the accommodation is ancillary.[4]

NOTES

1. See [**22**] above; e.g., treatment at a health farm: G.7.8. These benefits may include benefits to be provided by a third party, S.DA, s. 50 (1).

2. See [**23**] above.
3. See [**26**] below.
4. SDA, s. 46 (5).

Proviso

[**26**] The exception in relation to the provision of benefits etc. to persons using communal accommodation[1] does not apply when the provision of the benefits etc. falls within the scope of the employment provisions of the SDA[2] unless such arrangements as are reasonably practicable are made to compensate those members of the sex to whom such accommodation has been refused for any detriment caused by that refusal.[3]

NOTES
1. See [**22**] above.
2. See Chapter 6 below.
3. SDA, s. 46 (6).

INSURANCE

[**27**] Nothing in the SDA makes unlawful discriminatory treatment of a person in relation to an annuity, life assurance policy, accident insurance policy[1] or similar matter involving the assessment of risk, where the treatment was effected by reference to actuarial or other data from a source on which it was reasonable to rely, *and* was reasonable having regard to the data and any other relevant factors.[2]

NOTES
1. Note SDA, s. 29 (2) (*c*) which deals with the provision of insurance. See further Chapter 6, para. [**80**].
2. SDA, s. 45. It will, for example, be lawful for insurance companies to charge women lower premiums for life assurance on the grounds of their greater longevity. What is envisaged by "other relevant factors" is not clear.

ACTS DONE UNDER STATUTORY AUTHORITY

[**28**] Nothing in the SDA makes unlawful any act[1] done by a person if it was necessary for him to do it in order to comply with a requirement of an Act passed before the SDA[2] or of an instrument made or approved (whether before or after the passing of the SDA) by or under an Act passed before the SDA.[3]

NOTES
1. Act includes deliberate omission, SDA, s. 82 (1).
2. The SDA was passed on 12th November, 1975.
3. SDA, s. 51 (1). Where an Act passed after the SDA re-enacted (with or without modification) a provision of an Act passed before the SDA, nothing in the SDA shall render unlawful any act done by a person, if it was necessary for him to do it in order to comply with the requirements of that provision, SDA, s. 51 (2). An amusing illustration was the calling off of London's first women's wrestling match planned for 28th January, 1976 at the York Hall Baths, Bethnal Green between Blonde Bombshell, Mitzi Mueller and a German challenger, Lolita Lohn. A clause in the GLC licensing rules bans females from taking part in such a contest, and, as a piece of delegated legislation, overrode the SDA: *Evening News*, 28th January, 1976. It is to be noted that the exception is for *instruments* made, inter alia, *after* the SDA by or under an Act passed *before* the SDA. "Instrument" itself is not defined in the SDA; and would appear to have a wider meaning than that given to "Statutory

Instrument" by the Statutory Instruments Act 1946, s. 1, and to cover any category of delegated legislation. If this be right then e.g. local authorities can continue to make (if they do) discriminatory bye-laws.

Also if "instrument" has the extended meaning contended for, Oxford colleagues whose governing bodies have delegated power to make college statutes, under the Universities of Oxford and Cambridge Act 1923 subject to the statutes being laid before Parliament and approved by Her Majesty in Council, can continue with impunity to elect fellows of one sex only. For example the college statutes of Lady Margaret Hall provide "The Fellows of the College shall be women". In any event it does not appear that Fellows are employees of a College even within the broad definition given by the SDA, see [**35**] below. Oxbridge Colleges cannot, however, discriminate in their admission of pupils, see [**70**] below.

Generally this provision permits continued discrimination which is enshrined in the protective laws which govern the conditions of women working in factories, e.g. Factories Act 1961, The Employment of Women, Children and Young Persons Act 1920, and the Hours of Employment (Conventions) Act 1936. N.B. Power to amend these laws by Ministerial order under the Health and Safety at Work Act 1975: cf. SDA, s. 7 (1) (*f*); see [**42**] below. The commission have a duty to keep these laws under review: SDA, s. 55; see [**128**] below. On the subject of protective legislation see "Women Factory Workers" by Anna Coote (NCCL).

See *Mayes* v. *Commissioners of Inland Revenue,* I.T. 2632/76.

NATIONAL SECURITY

[**29**] Nothing in the SDA makes unlawful an act[1] done for the purpose of safeguarding national security.[2]

NOTES

1. Act includes "deliberate omission": SDA, s. 82 (1).
2. SDA, s. 52 (1). The exemption applies to discrimination by private employers, as well as to discrimination by the government or other public bodies, done for the purpose of national security. A certificate purporting to be signed by or on behalf of a Minister of the Crown and certifying that an act specified in the certificate was done for the purpose of safeguarding the national security shall be conclusive evidence that it was done for that purpose, SDA, s. 52 (2). A document purporting to be such a certificate shall be received in evidence and, unless the contrary is proved, shall be deemed to be such a certificate, SDA, s. 53 (3). Plender describes this provision as "baffling"; Bindman also has doubts about the need for it. It may be that the draftsman had Mata Hari in mind!

DISCRIMINATORY TRAINING BY CERTAIN TRAINING BODIES[1]

[**30**] (1) Where it appears to an eligible training body[2] that at any time within the previous twelve months there were no persons of one sex doing particular work in *Great Britain,* or that the number of persons of that sex doing such work in *Great Britain* was particularly small, it is not unlawful for that body to discriminate in or in connection with affording access to training for such work to that sex, or to take steps to encourage members of that sex to take advantage of opportunities for doing that work.[3]

(2) Where it appears to an eligible training body that at any time within the previous twelve months there were no persons of one sex doing particular work *in a particular area in Great Britain,* or that the number of persons of that sex doing such work in *such area* was particularly small, it is not unlawful for that body to discriminate in that way.[4]

(3) Where it appears to an eligible training body that there are persons in special need of training for employment because of the period for which they have been discharging domestic or family responsibilities to the

exclusion of regular full-time employment,[5] it is not unlawful for that body to discriminate in connection with affording access to training to those people.[6]

NOTES

1. The SDA does not generally allow "reverse discrimination", e.g. favouring women because of their past disadvantage. It does, however, permit positive action in certain circumstances. See also [31], [32], [33] below.

2. Eligible training body means an industrial training board established under s. 1 of the Industrial Training Act 1964, the Manpower Services Commission, the Employment Service Agency, and the Training Services Agency, or any other persons designated for the particular purpose by or on behalf of the Secretary of State for Home Affairs: SDA, s. 47 (4).

3. SDA, s. 47 (1).

4. SDA, s. 47 (2).

5. E.g. married women who have given up work to bring up a family and now wish to return to work: G.7.14.

6. SDA. s. 47 (3).

DISCRIMINATORY TRAINING BY EMPLOYERS

[31] Where particular work for an employer has at any time during the preceding twelve months been done exclusively by members of a particular sex or at any time during that period the number of persons of one sex doing that work for him has been small compared with the number of persons of the other sex doing it, it is not unlawful for the employer to discriminate in or in connection with affording access to training for that work to the disadvantaged sex, or to take steps to encourage members of that sex to take advantage of opportunities for doing that work.[1]

NOTE

1. SDA, s. 48 (1). This exception does not, however, make it lawful for the employer to discriminate at the point of selection for such work in order to achieve a balance between the sexes, G.7.16 (cf. the "racial balance" provisions of the RRA, s. 8 (2)), e.g. an employer with no women engineers could advertise specifically for women engineers but would have to see men candidates for a vacancy equally with women candidates, Hewitt, p. 18. Walker, p. 31, argues that it *could* not be discriminatory to encourage members of one sex to do certain work. This might, however, be construed as discrimination "in the way" in which access to opportunities for training are afforded.

MEMBERSHIP OF PROFESSIONAL OR TRADE ORGANISATION

[32] Nothing in the SDA makes unlawful any act[1] done by a Trade Union or employers organisation or any other body to which s. 12 of the SDA applies[2] in or in connection with encouraging persons of a particular sex only to become members of the body where at any time within the twelve months immediately preceding the doing of the act there were no persons of that sex among those members or the number of persons of that sex among the members was comparatively small.[3]

NOTES

1. Act includes deliberate omission: SDA, s. 82 (1).

2. See [47] below.

3. SDA, s. 48 (3).

ELECTIONS WITHIN PROFESSIONAL AND TRADE ORGANISATIONS ETC.

[**33**] Where in the opinion of a Trade Union or employers' associations or of any organisation to which s. 12 of the SDA applies[1] it is necessary to take special steps to ensure that the membership of an elected body within that organisation[2] contains a reasonable minimum[3] number of members of a particular sex it shall not be unlawful for it to take such steps *either* by reserving seats on the body for persons of that sex *or* by making extra seats on the body available (by election or co-option or otherwise) for persons of that sex on occasions when the number of persons of that sex in the other seats is below the minimum.[4]

NOTES

1. See [**47**] below.
2. E.g. a Committee.
3. What is reasonable must, it is submitted, be viewed objectively in terms of the needs of the organisation.
4. SDA, s. 49 (1). It is to be noted that it is still unlawful to discriminate in the arrangements for determining the persons entitled to vote in an election for members of the body, or otherwise to choose the persons to serve on the body, or to discriminate in any arrangements concerning membership of the organisation itself, SDA, s. 49 (2).

CHAPTER FOUR

EMPLOYMENT

INTRODUCTION

[**34**] The SDA makes it unlawful for an employer to discriminate on grounds of sex or marital status, or by way of victimisation in relation to recruitment or treatment of employees or contract workers (persons taken on under a contract with a third party). There are a number of specific broad exceptions. An employer may discriminate in relation to recruitment of employees where sex is a genuine occupational qualification for the job or for some of its duties: there are eight exclusive examples given. An employer may discriminate in relation to treatment of employees in the provision made for death or retirement; and in special treatment given to women in connection with pregnancy and childbirth. An employer may discriminate on grounds of sex or marital status but not by way of victimisation where the employment is in a private household or small firm. The SDA does not apply to work which is done wholly or mainly outside Great Britain, unless it is on a British ship, aircraft, or hovercraft. Some of the general exceptions listed in Chapter 3 (e.g. positive action by employers) are peculiarly appropriate to the field of employment. The SDA does not apply to the armed forces. It contains special provisions relating to midwives, police and prison officers and ministers of religion; and does not allow women to work as full-time underground miners. The SDA also makes unlawful discrimination in particular circumstances by partnerships of six or more partners in their treatment of partners or prospective partners; by trade unions and other organisations of workers, employers' organisations and professional bodies; by bodies granting licences or qualifications which affect employment opportunities; by vocational training bodies; by employment agencies (except where the employer could discriminate); and by the Manpower Services Commission; Employment Service Agency and the Training Services Agency.

EEC social affairs ministers have agreed to take measures to eliminate all forms of discrimination against women in employment and to ensure that legal redress is available to those who consider they have been denied equal treatment with men. Action will be taken on the basis of a draft directive submitted by the European Commission. The SDA, however, goes considerably beyond the Commission's proposals, and therefore amending legislation will not be required: *The Times*, 19th December, 1975. See now *Defrenne* v. *Sabena Belgian Airlines* (1976), *The Times*, 20th April.

SCOPE OF EMPLOYMENT COVERED

[35] It is unlawful for an employer to discriminate in specified circumstances[1] in relation to employment *by him* at an establishment[2] in Great Britain.[3] Employment comprises employment under a contract of service or apprenticeship or a contract personally to execute any work or labour.[4]

NOTES

1. See below, [38] and [39].
2. Where work is not done *at* an establishment it shall be treated as done at the establishment *from* which it is done (e.g., window cleaners or maintenance engineers will be treated as working at their employers' local office) and where it is not done from any establishment it shall be treated as done at the establishment with which it has the closest connection (e.g., commercial travellers or pools collectors will be treated as working at their employers' local office, SDA, s. 10 (4).
3. See [36] below.
4. SDA, s. 82 (1). No distinction is apparently drawn in this context between employment under a contract of service and employment under a contract for services, cf. RRA s. 3. However, where a person seeks to employ or employs an independent contractor who is not obliged personally to execute the work or labour contracted for but can procure its execution by his own employees or agents, or delegate its execution, he is not subject to this provision of the SDA. See further on "contract workers" SDA, s. 9: [41] below.

GREAT BRITAIN

[36] Employment is treated as being at an establishment in Great Britain unless the employee does his work wholly or mainly outside Great Britain.[1] Great Britain[2] includes such of the territorial waters of the United Kingdom as are adjacent to Great Britain.[3] An Order in Council may extend the scope of the SDA, in relation to employment concerned with the exploration of the sea bed or subsoil or the exploitation of their natural resources, to cover any area designated under the Continental Shelf Act 1964.[4]

NOTES

1. SDA, s. 10 (1).
2. Great Britain means England, Wales and Scotland: Union with Scotland Act 1706.
3. SDA, s. 82 (1).
4. SDA, s. 10 (5). The act will not include an area or part of an area in which the law of Northern Ireland applies *ibid*. The Order shall be of no effect unless a draft was laid before and approved by both Houses of Parliament, SDA, s. 10 (7).

SHIPS, HOVERCRAFT, AIRCRAFT

[37] Employment on board a ship[1] registered at a port of registry in Great Britain[2] *or* employment on an aircraft or hovercraft registered in the United Kingdom[2] and operated by a person who has his principal place of business[3] or is ordinarily resident in Great Britain[4] shall be treated as employment at an establishment in Great Britain and therefore within the scope of the SDA *unless* the employee does his work wholly outside Great Britain.[5]

NOTES

1. The ship is for this purpose deemed to be the establishment, SDA, s. 10 (3) and see SDA, s. 10 (4).
2. For registration of ships see Merchant Shipping Act 1894. For registration of aircraft

see Air Navigation Order 1960. For registration of hovercraft see Hovercraft (General Order) 1972, S.I. 1972 No. 674. *Note* that aircraft which are not registered in the United Kingdom register but are operated, for example, from overseas bases by subsidiaries of persons who have their principal place of business in the United Kingdom are not included. (Such aircraft would usually have foreign crews.)

3. The principal place of business of a firm, or office of a corporate body is where the general superintendance and management of the firm or body are carried out: *Palmer* v. *Caledonian Railway Co.*, [1892] 1 Q.B. 823, C.A.; *Davies* v. *British Geon, Ltd.*, [1957] 1 Q.B., C.A.

4. In *Levene* v. *Inland Revenue Commissioners*, [1928] A.C. 217, Viscount Cave said (at p. 225) that he thought the term ordinarily resident "connotes residence in the place with some degree of continuity and apart from accidental or temporary absence". Lord Warrington said (at p. 232) that if the term "has any definite meaning I should say it means according to the way in which a man's life is usually ordered". In *Inland Revenue Comrs.* v. *Lysaght*, [1928] A.C. 234, Lord Buckmaster said (at p. 248) "'Ordinarily resident' means in my opinion no more than that the residence is not casual and uncertain but that the person held to reside does so in the ordinary course of his life".

5. SDA, s. 10 (2).

DISCRIMINATION IN RECRUITMENT

[38] Subject to general[1] and particular[2] exceptions it is unlawful for an employer to discriminate when recruiting employees *either* in the arrangements he makes for the purpose of determining who should be offered the job[3] *or* in the terms on which he offers the job[4] *or* in refusing or deliberately omitting to offer the job.[5]

NOTES

1. See Chapter 3.
2. See [40]–[44], below.
3. SDA, s. 6 (1) (*a*). E.g. in interviews, application forms, instruction given to an employment agency, or, in the world of the theatre, the casting couch: also advertisements, see SDA, s. 38 in [9] above. A complaint can be made by a person deterred from applying for the job as well as by an applicant. See *McDonald* v. *Applied Art Glass Co., Ltd.*, [1976] I.R.L.R. 130.
4. SDA, s. 6 (1) (*b*). E.g. in relation to hours of work or time off. It also applies to offers of non-contractual terms as to payment, e.g. discriminatory bonuses; but *not* to offers of contractual terms as to payment, e.g. wages or salary unless, if the person accepted the offer, the term would be stuck down under the EPA. See generally Appendix I for a full discussion of this.
5. SDA, s. 6 (1) (*c*). Deliberate omission would, it is submitted, include deliberately failing to reply to a letter of application or pretending that a still unfilled vacancy had been filled. *Note* there is no requirement that the victim of discrimination should have been qualified for the job as there is in the RRA, s. 3.

DISCRIMINATION IN TREATMENT OF EMPLOYEES

[39] Subject to general[1] and particular[2] exceptions it is unlawful for an employer to discriminate *either* in the way in which he affords an employee access to opportunities for promotion, transfers or training,[3] or to any other benefits, facilities or services *or* by refusing or deliberately omitting to afford access to them[4] *or* by dismissing the employee[5] *or* by subjecting the employee to any other detriment.[6]

NOTES

1. See Chapter 3.
2. See [40]–[44] below, [31] above.
3. Training includes any form of education or instruction: SDA, s. 82 (2).
4. SDA, s. 6 (2) (*a*). Benefits etc. includes any benefits etc. which it is in the employer's power to have provided by a third party: SDA, s. 50 (1). Opportunity to earn overtime is a

benefit: *Baxter* v. *Glostal A.A. Ltd.*, I.T. 1168/76. It does not apply to benefits consisting of the payment of money when the provision of those benefits is regulated by the person's contract of employment: SDA, s. 6 (6). In these circumstances the EPA applies; see generally Appendix I for full discussion of this. Walker, p. 22 suggests that "Benefits consisting of the payment of money" is intended to refer to financial benefits *other* than wages or salaries, e.g. a travel or clothes allowance. It is submitted that this is too restrictive a view. Where the employer provides the public as well as his employees with any benefits, etc. he will be subject to the provisions of the SDA dealing with the provisions of goods, facilities, and services, SDA, s. 29, see Chapter 6 below. This means that any complaints will be dealt with by the Courts (see Chapter 10 below) and not by Industrial Tribunals. However the Industrial Tribunal will be the appropriate forum for dealing with complaints where *either* the provision to the public differs in a material respect from the provision to his employees (e.g. where a grocery store offers food to its employees at lower prices than those payable by customers) *or* where the provision is regulated by an employee's contract of employment (e.g. where the employer is obliged by the contract of employment to make the provision) *or* where the provision relates to training (including any form of education or instruction): SDA, s. 6 (7); e.g. an employee of a building society or bank cannot make a complaint to an Industrial Tribunal if he feels that he is being discriminated against as regards a loan when the building society or the bank makes like loans to the public at large. He must make a complaint to a county court under the provisions of the SDA dealing with goods, facilities and services, see Chapter 6 below. (Walker, p. 24 suggested that the employee has no claim at all. This is obviously wrong.) But if the building society gives concessionary rates of mortgages to its employees of one sex only, or the bank gives interest free loans to its employees of one sex only, then an employee of the other sex can make a complaint to an Industrial Tribunal.

5. SDA, s. 6 (2) (*b*). This may also constitute unfair dismissal pursuant to TULRA, Sch. 1, Part II. (N.B. in SDA the onus is on the employee to prove discrimination.) For a case of discrimination in favour of a woman on grounds of her sex see *Bills* v. *Kaye Shoes of Bilston* (1976),*The Times*, 13th March.

6. SDA, s. 6 (2) (*b*). Reducing overtime is a detriment: *Morris etc.* v. *Scott and Knowles*, I.T. 7673/76.

PREGNANCY, CHILDBIRTH, DEATH, RETIREMENT

[**40**] It is not unlawful for an employer to discriminate *either* by affording special treatment to women in connection with pregnancy or childbirth[1] *or* in the provision that he makes in relation to death or retirement.[2]

NOTES

1. SDA, s. 2 (2). *Note* under the Employment Protection Act 1975 women are entitled to six months maternity leave and to get their job back within 29 weeks of having a baby. See particularly ss. 35, 36 and 48 of that Act.

2. SDA, s. 6 (4). This allows an employer to discriminate in the provisions he makes in a pension scheme or in widows' benefits. It would not appear to entitle him to require one sex to retire earlier than another—this is hardly *provision* in relation to retirement (*contra* G.3.10). B.A. stewardesses have now been accorded the right to stay in employment until 55 like male cabin staff instead of being obliged to retire at 36 as they were previously: *The Times*, 13th December, 1975. As a result of the SDA, British Railways give female workers' husbands similar travel privileges to those enjoyed by male workers' wives. But they refused to give them to the husbands of retired workers on the ground of this "retirement" exception: *The Times*, 28th January, 1976. See also *Mayes* v. *Commissioners of Inland Revenue*, I.T. 2632/76.

Note. The Social Security Pensions Act 1975, ss. 53–56, contains provisions regarding equal access to occupational pension schemes from 1978.

PRIVATE HOUSEHOLD AND SMALL FIRMS

[**41**] It is not unlawful for a person to discriminate *except* by way of victimisation in recruitment for or treatment during employment *either*

for the purpose of a private household[1] *or* where the number of persons employed by the employer, added to the number employed by any associated employers[2] of his, does not exceed five (disregarding any persons employed for the purposes of a private household.[3]

NOTES

1. SDA, s. 6 (3) (*c*). It is submitted that this exception covers the employment of people *in* a private household such as domestic servants, au pairs or gardeners, cf. in relation to the analogous provision of the RRA, s. 8 (6): "within his own home someone may have only such employees . . . as he chooses": *Charter* v. *Race Relations Board*, [1973] 1 All E.R. 512 at p. 521 *per* Lord Morris of Borth-y-Gest. It is submitted that it does not cover persons sent *to* a private house to work such as television repairers to maternity nurses; see for rival arguments on the relevant provision of the RRA, s. 8 (6); Hepple, *Race, Jobs and the Law*, Penguin (2nd Edition), p. 123; Lester and Bindman, pp. 216–17. Discrimination against workers supplied by a third party is unlawful; and the "private households" exception does not apply: SDA, s. 9; see [45] below.

2. For the purposes of the SDA, two employers are to be treated as associated if one is a company of which the other (directly or indirectly) has control, or if both are companies of which a third person (directly or indirectly) has control: SDA, s. 82 (2). It is submitted that "persons employed by the employer" include persons employed otherwise than at the establishment in question as well as persons employed at it.

3. SDA, s. 6 (3) (*b*). (N.B. the figure of five can be reduced by statutory instrument: SDA, s. 80 (1) (*a*).) See *Marsh* v. *East Sussex Council on Alcoholism*, I.T. 3006/76.

GENUINE OCCUPATIONAL QUALIFICATION (GOQ)

[42] Sex discrimination (but *not* discrimination against married persons or victimisation) by an employer is *not* unlawful as regards *either* the arrangements he makes for the purpose of determining who should be offered the job[1] *or* a refusal or deliberate omission to offer the job[2] *or* the provision of opportunities for promotion or transfer to, or training for, that job,[3] if a person of a particular sex is genuinely required to fill the position.

NOTES

1. SDA, s. 7 (1) (*a*); see [38] n. 3 above.
2. SDA, s. 7 (1) (*a*); see [38] n. 5 above.
3. SDA, s. 7 (1) (*b*). *Note* that where a person actually offers to employ a person of a particular sex in a job, he must not discriminate in the terms on which he offers that person the job *or* by dismissing that person from it *or* by subjecting that person to any other detriment. The GOQ exceptions can be amended or added to by statutory instrument: SDA, s. 80 (1) (*a*).

The Criteria of Genuine Occupational Qualification

[43] A person's sex is a genuine occupational qualification *only* where:

(1) the job is one of two which are to be held by a married couple;[1] *or*

(2) subject to one proviso,[2] the essential nature of the job calls for a man (or woman) for reasons of physiology (excluding physical strength or stamina), *or*, in dramatic performance or other entertainment, for reasons of authenticity, so that the essential nature of the job would be materially different if carried out by a person of the other sex;[3] *or*

(3) the job needs to be held by a man (or a woman) to preserve decency or privacy because *either* it is likely to involve physical contact between the holder of the job and man (or woman) in circumstances

where they might reasonably object to the job being carried out by a person of the opposite sex *or* the holder of the job is likely to do his work in circumstances where persons of the opposite sex might reasonably object to the presence of a person of his or her sex because they are in a state of undress or are using sanitary facilities;[4] or

(4) the nature or location of the establishment makes it impracticable for the holder of the job to live elsewhere than in premises provided by the employer and the only available premises for persons holding that kind of job are lived in (or are normally lived in) by men (or women) and are not equipped with separate sleeping accommodation for each sex and sanitary facilities which could be used by one sex in privacy from the other (however, when it is reasonable to expect the employer either to equip those premises with such accommodation and facilities or to provide other premises entirely, he cannot rely on this genuine occupational qualification exception[5]); *or*

(5) the job is to be done in a single-sex or near single-sex hospital, prison or other establishment for persons requiring special care, supervision or attention, *or* in a single-sex or near single-sex part of such establishment, and the essential character of the establishment or the part of it within which the job is to be done is such that it is reasonable to require the job to be held by a person of the same sex as those catered for by the establishment or that part of it;[6] *or*

(6) the holder of the job provides individuals with personal services promoting their welfare and education or similar personal services, and those services can most effectively be provided by a person of a particular sex;[7] *or*

(7) the job needs to be held by a man because of restrictions imposed by the laws regulating the employment of women;[8] *or*

(8) the job needs to be held by a man because it is likely to involve the performance of duties outside the United Kingdom in a country whose laws or customs are such that the duties could not, or could not effectively, be performed by a woman.[9]

Note that often a job will not consist entirely of duties which fulfil the GOQ criteria. But, as long as some of the duties of which it consists do, the employer can rely upon the GOQ exception, subject to the proviso.[10]

NOTES

1. SDA, s. 7 (2) (*h*), e.g., married couples are often employed to manage public houses.
2. See [**44**] below.
3. SDA, s. 7 (2) (*a*). The first example in this category covers, e.g., models or bunny girls. The word "physiology" ("the science of the normal functions and phenomena of living things": Shorter OED) is inapt. Either physiognomy (which was presumably intended) or physique would be better. If the reason of physiology is physical strength or stamina, the case falls outside the example. It is submitted, however, that it is not unlawful to discriminate on grounds of physical strength or stamina as such. E.g., a fire authority can lawfully impose a condition of stamina or strength in respect of potential firemen (or firepersons). If a woman can satisfy this condition she is eligible for the job; if she cannot (which is more likely) she is not. What the fire authority cannot do is to claim the benefit of GOQ on the basis that the job calls for a man by reasons of physiology, i.e. physical strength or stamina, because the SDA says in effect that it cannot be *assumed* that a

man has the physical strength or stamina for the job, but that a woman does not. See SDA, s. 1 (1) (*b*) and notes; [2] above. The second example in this category covers, e.g. bass singers or ballerinas.

4. SDA, s. 7 (2) (*b*), e.g., lavatory attendants or masseurs. This example does not make lawful discrimination against, e.g., women doctors because men could not "reasonably object" to their presence. Women could, however, object to male midwives; see [67] below.

5. SDA, s. 7 (2) (*c*), e.g., oil rigs, ships, lighthouses or remote construction sites. It is submitted that the phrase "normally lived in" is to cover the case, e.g., of a ship before it is launched on its first voyage. See further [22] to [25] on communal accommodation. SDA, s. 7 (2) does not apply to firemen who do not live at the fire station but only work there.

6. SDA, s. 7 (2) (*d*), e.g., hospital staff in a one-sex establishment like the Elizabeth Garret Anderson Hospital for women in London (which is to be closed, *The Times*, 13th February, 1976). E.g. Prison officers, who supervise and witness all aspects of prisoners' lives and so should be of the same sex as the prisoners, but not prison cooks, and see [65] below for Prison Governors. Walker, p. 77 says that the tribunal can consider whether it would be reasonable to refuse to employ a woman as governor of a men's prison; but see SDA, s. 18 (2) for the reverse situation. It is submitted that the phrase "other establishment etc." in SDA, s. 7 (2) (*d*) (ii) covers, e.g., schools for maladjusted children or homes for unmarried mothers.

7. SDA, s. 7 (2) (*e*), e.g., a female probation officer in a mixed team; or a married tutor in a Cambridge women's college. See *Roadburg* v. *Lothian R.C.*, I.T. (Scot.) S/91/76.

8. SDA, s. 7 (2) (*f*), e.g., see Factories Act, Hours of Employment Convention Act 1936 and Mines and Quarries Act 1954. See also SDA s. 51. See [28] and s. 55.

9. SDA, s. 7 (2) (*g*), e.g., export salesman to a Muslim country.

10. SDA, s. 7 (3), e.g., an assistant in a tailor's shop may *sometimes* need to measure, etc. customers in the changing room. This part of his job, although not all of it, involves considerations of decency and privacy. See *Cartwright* v. *John Collier* (1976), *Daily Express*, 1st April where it was held respondents lawfully dismissed applicant whom they would not allow to measure men's inside trouser legs.

Proviso

[44] An employer *cannot* rely upon the GOQ exception where an employer already has employees of the appropriate sex who are capable of carrying out the duties to which the GOQ criteria would apply, whom it would be reasonable to employ on those duties and whose numbers are sufficient to meet the employer's likely requirements in respect of those duties without undue inconvenience.[1]

NOTE

1. SDA, s. 7 (4). E.g., a business man in the export field could not necessarily rely on the GOQ exception to refuse to employ any women on the grounds that they might on occasion need to travel to a Muslim country. Once he had sufficient male salesmen to carry out those visits, he could not discriminate against women applicants for the job on that ground. E.g. an employer wishes to fill a vacancy for a salesman of male underclothing. Prima facie the job needs to be held by a man because of consideration of decency and privacy, see [43] above. However, if the employer already has male employees who are capable of doing that part of the job that involves, e.g., the actual fitting of underwear, and whom it would be reasonable to employ on those duties and whose numbers are sufficient to meet the employer's likely requirements in respect of those duties without undue inconvenience, then he is not entitled to refuse to fill the vacancy with a woman, who can perform the other parts of the job, e.g., recording sales made, assisting at the counter, etc., where no consideration of decency or privacy exists.

CONTRACT WORKERS

[45] Subject to general[1] and particular[2] exceptions, it is unlawful for a person ("the principal") who contracts with another person for the services of workers ("the contract workers") employed by that other person, to discriminate against a contract worker of a particular sex either in the

terms on which he allows the contract worker to do that work *or* by not allowing the contract worker to do it or continue to do it *or* in the way he affords the contract worker access to any benefits,[3] facilities or services *or* by refusing or deliberately omitting to afford the contract worker access to them *or* by subjecting the contract worker to any other detriment.[4]

NOTES

1. See Chapter 3.

2. It is not unlawful for a principal to refuse to allow a contract worker to do work, or to continue to do it where, if it were work done by a person taken into his employment, the GOQ exception would apply to the job: SDA, s. 9 (3). For GOQ exception see **[43]** above.

3. Benefits etc. includes any benefit etc. by which it is in the principal's power to have provided by a third party: SDA, s. 50 (1).

Where the principal provides the public as well as his contract workers with any benefits etc., he shall be subject to the provisions of the SDA dealing with the provisions of goods, facilities or services, SDA, s. 29, see below *unless* the provisions to the public differs in a material respect from the provision to his employees: SDA, s. 9 (4); see **[39]**, n. 4 above.

4. SDA, s. 9. Temporary staff supplied by an employment agency come within this provision.

PARTNERSHIPS

[46] Subject to general[1] and particular[2] exceptions it is unlawful for a firm[3] consisting of six or more partners[4] to discriminate *either* in the arrangements it makes for determining who should be offered a partnership[5] *or* by refusing or deliberately omitting to offer a partnership[6] *or* in the terms on which it offers a partnership[7] *or* in affording a partner access to any benefits, facilities or services,[8] *or* by refusing or deliberately omitting to afford a partner access to them *or* by expelling a partner *or* by subjecting a partner to any other detriment.[9]

NOTES

1. See Chapter 3.

2. It is not unlawful to discriminate against a partner or a potential partner when, if the position as partner were employment, the GOQ exception would apply to the job: SDA, s. 11 (3). For the GOQ exception see **[43]** above.

3. In the SDA "firm" has the meaning given by the Partnership Act 1890, s. 4: SDA, s. 82 (1).

4. The Secretary of State may, by an order, the draft of which has been approved by each house of Parliament, alter this number: SDA, s. 80 (1) (*d*). In the case of a limited partnership, only general partners (i.e., partners liable for all debts and obligations of the firm) count for this purpose: SDA, s. 11 (5). The provisions also apply to persons proposing to form themselves into a firm as they apply in relation to a firm itself. Firms of solicitors, architects, accountants, etc. are covered by these provisions. The Bar, however, is not, as it does not permit partnerships, and the traditional discrimination against aspirant female barristers will continue untouched by the SDA. See Plender, p. 12.

5. SDA, s. 11 (1) (*a*); see **[38]**.

6. SDA, s. 11 (1) (*c*); see **[38]**.

7. SDA, s. 11 (1) (*b*). But not where the terms consist of provisions made in relation to death or retirement: SDA, s. 11 (4): see **[40]**, n. 2. See also SDA, s. 77 for partnership agreements.

8. SDA, s. 11 (1) (*d*) (i). But not where the benefits, facilities or services consist of provision made in relation to death or retirement: SDA, s. 11 (4). Benefits etc. includes any benefits etc. which it is in the firm's power to have provided by a third party: SDA, s. 50 (1).

9. SDA, s. 11 (*d*) (ii). But not where the detriment relates to provisions made in relation to death or retirement: SDA s. 11 (4); see **[40]**, n. 2.

TRADE UNIONS, PROFESSIONAL AND TRADE ORGANISATIONS

[47] Subject to general[1] and particular[2] exceptions, it is unlawful for any of the following organisations[3] to discriminate against a person *either* in the terms on which it is prepared to admit a person to membership[4] *or* by refusing or deliberately omitting to accept an application for membership[5] *or* in the way in which it affords a member access to any benefits, facilities or services[6] *or* by refusing or deliberately omitting to afford a member access to them[6] *or* by depriving a member of membership[7] *or* varying the terms of membership *or* by subjecting a member to any other detriment[8].

The organisations referred to are any organisation of workers,[9] any organisation of employers,[10] or any other organisation whose members carry on a particular profession[11] or trade[12] for the purposes of which the organisation exists.[13]

NOTES

1. See Chapter 3 above and SDA, ss. 48 (2), (3), 49.
2. See below, [48], [49], [50].
3. See below nn. 9–13.
4. SDA, s. 12 (2) (*a*). This does not apply to provision made in relation to the death or retirement from work of a member: SDA, s. 12 (4); see [40] n. 2.
5. SDA, s. 12 (2) (*b*). A complainant must actually have applied; *contra* one under SDA, s. 12 (2) (*a*).
6. SDA, s. 12 (3) (*a*). This does not apply to provision made in relation to the death or retirement from work of a member, SDA, s. 12 (4), see [40] n. 2. Benefits etc. includes any benefits which it is in the power of the organisation to have provided by a third party, SDA, s. 50 (1).
7. SDA, s. 12 (3) (*b*). This does not apply to provision made in relation to the death or retirement from work of a member, SDA, s. 12 (4): see [40], n. 2.
8. SDA, s. 12 (1) (*c*).
9. It is submitted that not only Trade Unions but any organisation of workers (e.g., an employees' pension, fund run by employees for the benefit of the employees of a particular concern) will be within the scope of this provision.
10. E.g. the Confederation of British Industry: but not a Chamber of Commerce, the members of which are not necessarily employers and do not carry on a common trade: Walker, p. 63.
11. Profession includes any vocation or occupation, SDA, s. 82 (1). E.g., The Law Society, the British Medical Association.
12. Trade includes any business: SDA, s. 82 (1). E.g., the City Guilds.
13. SDA, s. 12 (1). Since the organisation must exist for the purposes of the particular profession or trade it is submitted that social or sports clubs whose members carry on a particular profession or trade would not be within the scope of the provision.

Temporary Exceptions: Subscriptions etc. Pre 1978

[48] It is not unlawful for such an organisation to discriminate in relation to contributions or other payments falling to be made to the organisation by its members or by a person seeking membership *or* to financial benefits accruing to members of the organisation by reason of their membership where the payment falls to be made, or the benefit accrues before 1st January, 1978 under the rules of the organisation made before the passing of the SDA.[1]

NOTE

1. SDA, Sch. 4, para. 1.

Exception: Single Sex Organisations in the Teaching Profession Pre 1978

[49] Until 1st January, 1978, the rules prohibiting sex discrimination by such an organisation do not apply to any organisation of members of the teaching profession where at the passing of the SDA the organisation is an incorporated company with articles of association, which restrict membership to persons of one sex (disregarding any minor exceptions) and there exists another organisation, being an incorporated association with like articles, which is for persons of the other sex and has objects, as set out in its memorandum of association, which are substantially the same as those of the organisation, subject only to differences consequential on the difference of sex.[1]

NOTE
1. SDA, Sch. 4, para. 2. The SDA was passed on 12th November, 1975.

Exception: Office in the Organisation

[50] It is not unlawful for such an organisation *either* to afford persons of one sex only in the organisation access to facilities for training which would help to fit them for holding a post of any kind in the organisation *or* to encourage persons of one sex only to take advantage of opportunities for holding such posts in the organisation, where at any time within the previous twelve months there were no persons of the sex in question among persons holding such posts in the organisation or the number of persons of that sex holding such posts was comparatively small.[1]

NOTE
1. SDA, s. 48 (2). (Although this is classified under the heading GENERAL EXCEPTIONS it has only this special applicability.) This provision would enable, for example, a Trade Union to encourage and train women to become shop stewards in a situation where female shop stewards were in a minority. It would *not* enable them to discriminate in the appointment of shop stewards when it actually came to appointing members to such positions.

QUALIFYING BODIES

[51] Subject to general[1] and particular[2] exceptions it is unlawful for an authority or body which can confer[3] an authorisation or qualification[4] which is needed for, or facilitates engagement in, a particular profession[5] or trade[6] to discriminate against a person of a particular sex *either* in the terms on which it is prepared to confer an authorisation or qualification;[7] *or* by refusing or deliberately omitting to grant such authorisation or qualification;[8] *or* by withdrawing it or varying the terms on which it is held.[9]

NOTES
1. See Chapter 3 above.
2. See [52] below.
3. "Confer" includes renew or extend: SDA, s. 13 (3) (*b*).
4. "Authorisation or qualification" includes recognition, registration, enrolment, approval and certification: SDA, s. 13 (3) (*a*).
5. "Profession" includes any vocation or occupation: SDA, s. 82 (1).
6. "Trade" includes any business: SDA, s. 82 (1).

7. SDA, s. 13 (1) (*a*).

8. SDA, s. 13 (1) (*b*). The infelicitous expression in the SDA is "grant her application for it" (*sic*).

9. SDA, s. 13 (1) (*c*). This provision would apply to the Law Society, Inns of Court, British Medical Association, licensing justices, the Jockey Club, etc. Walker, p. 71 suggests that the provision also "covers trade union, membership of which is, in practice, often a prerequisite to engaging in employment in a particular trade, certainly when a 'closed shop' is operating". For appeals against a decision of a qualifying body, see [99], n. 1.

Note. Unlawful discrimination by specified bodies in charge of educational establishments or by local education authorities fall outside the scope of the provisions dealing with qualifying bodies and is separately dealt with: SDA. s. 13 (4); see Chapter 5. Walker, p. 73 suggests that accordingly "universities will be able to continue to confer degrees, even where such degrees effectively control entrance to a profession or vocations, in a manner which discriminates between the sexes". This conclusion appears to ignore the provisions of SDA, s. 22 itself; see [70] below.

Exception: Discrimination by Qualifying Bodies in the Field of Religion

[52] It is not unlawful to discriminate as regards an authorisation or qualification[1] for purposes of an organised religion[2] where the authorisation or qualification[1] is limited to one sex so as to comply with the doctrines of the religion or to avoid offending the religious sensibilities of a significant number of its followers.[3]

NOTES

1. See [51], n. 4.

2. Organised religion is not defined in the SDA. Scientology is not a religion: *R.* v. *Registrar-General, ex p. Segerdal*, [1970] 2 Q.B. 697.

3. SDA, s. 19 (2). This exception applies e.g. to ordination for the priesthood.

FURTHER OBLIGATION OF QUALIFYING BODIES

[53] Where an authority or body is required by law[1] to satisfy itself as to the good character of a person before conferring on such a person an authorisation or qualification[2] which is needed for, or facilitates their engagement in any profession[3] or trade[4] then, without prejudice to any other duty to which it is subject, that requirement shall be taken to impose on the authority or body a duty to have regard to any evidence tending to show that he, or any of his employees or agents (whether past or present) had practised unlawful discrimination in, or in connection with the carrying on of any profession[3] or trade.[4,5]

NOTES

1. See, e.g., Solicitors Act 1974, s. 3 "no person shall be admitted as a solicitor unless . . . the Society . . . is satisfied as to his character and his suitability to be a solicitor". Licensing justices would also be covered by this provision.

2. See [51], n. 4.

3. Profession includes any vocation or occupation: SDA, s. 82 (1).

4. Trade includes any business: SDA, s. 82 (1).

5. SDA, s. 13 (2); cf. Consumer Credit Act 1974, s. 25 (2) (*c*), which requires the Director of Fair Trading to have regard to discrimination in terms, *inter alia*, of sex in relation to fitness for a licence for credit or for a business.

VOCATIONAL TRAINING BODIES

[54] Subject to general[1] and particular[2] exceptions it is unlawful for any of the following vocational training bodies to discriminate against a

person seeking or undergoing training[3] which would help to fit her for any employment[4] *either* in the terms on which that person affords access to any training courses or other facilities[5] *or* by refusing *or* deliberately omitting to afford such access[6] *or* by terminating the training.[7]

The vocational training bodies referred to are: industrial training boards established under s. 1 of the Industrial Training Act 1964;[8] the Manpower Services Commission;[9] the Employment Service Agency;[9] the Training Services Agency;[9] any association which comprises employers and has as its principal object, or one of its principal objects, affording their employees access to training facilities;[10] any other person providing facilities for training for employment, being a person designated for this purpose in an order made by or on behalf of the Secretary of State.[11]

NOTES
    1. See Chapter 3 and SDA, s. 47.
    2. See Exceptions 1 and 2 below.
    3. Training includes any form of education or instruction: SDA, s. 82 (1).
    4. Employment means employment under a contract of service or of apprenticeship or a contract personally to execute any work or labour: SDA, s. 82 (1).
    5. SDA, s. 14 (1); facilities, etc. includes such facilities as it is in the power of the Qualifying Body to have provided by a third party: SDA, s. 50 (1).
    6. SDA, s. 14 (1) (*b*).
    7. SDA, s. 14 (1) (*c*).
    8. SDA, s. 14 (2) (*a*).
    9. SDA, s. 14 (2) (*b*).
    10. SDA. s. 14 (2) (*c*).
    11. SDA, s. 14 (2) (*d*).

Exception 1: Discrimination by Certain Vocational Training Bodies in the Educational Field

Unlawful discrimination by specified bodies in charge of educational establishments or by local education authorities falls outside the scope of the provisions dealing with vocational training bodies and is separately dealt with.[1]

NOTE
    1. SDA, s. 14 (3); see SDA, s. 22 and s. 23, and see Chapter 5. The practical effect of this is to ensure that complaints are dealt with not by Industrial Tribunals but under the education enforcement procedures: see Chapter 9.

Exception 2: Training Midwives

It is not unlawful for a vocational training body to discriminate in respect of training of midwives.[1]

NOTE
    1. SDA, s. 20 (3); see for midwives [67].

EMPLOYMENT AGENCIES

[55] Subject to general[1] and particular[2] exceptions and to a statutory defence[3] it is unlawful for an employment agency[4] to discriminate *either* in the terms on which the agency offers to provide any of its services,[5] *or*

by refusing or deliberately omitting to provide any of its services[6] *or* in the way it provides any of its services.[7]

NOTES

 1. See Chapter 3 above.
 2. See [**57**].
 3. See [**58**].
 4. "An employment agency" means a person who, for profit or not, provides services for the purposes of finding employment for workers or supplying employers with workers: SDA s. 82 (1). E.g., university appointments boards, commercial agencies such as Alfred Marks or Brook Street Bureau, or the Employment Services Agency or the Manpower Services Commission: SDA, s. 16 (2) (*b*).
 5. SDA, s. 15 (1) (*a*). "Services" include guidance on careers and any other services related to employment: SDA, s. 15 (3).
 6. SDA, s. 15 (1) (*b*).
 7. SDA, s. 15 (1) (*c*).

LOCAL EDUCATION AUTHORITIES AND s. 8 OF THE EMPLOYMENT AND TRAINING ACT 1973

[**56**] Subject to general[1] and particular[2] exceptions it is unlawful for a local education authority or an education authority[3] to discriminate in the performance of its functions under s. 8 of the Employment and Training Act 1973.[4]

NOTES

 1. See Chapter 3.
 2. See [**58**] below.
 3. In relation to Scotland has the same meaning as in s. 145 (16) of the Education (Scotland) Act 1962: SDA, s. 82 (1).
 4. SDA, s. 15 (2). The practical effect of locating this obligation in Part II of the SDA (employment) and not Part III of the SDA (education) is that complaints of this type of discrimination must be made to the Industrial Tribunal.

Exception: No Discrimination by Employer

[**57**] It is not unlawful for an employment agency,[1] education authority[2] or local education authority to discriminate in the case of employment which the employer could lawfully refuse to offer the applicant.[3]

NOTES

 1. See [**55**], n. 4.
 2. See [**56**], n. 3.
 3. SDA, s. 15 (4), e.g. because of the Private Households and Small Firms exception (see [**41**] above) or the GOQ exception (see [**42**] above) applied to it.

Defence: Reliance on Employer's Statement

[**58**] An employment agency,[1] education authority or local education authority[2] shall not be subject to any liability for discrimination[3] if it proves *both* that it acted in reliance on a statement made to it by the employer to the effect that its action would not be unlawful because the discrimination only concerned employment which the employer could lawfully refuse to offer the applicant[4] *and* it was reasonable for it to rely on the statement.[5]

    1. See [55], n. 4.
    2. See [56], n. 3.
    3. I.e. of the prohibited kind: see [55] and [56], above.
    4. See [57], n. 3.
    5. SDA, s. 15 (5). It is a criminal offence knowingly or recklessly to make such a statement: SDA, s. 15 (6).

MANPOWER SERVICES COMMISSION

[59] Subject to general[1] and particular[2] exceptions it is unlawful for any of the following bodies to discriminate in the provision of facilities or services under s. 2 of the Employment and Training Act 1973.[3] The bodies referred to are the Manpower Services Commission and its agencies; the Employment Services Agency; the Training Services Agency.

NOTES
    1. See Chapter 3.
    2. See Exception, below.
    3. SDA, s. 16 (1). By s. 2 (1) of the Employment and Training Act 1973 it is the duty of the Manpower Services Commission to make arrangements in connection with assisting persons to select, train for, obtain and retain employment suitable for their ages and capacities, and to obtain employees (including partners and other business associates). By s. 2 (4) of the same Act it is the duty of each of the two specified agencies to exercise on behalf of the Commission such of the Commission's functions as the Commission directs the agency to exercise, and to give effect to any directions given to it by the Commission otherwise than in pursuance thereof. Walker, p. 56 suggests that but for this provision the Manpower Services Commission etc. could validly discriminate pursuant to their statutory powers under the Employment and Training Act 1973 because of SDA, s. 51 (see [28] above) which exempts all acts which are necessary in order to comply with an Act passed before the SDA. However, this Act (unlike e.g. the Factories Acts) does not purport to discriminate between men and women. But SDA, s. 51 is dominant, so SDA, s. 16, would be incapable of overruling it!

Exception: Functions as Training Body and Employment Agency

The foregoing provision does not apply where the Manpower Services Commission or either of its agencies is acting as a vocational training body or as an employment agency.[1]

NOTE
    1. SDA, s. 16 (2), see SDA, s. 14 ([54] above) and SDA, s. 15 ([55] above). In fact most of its activities fall within the scope of these other provisions! The other sections are much wider in their scope, and the purpose of this exception is to ensure that the widest possible check is put on the ability of the Manpower Services Commission lawfully to discriminate.
    The Training Services Agency has prepared plans to improve women's chances of obtaining decent jobs. These range from incentives to engineering firms for training of girl engineering technicians to the study of refresher courses facilities for married professional women and "self-presentation courses", courses aimed at equipping women returning to work with the confidence and skill to cope successfully both with the recruitment process and relationships at work: *The Times*, 30th December, 1975.

GOVERNMENT SERVICE

[60] Subject to a particular exception,[1] the employment provisions of the SDA apply to acts[2] done by or for the purposes of a Minister of the Crown or Government Department or to acts done on behalf of the Crown[3] by a statutory body[4] or a person holding statutory office[5] in the

same way as they apply to acts done by a private person (i.e. with the same exceptions, etc.).[6] They also apply to service for the purposes of a Minister of the Crown or Government Department[7] (other than service on behalf of a person holding statutory office[5]) *or* service on behalf of the Crown[8] for the purpose of a person holding statutory office[5] or for the purposes of a statutory body and (by virtue of the Employment Protection Act 1975) to service on the staff of the House of Commons in the same way as they apply to employment by a private person (i.e. with the same exceptions, etc.).[9]

NOTES
    1. See [62] below.
    2. "Act" includes a deliberate omission: SDA, s. 82 (1).
    3. The Crown means the organs of central Government. The B.B.C. is not part of the Crown: *B.B.C.* v. *Johns*, [1965] Ch. 32. The N.H.S. is part of the Crown: *Pfizer Corporation* v. *Ministry of Health*, [1965] A.C. 512. See Garner, *Public Corporations in the U.K. Government Enterprise* (ed. Fridman & Garner, Stevens, 1970).
    4. Statutory body means a body set up by or in pursuance of an enactment: SDA, s. 85 (10).
    5. Statutory office means an office set up by or in pursuance of an enactment: SDA, 85 (10).
    6. SDA, s. 85 (1). This provision looks at the matter from the point of view of the discriminator. Note special provisions on the police (SDA, s. 17) which are unaffected by this provision: SDA, s. 85 (3). See [63].
    7. Service "for the purpose of" a Minister of the Crown of Government Department does not include service in any office in Schedule 2 (Ministerial offices) to the House of Commons Disqualification Act 1975 as for the time being in force: SDA., s. 85 (10).
    8. SDA, s. 85 (2). This provision looks at the matter from the point of view of the victim of discrimination. Note special provisions on the police which are unaffected by this provision: SDA, s. 85 (3). See [63].
    9. For private persons, see above esp. [38] and [39].

PUBLIC APPOINTMENTS

    [61] Where a Minister of the Crown or Government Department appoints someone to an office or post and the appointment does not constitute employment,[1] the Minister or department is under an obligation not to discriminate in the way in which the appointment or the arrangements for determining who should be offered the appointment is made in the same way as if the appointment did constitute employment.[2]

NOTES
    1. I.e. when there is no contract of service.
    2. SDA, s. 86 (2). This applies e.g. to members of the Commission itself, Governors of the B.B.C., members of the Boards of nationalised industries, etc.: Hewitt, p. 19.

ARMED SERVICES

    [62] Nothing in the SDA applies to service in the navy, army or airforce or any women's service administered by the Defence Council,[1] or to employment in which the employee may be required to serve in support of the armed forces.[2] Nor does the SDA apply to admission to the Army Cadet Force, Air Training Corps, Cadet Corps or Combined Cadet Force or any other cadet training corps for the time being administered by the Ministry of Defence.[3]

NOTES
    1. SDA, s. 85 (4).
    2. SDA, s. 85 (6).
    3. SDA, s. 85 (5).

THE POLICE

[**63**] For the purposes of the SDA, the holding of the office of constable is treated as employment by the chief officer of police[1] as respects any act done by the chief officer in relation to a constable or his office and by the police authority[2] as respects any act done by them in relation to a constable or his office.[3]   Corresponding provision is made with respect to police cadets.[4]   Proceedings[5] which would accordingly lie against a chief officer of police under the SDA shall be brought against the chief officer of police *for the time being*, or, in the case of a vacancy in that office, against the person for the time being performing the functions of that office.[6]   Any compensation, costs or expenses awarded against a chief officer of police in any such proceedings, *and* any costs or expenses incurred by him in any such proceedings so far as not recovered by him in the proceedings, *and* any such sum required by a chief officer of police for the settlement of any claim made against him under the SDA (if the settlement is approved by the police authority[2]) shall be paid out of the police fund.[7]

NOTES
     1. Chief Officer of Police: if the appointment is made under the Metropolitan Police Act 1829, the City of London Police Act 1839 or the Police Act 1964, then the definition is contained in Schedule 8 of the Police Act 1964.   In relation to any other person or appointment it means the officer who has the direction and control of the body of constables in question: SDA, s. 17 (7); for Scotland, see SDA, s. 17 (8).
     2. Police authority: this has the same meaning as in the Police Act 1964 in relation to a person appointed or an appointment falling to be made under the Metropolitan Police Act 1829, the City of London Police Act 1839 or the Police Act 1964.   In relation to any other person or appointment it means the authority by whom the person in question is or on appointment would be, paid: SDA, s. 17 (7); for Scotland, see SDA, s. 17 (8).
     3. SDA, s. 17 (1).
     4. SDA, s. 17 (6).   "Police cadet" means any person appointed to undergo training with a view to becoming a constable: SDA, s. 17 (7); for Scotland, see SDA, s. 17 (8).
     5. I.e., in the Industrial Tribunal; see Chapter 8 below.
     6. SDA, s. 17 (5).
     7. SDA, s. 17 (4).   In relation to a chief officer of police falling within Police Act 1964, Schedule 8, column 3, the police fund is the fund specified in column 4 of that Schedule.   In any other case the police fund means money produced by the police authority: SDA, s. 17 (7); for Scotland, see SDA, s. 17 (8).

Police Regulations

[**64**] Regulations made under ss. 33, 34 or 35[1] of the Police Act 1964[2] shall not treat men and women differently *except* as to requirements relating to height, uniform or equipment,[3] *or* allowances in lieu of uniform or equipment,[3] *or* so far as special treatment is accorded to women in connection with pregnancy or childbirth,[4] *or* in relation to pensions to or in respect of special constables or police cadets.[5]   Any such discriminatory regulations shall not be unlawful.[6]

NOTES
     1. These sections empower the Secretary of State for the Home Department to make regulations as to the government administration and conditions of service in the police forces.
     2. For Scotland the reference is to the Police (Scotland) Act 1967, ss. 26 and 27.
     3. SDA, s. 17 (2) (*a*).
     4. SDA, s. 17 (2) (*b*), and see SDA, s. 2 (2).
     5. SDA, s. 17 (2) (*c*).
     6. SDA, s. 17 (3).   And see SDA, s. 51 which would appear to make acts done in pursuance of such regulations lawful in any event.

PRISON OFFICERS

[65] It is not unlawful to discriminate between male and female prison officers as to requirements relating to height.[1]

NOTE
    1. SDA, s. 18 (1). *Cf.* SDA, s. 1 (1) (*b*).

MINISTERS OF RELIGION ETC.

[66] It is not unlawful to discriminate in respect of employment for the purposes of an organised religion[1] where employment is limited to one sex so as to comply with the doctrines of the religion or avoid offending the religious susceptibilities of a significant number of its followers.[2]

NOTES
    1. There is no definition of organised religion. Scientology is not a religion: *R.* v. *Registrar General, ex parte Segerdal*, [1970] 2 Q. B. 697.
    2. SDA, s. 19 (1); i.e., it will not be unlawful for the Church of England to refuse to ordain women. These bodies which can lawfully refuse to grant authorisation or qualifications to persons by reason of this section will not be liable for discrimination in this respect under SDA, s. 13: SDA, s. 19 (2); see **[51]** above.

MIDWIVES

[67] It is not unlawful to discriminate in respect of employing someone as a midwife[1] or in respect of promotion, transfer or training as a midwife.[2]

NOTES
    1. SDA, s. 20 (1). Thus the mother's choice is preserved.
    2. SDA, s. 20 (2). Note vocational training bodies can discriminate as regards training as a midwife: SDA, s. 20 (3); see **[54]** above: but a man can now be enrolled and certified as a midwife, see **[68]** below.

EMPLOYMENT: ENLARGEMENT OF OPPORTUNITIES

[68] (1) A man can now become a Governor of a woman's prison.[1]

(2) Subject to certain transitional arrangements[2] a man can now be enrolled and certified as a midwife.[3]

(3) A woman can now be employed below ground in a disused mine or in a job which involves occasional underground duties in an active mine, but *not* in a job whose duties ordinarily require the employee to spend a significant proportion of his time underground in an active mine.[4]

NOTES
    1. SDA, s. 18 (2). This may solve the problem of the producers of ITV's serial "Within these Walls" now that Googie Withers has gone back to Australia. Mr. M. V. Roberts has become the first deputy Governor of Holloway Prison by virtue of this provision.
    2. SDA, Sch. 4, para. 3.
    3. SDA, s. 20 (4); for Scotland, see SDA, s. 20 (5). But note that a male midwife can still find himself out of a job, or denied opportunities for promotion, transfer or training as a midwife: see **[67]** above. Mr. Norman Imms plans to be England's first male midwife: *Evening Standard*, 15th April, 1976.
    4. SDA, s. 21 (1). In consequence regulations for the number of hours which may be worked by miners are extended to cover women: SDA, s. 21 (2).

CHAPTER FIVE

DISCRIMINATION IN EDUCATION

INTRODUCTION

[**69**] The SDA makes unlawful discrimination in the field of education on the grounds of sex or by way of victimisation. References in this chapter to discrimination are references to discrimination on either of these grounds save where it is otherwise stated. Bodies responsible for educational establishments at all levels, primary, secondary or tertiary, both in the private and public spheres, are prohibited from discrimination as regards admission or their treatment of pupils or students. In addition local education authorities have certain further duties not to discriminate; and there is a general duty not to discriminate in the public sphere of education.[1] (There are considerable overlaps in these provisions.) Certain bodies providing education fall outside the scope of these provisions, but within the scope of the provisions dealing with goods, facilities and services.[2] Exceptions are made for single-sex establishments and establishments with boarding accommodation for one sex; but there are provisions to encourage such establishments to become fully co-educational. Exceptions are also made for physical training courses in the field of further education. The enforcement procedures in the field of education are complex; and the SDA contains specific provisions to avoid overlap between the education provisions and other provisions with relevance to the educational field, e.g. those dealing with employment or the provision of goods, facilities and services.

NOTES
    1. For modification of educational trusts, see [**20**], n. 2.
    2. See Appendix V, Discrimination in Education, p. 89, *post*.

DISCRIMINATION BY BODIES IN CHARGE OF EDUCATIONAL ESTABLISHMENTS

[**70**] Subject to general[1] and particular[2] exceptions it is unlawful for the responsible body[3] in charge of an educational establishment[4] to discriminate *either* as regards terms of admission to the establishment[5] *or* by refusing or deliberately omitting to accept an application for admission[6] *or* in the way it affords a pupil access to any benefits, facilities or services[7] *or* by refusing or deliberately omitting to afford such access[8] *or* by excluding the pupil from the establishment[9] *or* by treating the pupil unfavourably in any other way.[9]

NOTES

1. See Chapter 3.
2. See [74], [75], [76] and [77] below.
3. See [71] below.
4. See [71] below. It does not include establishments such as commercial language colleges or institutions offering correspondence courses. These are, however, covered by the provisions of the SDA dealing with goods, facilities and services, see [80] below.
5. SDA, s. 22 (*a*).
6. SDA, s. 22 (*b*). Responsible bodies for educational establishments which are of the opinion that on the date on which it becomes unlawful for them to discriminate by refusing applications for admission (1st September, 1976) it will be impracticable for them to comply with that requirement of the SDA can apply for a transitional exemption order authorising discriminatory admissions during the period specified in the order. SDA, Schedule 4, para. 4. For procedure as to application for transitional exemption orders see SDA, Schedule 2. For effect see SDA, s. 27 (2)–(5). Note especially: (i) that the exemption from liability commences from the time the application is made SDA, s. 27 (5); (ii) that any exemption resulting from a successful application is dependent upon compliance with any conditions of the transitional exemption order SDA, s. 27 (3).
7. SDA, s. 22 (*c*) (i). Benefits etc. include any benefit etc. which it is in the responsible body's power to have provided by a third party: SDA, s. 50 (1).
8. *Ibid.* A Department of Education and Welsh Office circular has correctly informed local education authorities that in mixed schools boys must be admitted to, e.g., cooking classes and girls to, e.g. woodwork classes, *Daily Telegraph*, 21st January, 1976.
Hewitt p. 26 suggests that the provision of books in which women are put at a disadvantage (e.g. by showing them only in domestic roles) may amount to sex discrimination. Such provision does not however amount to discrimination where the books are provided on an equal basis to both sexes! The EOC, however, are hostile to such books, see [128] below. The Inner London Education Authority has sent a booklet to 13,000 heads, principals, managers and governors, stating that "myths and taboos" in "sexist" reading books which impress on small children the dominant role of boys must be attacked: *The Times*, 30th December, 1975.
9. SDA, s. 22 (*c*) (ii). The Sex Discrimination Act (Commencement) Order 1975, S.I. 1975 No. 1845, art. 5 creates a transitional provision to this section and s. 25 relating to the admission of pupils to educational establishments. The sections shall not apply to offers of, or applicants for, admissions on a date before 1st September, 1976.

EDUCATIONAL ESTABLISHMENTS AND RESPONSIBLE BODIES

[71] The Educational establishments and their responsible bodies, referred to in [70] above are listed in the following table. Those establishments identified in the table with an asterisk (thus *) are in the public sector of education.

TABLE

Establishment	*Responsible body*
ENGLAND AND WALES	
*1. Educational establishment maintained by a local education authority	Local education authority or managers or governors, according to which of them has the function in question
2. Independent school[1] not being a special school[2]	Proprietor[3]
*3. Special school not maintained by a local education authority	Proprietor[3]

TABLE (*continued*)

Establishment	*Responsible body*

ENGLAND AND WALES

| 4. University[4] | Governing body |
| 5. Establishment (not falling within paragraphs 1 to 4) providing full-time or part-time education, being an establishment designated under section 24 (1)[5] | Governing body |

SCOTLAND

*6. Educational establishment[6] managed by an education authority	Education authority[6]
*7. Educational establishment[6] in respect of which the managers are for the time being receiving grants under section 75 (*c*) or (*d*) of the Education (Scotland) Act 1962	Managers of the educational establishment[7]
8. University	Governing body
9. Independent school[1]	Proprietor[3]
10. Any other educational establishment[6] (not falling within paragraphs 6, 7 and 9) providing full or part-time school education or further education	Managers[7] of the educational establishment

NOTES

1. Independent school has the meaning given by s. 114 (1) of the Education Act 1944 and in Scotland has the meaning given by s. 145 (26) of the Education Act 1962, e.g. Eton, Heathfield, Dartington Hall.

2. E.g. a school for handicapped children.

3. Proprietor has the meaning given by s. 114 (1) of the Education Act 1944 and in Scotland has the meaning given by s. 145 (37) of the Education (Scotland) Act 1962.

4. "University" includes a university college (e.g. the University College at Buckingham) and the college, school or hall of a university (e.g. Magdalen College, Oxford).

5. The Secretary of State may by order designate an establishment which is *either* recognised by the Secretary of State as a polytechnic *or* is an establishment in respect of which grants are payable out of money provided by Parliament *or* is assisted by a local education authority in accordance with a scheme approved under s. 42 of the Education Act 1944 *or* provides full-time education for persons who have attained the upper limit of compulsory school age (upper age limit of compulsory school age is 16: the Raising of the School Leaving Age Order 1972, S.I. 1972 No. 444) but not the age of 19: SDA, s. 24 (1) (2). Such a designation remains in force until revoked: SDA, s. 24 (3). The Secretary of State has made an order designating *(1) certain independent polytechnics in London, *(2) certain establishments which receive grants from the Department of Education and Science, (3) certain establishments which receive grants from the University Grants Committee, *(4) certain establishments which are assisted by local education authorities, (5) certain independent establishments of further education. See S.I. 1975 Nos. 1902, 2113 for a full list.

6. Education authority and educational establishment in relation to Scotland have the same meaning as they have respectively in s. 145 (16) and (17) of the Education (Scotland) Act 1962.

7. Managers have the same meaning for Scotland as in s. 145 (26) of the Education (Scotland) Act 1962.

OTHER DISCRIMINATION BY LOCAL EDUCATION AUTHORITIES

[72] It is unlawful for a local education authority in England and Wales or an education authority in Scotland to discriminate in the performance of those of its functions under the Education Acts 1944 to 1975 or the Education (Scotland) Acts 1939 to 1974 which do not fall within [70].[1]

NOTE

1. SDA, s. 23 (1). For example a local education authority must not discriminate in the award of discretionary grants under s. 2 of the Education Act 1962 or the provision of facilities for social and physical recreation under section 53 of the Education Act 1944.

GENERAL DUTY IN THE PUBLIC SECTOR OF EDUCATION

[73] Subject to general[1] and particular[2] exceptions there is a duty on responsible bodies for educational establishments in the public sector of education[3] to secure that facilities for education provided by them, and any ancillary benefits or services,[4] are provided without sex discrimination.[5]

NOTES

1. Chapter 3.
2. [74] to [77] below.
3. The establishments are those identified by an asterisk in [71] and [71], n. 5 above.
4. Does this apply to benefits, etc., which it is in the power of the body to have provided by a third party (SDA, s. 50 (1)? That section speaks of references in the SDA to the "affording" by any person of access to benefits etc. The reference in this section is to the "securing" of benefits etc. Probably SDA, s. 50 (1) does not, therefore, come into play.
5. SDA, s. 25 (1) see also [70], n. 8 and, for commencement, n. 9.

EXCEPTIONS

Single-Sex Establishments

[74] It is not unlawful for single-sex establishments to discriminate in admissions or terms of admission.[1] Single-sex establishments are those which admit pupils of one sex only (disregarding any pupils of the opposite sex whose admission is exceptional *or* whose numbers are comparatively small and whose admission is confined to particular courses of classes). Nor is it unlawful for single-sex establishments which admit comparatively small numbers of pupils of the opposite sex for the purpose of particular courses or classes to discriminate by confining particular courses or classes to pupils of one sex.[2]

NOTES

1. SDA, s. 26 (1). Responsible bodies for single-sex establishments which wish to alter their admission arrangements so as to become fully co-educational may apply for a transitional exemption order authorising discriminatory admissions during the period specified in the order: SDA, s. 27 (1). For procedure and effect see [70], n. 6.

2. SDA, s. 26 (2). For example some boys, public schools admit girls to classics courses in the sixth form because of the superior teaching available in such schools. It will not by virtue of this provision be open to girls to claim admission, say, in the modern language course. Note that this provision is only concerned with single-sex classes which admit a comparatively small number of persons of the opposite sex for the purpose of particular courses or classes. Those that admit them exceptionally but without specifically confining their admission to such courses or classes cannot discriminate, e.g. The Dragon School, Oxford which admits a small number of girls. Boys exceptionally admitted to infant classes of a girls' school are entitled to enjoy the same treatment as the female majority: G.4.ii.

Physical Training

[**75**] It is not unlawful for any responsible body for an educational establishment[1] concerned with further education[2] to discriminate as regards further education courses in physical training or courses designed for teachers of physical training.[3]

NOTES
1. See [**71**] above.
2. Further education has the meaning given by s. 41 (*a*) of the Education Act 1944 and in Scotland has the meaning given by s. 145 (21) of the Education (Scotland) Act 1962.
3. SDA, s. 28. Note too the general exception as to "sport": SDA, s. 44, [**21**] above.

Benefits etc. Outside Great Britain

[**76**] It is not unlawful for any responsible body for an educational establishment to discriminate in respect of benefits,[2] facilities or services to be provided outside Great Britain[3] *except* as regards travel on a ship registered at a port of registry in Great Britain[4] *or* benefits, facilities or services provided on a ship so registered.[5]

NOTES
1. See [**71**] above.
2. E.g. School travel outings abroad. Benefits to include any benefits which it is in the power of the responsible body to have provided by a third party: SDA, s. 50 (1).
3. Great Britain includes such of the territorial waters of the United Kingdom as are adjacent to Great Britain: SDA, s. 82 (1).
4. See [**37**], n. 2.
5. SDA, s. 36 (5).

Single-Sex Boarding Accommodation

[**77**] It is not unlawful for co-educational schools with boarding accommodation for one sex only (disregarding any pupils of the opposite sex whose numbers are comparatively small) to discriminate in admissions of boarders or the provision of boarding facilities.[1]

NOTE
1. SDA, s. 26 (2). Responsible bodies for such schools which wish to alter their admissions arrangements so as to become fully co-educational may apply for a transitional exemption order authorising discriminatory admissions during the period specified in the Order SDA: s. 27 (1). For procedure and effect see [**70**], n. 6. "School" has the meaning given by s. 114 (1) of the Education Act 1944, and in Scotland has the meaning given by s. 145 (2) of the Education (Scotland) Act 1962: SDA, s. 82 (1). Note that [**77**] applies to schools only, whereas [**74**] applies to all educational establishments. Note too the general exception as to "communal accommodation" (SDA, s. 46, [**22**] above) which applies *inter alia*, to establishments (including schools) which provide boarding accommodation for both sexes. King's College School, Cambridge are admitting day girls in September 1976 but they will not be choristers. The duties and work of choristers make it essential that they should be boarders: *The Guardian*, 2nd March, 1976.

CHAPTER SIX

DISCRIMINATION IN THE PROVISION OF GOODS, FACILITIES AND SERVICES, AND THE DISPOSAL AND MANAGEMENT OF PREMISES

INTRODUCTION

[**78**] The SDA makes unlawful discrimination in the provision of goods, facilities or services, and in the disposal and management of premises on the grounds of sex or by way of victimisation. References in this chapter to discrimination are references to discrimination on either of these grounds save where it is otherwise stated. The main exceptions are where the facilities, or services are to be provided at establishments for persons requiring special care, supervision or attention or at places used for religious purposes; where decency and privacy demand; where voluntary bodies restrict their membership and the benefits of membership to persons of one sex; where political parties make special provision for one sex in their constitution or organisation; where the facility consists of accommodation in small premises. There are also exceptions where the premises to be disposed of or managed are small premises; or where a voluntary body restricts disposal or user of its premises to one sex. The scope of this part of the SDA too is limited essentially to Great Britain. Individuals can enforce its provisions in the courts.

DISCRIMINATION IN THE PROVISION OF GOODS, FACILITIES AND SERVICES

[**79**] Subject to general[1] and particular[2] exceptions it is unlawful for any person concerned with the provision (whether for payment or free of charge) of goods, facilities[3] or services[4] to the public or a section of the public[5] to discriminate *either* by refusing or deliberately omitting to provide them[6] *or* by refusing or deliberately omitting to provide them of like quality,[7] in the like manner and on the like terms as he normally provides them.[8]

NOTES
1. See Chapter 3.
2. See [**82**], [**83**], [**84**] and [**85**] below.
3. The opportunity to be considered for membership of a club is not included among the "facilities" provided by the club: *Race Relations Board* v. *Charter*, [1972] 1 Q.B. 545 at 555, 560; [1972] 1 All E.R. 556 at 559. Foster parents taking children from a local authority are

49

concerned with facilities. *Applin* v. *Race Relations Board*, [1974] 2 All E.R. 73. And see "Boys' Lib! It beats the junk shop sex ban": *Evening Standard*, 9th June, 1976.

4. Does this include benefits etc. which it is his power to have provided by a third party? See [**73**], n. 4 above.

5. The words "the public or a section of the public" are words of limitation. The word "public" is used in contrast to "private". *Charter* v. *Race Relations Board*, [1973] 1 W.L.R. 512 at 515, 516, 524, 527, 529, 531 and 532. A members' club is not within the scope of the Act if it has rules which provide for a genuine selection of persons to be members on grounds of their acceptability and the rules are in practice complied with, *ibid*. 516, 525, 529, 534. Nor are guests and associates of such a club a "section of the public". *Dockers Labour Club & Institute, Ltd.* v. *Race Relations Board*, [1974] 3 All E.R. 592. Foster parents to whom children are allocated by a local authority are concerned with the provision of facilities to a "section of the public", i.e. to the children in care of the local authority, coming haphazard from the public at large: *Applin*, v. *Race Relations Board* above.

6. SDA, s. 29 (1) (*a*). In *Morris* v. *Duke Cohan & Co.* (1975), 119 Sol. Jo. 826, Caulfield, J., said that when a husband and wife are both clients of the same solicitor "the solicitor should not have taken instructions from the wife when the husband was available, for a sensible wife did not normally make major decisions". A solicitor who acted in accordance with that dictum would be in clear breach of the SDA!

7. Walker, p. 137 points out that "in all the earlier references to facilities and service there is no mention of quality, and to that extent it would appear that the general public in their capacity as customers or clients are to be treated better than employees, partners and members of trade unions and other bodies". It is submitted that the distinction is not a material one in practical terms.

8. SDA, s. 29 (1) (*b*). It is suggested "There must be no special deference, no ostentatious holding open of doors, or so it would seem": Bennion, p. 40. Perhaps the *de minimis* doctrine would apply. British rail are planning to remove from their season tickets the letter W which identifies them as the property of a woman. The purpose is to stop unlawful transfer: *Daily Telegraph*, 19th January, 1976. This is arguably the provision of a service "in a different manner", but again might not the *de minimis* rule apply?

Note: a person with a particular skill which is commonly exercised in a different way depending on the sex of the customer (e.g. a man's tailor or a woman's hairdresser) who normally exercises it for one sex only can insist that he exercises it for a member of the other sex in accordance with his normal practice or if he reasonably considers it impracticable to do that, can refuse or deliberately omit to exercise it: SDA, s. 29 (3). In other words a barber can say to a lady customer "Short back and sides or get out". The matter may be complicated by the development of unisex styles in clothing and hairdressing.

SPECIFIC EXAMPLES OF GOODS, FACILITIES AND SERVICES

[80] Specific examples (which are *not* exclusive) of the facilities, or services in respect of which it is unlawful to discriminate[1] are: (a) access to and use of any place which members of the public or a section of the public are permitted to enter;[2] (b) accommodation in a hotel, boarding house or other similar establishment;[3] (c) facilities by way of banking or insurance or for granting loans, credit or finance;[4] (d) facilities for education;[5] (e) facilities for entertainment, recreation or refreshment;[6] (f) facilities for transport or travel;[7] (g) the service of any profession[8] or trade or any local or other public authority.

NOTES

1. SDA, s. 29 (2); and see [**79**] above.

2. Members of the public can be admitted to a private place for this purpose, see *Race Relations Board* v. *Bradmore Working Men's Club* (1970), *The Times*, 10th April: Birmingham County Court. (Private club hired out hall for a party to employees of telephone exchange; tickets were sold to employees who were permitted to bring relatives and friends; refusal of admission to employee and friends on the ground of colour held to be unlawful.) Cf. *Sewell* v. *Taylor* (1859), 5 C.B.N.S. 160 (public auction in private house and garden); *Glynn* v. *Simmonds*, [1952] 2 All E.R. at p. 48, D.C., *per* Lord Goddard (meaning of "place of public resort" under the Vagrancy Act 1824, s. 4); *Russell* v. *Thompson* (1953), N.I. at p. 56, C.A. *per* Lord Macdermott, C.J. (general meaning of "place to which the public have or are permitted to have access" under Northern Irish legislation).

3. At common law innkeepers are under a duty to serve all customers without arbitrary discrimination: see Halsbury's Laws, 3rd Edition, Vol. 21, para. 938. El Vino's, the Fleet Street wine bar, refuses to serve unescorted women, and women who stand at the bar. This is unlawful discrimination, which was challenged on the first day the SDA came into force: *The Times*, 31st December, 1975.

4. See insurance exception, [27] above. Also it is not unlawful to discriminate in respect of facilities by way of banking or insurance for grants, loans, credit or finance when they are for a purpose to be carried out outside Great Britain or in connection with risks wholly or mainly arising outside Great Britain: SDA, s. 36 (1) (*b*).

5. Education includes any form of training or instruction: SDA, s. 82 (1). This provision applies to commercial language courses, colleges offering correspondence courses, the Inns of Court.

6. See note 3 above.

7. At common law common carriers are under a duty to serve all customers without arbitrary discrimination. See Halsbury's Laws, 4th Edn., Vol. 5, paras. 301 *et seq*.

8. "Profession" includes any vocation or occupation. Trade includes any business: SDA, s. 82 (1).

TERRITORIAL AMBIT OF PROVISIONS DEALING WITH GOODS, FACILITIES OR SERVICES

[81] With certain exceptions it is not unlawful to discriminate in the provision of goods, facilities or services outside Great Britain.[1] The exceptions are: (i) facilities for travel outside Great Britain;[2] (ii) goods, facilities (including facilities for travel outside Great Britain) services on or in relation to any ship registered at a port of registry in Great Britain[3] *or* any aircraft or hovercraft registered in the United Kingdom and operated by a person who has his principal place of business or is ordinarily resident in Great Britain[4] *or* any ship, aircraft or hovercraft belonging to or possessed by the Government of the United Kingdom,[5] even where the ship, aircraft or hovercraft is outside Great Britain.[6]

Note: It will not be unlawful under the SDA to discriminate in or in the air spaces over a country outside Great Britain or in the air space over its territorial waters for the purposes of complying with the laws of that country.[7]

NOTES

1. SDA, s. 36 (1) (*a*). "Great Britain" includes such of the territorial waters of the United Kingdom as are adjacent to Great Britain: SDA, s. 82 (1).

2. SDA, s. 36 (2) where the discrimination occurs inside Great Britain or on a ship, aircraft or hovercraft (see nn. 3–6 below). This means that the SDA covers, e.g., the activities of travel agents who provide foreign package tours.

3. SDA, s. 36 (3) (*a*); see [37], n. 2.

4. SDA, s. 36 (3) (*b*); see [37], n. 2.

5. SDA, s. 36 (3) (*c*).

6. SDA, s. 36 (3).

7. SDA, s. 36 (4).

EXCEPTIONS

Establishments for Persons Requiring Special Care, Supervision or Attention

[82] It is not unlawful to restrict facilities or services to one sex where they are provided at, or at part of, an establishment for persons requiring

special care, supervision or attention, such as a hospital or a reception centre provided by the Supplementary Benefits Commission.[1]

NOTE
1. SDA, s. 35 (1) (*a*).   Another example would be a voluntary reception centre provided by the Salvation Army.

Places Used for Religious Purposes

[83] It is not unlawful to restrict facilities or services to one sex where they are provided at a place which is used (whether permanently or for the time being) for the purposes of an organised religion;[1] and such restriction is required so as to comply with the doctrines of that religion or avoid offending the religious sensibilities of a significant number of its followers.[2]

NOTES
1. See [66], n. 1.
2. SDA, s. 35 (1) (*b*).

Decency and Privacy

[84] It is not unlawful to restrict facilities or services *either* where they are provided for, or likely to be used by, two or more persons at the same time, and the nature of the facilities or services is such, or the users are such, that male users are likely to suffer serious embarrassment at the presence of a woman (or vice versa),[1] *or* if the users are likely to be undressed and a male user might reasonably object to a female user (or vice versa),[2] *or* where physical contact between the user of the facilities or services and another person is likely and the other person (if a man) might reasonably object if the user were a woman (or vice versa).[3]

NOTES
1. SDA, s. 35 (1) (*c*) (i), e.g. homosexual group therapy.   British Railways intend (in reversal of an earlier decision): *The Times*, 28th January, 1976) to keep ladies-only waiting rooms on stations and ladies-only carriages on trains on the basis that this provision applies to these facilities.   It would appear that this is stretching the sense of the provision save in cases, possibly, where a ladies' room has a toilet annexed to it.   Maybe, however, British Railways can pray in aid SDA, s. 51; [28] above.   Walker, p. 135 states that "what is noticeable is that neither here nor in s. 7 [i.e. GOQ] is there any exception relating to the sale of ladies' underwear, or of sanitary appliances to either sex, to be carried out by a member of the same sex as the buyer".   It is submitted, however, that it is lawful to employ someone of a particular sex to serve others of the same sex underwear etc., see [43], n. 4 above.   Nor could a male customer complain that he was being sold underwear by a male rather than a female assistant unless he argued (which is in the real world unlikely anyway) that the goods were being provided to him "in a different manner".
2. SDA, s. 35 (1) (*c*) (ii), e.g., cubicles and dressing rooms for changing clothes in shops, sport grounds, swimming pools, Turkish baths, hospitals or clinics.   But saunas are often advertised with illustrations of nude couples enjoying them together.
3. SDA, s. 35 (2).   Note that it is the other person (e.g., the provider of the service) and *not* the user who is entitled to make the objection.

Political Parties

[85] It is not unlawful for a political party to discriminate by the special provision for persons of one sex[1] only in the constitution, organisation or administration, or by anything done to give effect to such a provision.[2]

NOTES
1. A political party is within the ambit of this exception if it has as its main (or one of its main) objects the promotion of parliamentary candidatures for the United Kingdom Parliament or is an affiliate of *or* has as an affiliate *or* has similar formal links with such a political party: SDA, s. 33 (1). But what if there were devolution and separate assemblies for Scotland and Wales?
2. SDA, s. 33 (2) and (3). The Women's Section of the National Executive Committee of the Labour Party is among the groups saved from extinction.

DISCRIMINATION IN THE DISPOSAL OF PREMISES

[86] Subject to general[1] and particular[2] exceptions it is unlawful for a person who has power to dispose[3] of premises[4] in Great Britain[5] to discriminate *either* in the terms on which he offers those premises;[6] *or* by refusing an application for those premises;[7] *or* in his treatment of people in relation to any list of persons in need of premises of that description.[8]

NOTES
1. See Chapter 3 above.
2. See [87], [89], [91] and [92] below.
3. Power to dispose in relation to premises includes granting a right to occupy the premises: SDA, s. 82 (1). To have power to dispose of premises it is not necessary that those premises should have been completed: *R.R.B.* v. *Geo. H. Haigh and Co., Ltd.* (1969), 119 New Law J. 858.
4. Premises, it is submitted, includes any house, flat or office. *Quaere* whether it includes land: Bindman, p. 8. In the *R.R.A.*, s. 5, the reference is to "land" not "premises".
5. Great Britain includes such of the territorial waters of the United Kingdom as are adjacent to Great Britain: SDA, s. 82 (1).
6. SDA, s. 30 (1) (*a*); e.g. by charging more, or by imposing special conditions of tenancy.
7. SDA, s. 30 (1) (*b*).
8. SDA, s. 30 (1) (*c*). In *Ealing London Borough Council* v. *Race Relations Board*, [1972] A.C. 342, H.L., it was conceded that a list of persons in need of accommodation includes a local authority housing list. Such people as estate agents who fail to provide lists of premises available would fall within s. 29 as failing to provide facilities and services rather than within s. 30 (1) (*c*): *R.R.B.* v. *London Accommodation Bureau* (Rep. of R.R.B., 1973, p. 44).

Exception: For An Occupant

[87] It is not unlawful for a person who owns an estate or interest[1] in the premises[2] and wholly occupies[3] them to discriminate in any of the said ways unless he uses the services of an estate agent[4] for the purposes of the disposal[5] of the premises or published or causes to be published an advertisement[6] in connection with the disposal.[7]

NOTES
1. Is a licence an interest in premises? See Megarry and Wade, The Law of Real Property (4th Edn.), pp. 776ff, and see for premises [86], n. 4 above.
2. I.e., in Great Britain, see [86], n. 5 above.
3. It is submitted that this means, in this context, himself lives in.
4. "Estate agent" means a person who by way of profession or trade, provides services for the purpose of finding premises for persons seeking to acquire them or assisting in the disposal of premises: SDA, s. 82 (1).
5. See [86], n. 3 above.
6. "Advertisement" includes every form of advertisement, whether to the public or not, and whether in a newspaper or other publication, by television or radio, by display of notices, signs, labels, show cards or goods, by distribution of samples, circulars, catalogues, price lists or other material, by exhibition of pictures, models or films, or in any other way: SDA, s. 82 (1).
7. SDA, s. 30 (3). The advertisement too will be unlawful, and the publisher of it separately liable: SDA, s. 38 (1). Walker, p. 147 says: "It is not so clear why the exception

should apply to any owner-occupier disposing of a freehold or leasehold house or flat with vacant possession on the completion of the sale, as it undoubtedly does, nor why the exception should only be available if an estate agent is not used and the premises are not advertised." It is submitted that the intention is to preserve the licence to discriminate in a purely private transaction. He also says, p. 148, that this subsection "is an attempt to permit discrimination by owner-occupiers of boarding houses and private hotels, since they are the principal people who can be said to 'wholly occupy' premises if they have let them in the past. A boarder or lodger is, in law, a mere licensee, and the landlady (or landlord) does not part with possession of their room or, technically, cease to occupy it but has the right to enter at will". It is submitted that the courts will not look at the matter technically and will construe occupation as meaning "living in".

DISCRIMINATION IN THE MANAGEMENT OF PREMISES

[88] Subject to general[1] and particular[2] exceptions it is unlawful for a person who manages premises[3] to discriminate against an occupant of the premises *either* in the way in which he affords access to any benefits or facilities,[4] *or* by refusing or deliberately omitting to afford access to them,[4] *or* by evicting the occupant or by subjecting the occupant to any other detriment.[5]

NOTES
1. See Chapter 3 above.
2. See [89], [91] and [92] below.
3. See [86], n. 4. There appears to be no territorial restriction; *cf.* [86], n. 5. Nor need the manager own or have power to dispose of the premises. An agent who merely collects rent does not manage.
4. SDA, s. 30 (2) (*a*); e.g., use of a bath at a certain time. Benefits etc. include benefits which it is in the power of the manager to have provided by a third party: SDA, s. 50 (1); see [39], n. 4.
5. SDA, s. 30 (2) (*b*).

Exception: Small Dwellings

[89] It is not unlawful for a person to discriminate in the provision or disposal[1] of premises if that person or a near relative[2] of his resides,[3] and intends to continue to reside, on the premises and shares accommodation (other than storage accommodation or means of access) with other persons residing there who are not members of his household;[4] and when the premises are small premises.[5]

NOTES
1. Disposal includes granting a right to occupy the premises, SDA, s. 82 (1).
2. A near relative is a wife or husband, a parent or child, or grandparent or grandchild, or a brother or sister (whether of full blood or by affinity) and "child" includes an illegitimate child and the wife or husband of an illegitimate child: SDA, s. 82 (5). It is not clear why the definition is extended to the wife or husband of an illegitimate child, but *not* the wife or husband of a legitimate child.
3. Resides: In *Stoke-on-Trent Borough Council* v. *Cheshire C.C.*, [1915] 3 K.B. 699, Lord Reading, C.J., said at pp. 704–5 that a place where a person resides is a place "where a person lives, that is where he has his bed, and where he dwells". In *Bailey* v. *Bryant* (1858), 1 E. & E. 340, it was held that a person may be resident in a flat although absent from time to time, and that a person may be resident in more than one place at a time.
4. Household, it is submitted, comprises family and resident domestic staff.
5. SDA, s. 32 (1). Small premises: see [90] below. If a person lets off a room in a house as a bed-sitter, and the occupant does not share any of the rest of the accommodation in the house other than hall, stairs, landing, and use of a storeroom then it will be unlawful for him to discriminate.

Definition of Small Dwelling

[**90**] Small premises are, in the case of premises comprising residential accommodation for one or more households[1] in addition to the accommodation occupied by the provider of that accommodation or a near relative of his ("the relevant occupier")[2], those where there is not normally residential accommodation for more than two such households *and* only the relevant occupier and members of his household reside in the accommodation occupied by him.[3] Small premises are in any other case premises where there is not normally residential accommodation for more than six persons, ignoring the relevant occupier and any members of his household.[4]

NOTES

1. See [**89**], n. 4 above. The accommodation can be let under a separate letting or similar agreement, SDA, s. 32 (2) (*a*).
2. See [**89**], n. 2 above.
3. SDA, s. 32 (2) (*a*). In other words if a person can tolerate strangers in his own accommodation, he cannot discriminate in respect of the remainder of the premises!
4. SDA, s. 32 (2) (*b*).

EXCEPTIONS

Voluntary Bodies

[**91**] It is not unlawful for a body whose activities are carried on otherwise than for profit and which was not set up by statute[1] *either* to restrict its membership,[2] or the benefits, facilities or services it provides to its members,[3] to one sex (disregarding any minor exception), notwithstanding that membership of the body is open to the public, or to a section of the public. Nor is it unlawful for any such body, whose main object is to confer benefits on one sex (disregarding any exceptional or relatively insignificant provision to persons of the other sex) to have a provision embodying that object or to do anything necessary to give effect to that object.[4]

NOTES

1. SDA, s. 34 (1); e.g., learned societies or the YMCA or single-sex housing associations. In 1962 the author successfully moved that women be admitted as full members of the Oxford Union Society. Had the society chosen, however, to remain an all-male club, this provision would have enabled it to do so.
2. SDA, s. 34 (2) (*a*).
3. SDA, s. 34 (2) (*b*). Does this include benefits which it is in the power of the body to have provided by a third party? See [**73**], n. 4.
4. SDA, s. 34 (3), (4); e.g. Women's Institutes.

Avoidance of Overlap

[**92**] Discrimination which is unlawful (or would be unlawful if it were not for an exception) under the employment or education provisions is not unlawful as well, or alternatively, under the provisions dealing with the provision of goods, facilities or services or the disposal or management of premises.[1]

NOTE

1. SDA, s. 35 (3). The reason is that discrimination under the provisions dealing with

the provision of goods etc. is redressable in the county courts: see Chapter 10 below; discrimination in employment is redressable in Industrial Tribunals: see Chapter 8 below; and the relevant discrimination in education is redressable by the Secretary of State. The provisions in respect of which overlap is avoided are set out in the following table:

Provision creating illegality	*Exception*
Part II	Sections 6 (3), 7 (1) (*b*), 15 (4), 10 and 20 Schedule 4, paragraphs 1 and 2
Section 22 or 23	Sections 26, 27 and 28 Schedule 4, paragraph 3

DISCRIMINATION IN GRANTING CONSENT FOR ASSIGNMENT OR SUBLETTING

[93] Where a tenant requires the consent or licence of the landlord to assign or sub-let premises[1] in Great Britain[2] comprised in a tenancy[3] to another person, it is unlawful for the landlord to discriminate against the prospective assignee or sub-lessee by withholding the consent or licence.[4]

NOTES

1. See **[86]**, n. 4 above.
2. See **[86]**, n. 5 above.
3. Tenancy means a tenancy created by a lease or sub-lease, by an agreement for a lease or sub-lease or by a tenancy agreement or in pursuance of any enactment: SDA, s. 31 (3). The provision applies to tenancies created before the passing of the SDA, s. 31 (4); *cf*. Landlord and Tenant Act 1927, s. 19 which requires that consent should not be unreasonably withheld in a case where there is a covenant in a lease requiring consent for assignment; and see *Mills* v. *Canon Brewery Co., Ltd.*, [1920] Ch. 38.
4. SDA, s. 31 (1). This provision is also subject to a small-dwellings exception: SDA, s. 31 (2); see **[89]** above.

APPLICATION TO THE CROWN

[94] This part of the SDA applies to acts done by or for the purposes of a Minister of the Crown[1] or government department, or on behalf of the Crown by statutory body[2] or person holding a statutory office[3] in the same way as it applies to acts done by a private person.[4] Admissions to the Army Cadet Force, Air Training Corps, Sea Cadet Corps or Combined Cadet Force, or any other Cadet Training Corps for the time being administered by the Ministry of Defence are outside the scope of the SDA.[5]

NOTES

1. See **[60]**, n. 3.
2. Statutory body means a body set up by or in pursuance of an enactment: SDA, s. 85 (10).
3. Statutory office means an office set up by or in pursuance of an enactment: SDA, s. 85 (10).
4. SDA, s. 85 (1).
5. SDA, s. 85 (5).

CHAPTER SEVEN

ENFORCEMENT: THE GENERAL SCHEME

INTRODUCTION

[95] The SDA (unlike the RRA 1968) provides the right of individual access to legal remedies. The Equal Opportunities Commission (the Commission) has a strategic role and also enforces those parts of the law that have a primarily public dimension. Certain qualifying bodies also have a role to screen applicants for qualifications to see whether or not they have been guilty of discrimination.[1] Contravention of the SDA invites only such sanctions, civil or criminal, as the SDA itself provides.[2]

NOTES
1. See for these duties of qualifying bodies [51] above.
2. SDA, s. 62 (1). The prerogative orders are not considered to be sanctions for this purpose: SDA, s. 62 (2). It is made clear that a person (whether the alleged victim or the alleged perpetrator of discrimination) cannot go to the High Court and seek a declaration that an act of discrimination has/has not been committed: *cf.* on the RRA, *Ealing London Borough Council* v. *Race Relations Board*, [1972] A.C. 342, H.L. See also RRB, Sch. 4, para. 1.

INDIVIDUAL ACCESS

[96] An individual who has been the object of unlawful discrimination (other than discriminatory practices or advertising or pressure or instructions to discriminate) has a right to institute proceedings in an industrial tribunal (if the complaint is in the fields of employment)[1] *or* in a county or sheriff court (if the complaint is in the field of education or of provision of goods, facilities or services or of the disposal or management of premises).[2] However, an individual may not institute proceedings in respect of discrimination by responsible bodies for educational establishments in the public sector unless he or she has notified the complaint to the appropriate Education Minister and the Minister has had time to consider the matter.[3] Moreover, the general duty not to discriminate in the public sector of education is enforceable in England only by the Secretary of State.[4]

NOTES
1. SDA, s. 63.
2. SDA, s. 66.
3. SDA, s. 66 (5); see [109], n. 3 below.
4. SDA, s. 25 (2), (3). The Minister also has like provision in respect of other discrimination in the public sector (*ibid.*).

ENFORCEMENT: A GENERAL ILLUSTRATION

Type of discrimination	Right to seek enforcement	Power to enforce	Remedies	Relevant sections of SDA
Discrimination by employers and related bodies (SDA, Pt. II)	Individual	Industrial tribunal	Declaration: compensation: recommendation of action	63 (Jurisdiction of industrial tribunals): 64 (Conciliation in employment cases): 65 (Remedies): 76(1), (5), (6) (Time limits)
Discrimination by bodies in charge of educational establishments (SDA, ss. 22, 24)	Individual or Minister	Public sector: Minister or county court / Private sector: county court	Ministerial order or declaration, damages or injunction	25(2) (Power of Minister): 66(5) (Duty to refer to Minister): 66 (Claims in county court): 76(2), (5), (6) (Time limits)
Other discrimination by local education authorities (SDA, s. 23)	Individual or Minister	Minister or county court	Ministerial order or declaration, damages or injunction	25(2) (Power of Minister): 66(5) (Duty to refer to Minister): 66 (Claims in county court): 76(2), (5), (6) (Time limits)
Breach of general duty in public sector of education (SDA, s. 25)	Individual or Minister	Minister	Ministerial order	25(2) (Power of Minister)
Discrimination in the provision of goods, facilities or services, or in the disposal or management of premises (SDA, ss. 29, 30)	Individual	County court	Declaration, damages or injunction	66 (Claims in county court): 76(2), (5), (6) (Time limits)
Discriminatory practices (SDA, s. 37)	Commission	Commission	Non-discrimination notice	67–70 (Non-discrimination notices)
Discriminatory advertisements (SDA, s. 38)	Commission	Industrial tribunal (employment) County court (other fields)	Declaration	72 (Enforcement of ss. 38–40): 73 (Preliminary action in employment cases): 76(3) (Time limits)
Instructions to discriminate (SDA, s. 39)	Commission	ditto	ditto	ditto
Pressure to discriminate (SDA, s. 40)	Commission	ditto	ditto	ditto
Persistent discrimination (SDA, s.71)	Commission	County court	Injunction	71 (Persistent discrimination): 73 (Preliminary action in employment cases)

THE ROLE OF THE EQUAL OPPORTUNITIES COMMISSION (EOC OR COMMISSION)

[97] The EOC has four main functions in relation to enforcement of the SDA:

(i) the EOC can conduct formal investigations into any matter, and where it finds that there has been discrimination, can issue a non-discrimination notice;[1]

(ii) the EOC can institute legal proceedings in respect of persistent discrimination;[2]

(iii) the EOC has the sole power to institute proceedings in respect of discriminatory practices and advertisements, and instructions and pressure to discriminate;[3]

(iv) the EOC can in appropriate circumstances assist individual litigants.[4]

NOTES

1. SDA, ss. 57ff, 67ff; see [131] and [138] below.
2. SDA, s. 71; see [144] below.
3. SDA, s. 73; see [146] and [147] below.
4. SDA, s. 75; see [148] below.

HELP FOR PERSONS SUFFERING DISCRIMINATION: HOW TO OBTAIN INFORMATION

[98] The Secretary of State for Home Affairs has prescribed forms by which a person who believes himself the object of discrimination may question a potential respondent on any relevant matter relating to his treatment (and by which a respondent may reply) so as to help that person to decide whether to institute proceedings and, if he does so, to formulate and present his case in the most effective manner.[1] Subject to the normal rules relating to the admissibility of evidence[2] and provided that the questions are put within the prescribed time[3] the questions and answers (whether on the prescribed forms or not) are admissible in evidence in court or tribunal proceedings under the SDA.[4] If it appears to the court or tribunal that the respondent deliberately, and without reasonable excuse omitted to reply within a reasonable period or that his reply is evasive or equivocal, the court or tribunal may draw any inference from that fact that it considers just and equitable to draw, including an inference that the respondent committed an unlawful act.[5]

NOTES

1. SDA, s. 74 (1). See generally S.I. 1975 No. 2048 for form, manner of service, etc.
2. SDA, s. 74 (5); e.g., rules as to privilege, hearsay, etc.
3. SDA, s. 74 (3) (a).
4. SDA, s. 74 (2) (a).
5. SDA, s. 74 (2) (b). This is a novel procedure which has affinities with discovery or interrogatories (these procedures are, of course, retained: SDA, s. 74 (5)). Experience in operating the RRA showed how difficult it was for the person who believed himself the victim of discrimination to discover whether or not he had a case, and, if so, how strong a one in face of a respondent who simply refused to co-operate with him or with the officers of the Race Relations Board. The new procedures should help to avoid unnecessary litigation as well as assist the complainant. However it falls short of the solution in unfair dismissal cases of shifting the burden of proof (i.e., disproof) to the respondent: TULRA, Sch. 1, Pt. II.

CHAPTER EIGHT

ENFORCEMENT : THE FIELD OF EMPLOYMENT

[99] All complaints about discrimination in the employment field (including acts treated as being unlawful in this field by virtue of the provisions dealing with aiding unlawful acts and vicarious liability) are dealt with by an industrial tribunal (except certain complaints about discrimination in the granting of authorisations or qualifications by qualifying bodies[1]). The remedies are a declaration, compensation, or recommendation of a course of action (with compensation if default is made in complying with it).

Exception

There is no complaint in respect of discrimination by a qualifying body to an industrial tribunal where there is a statutory right of appeal.[1]

NOTE
1. SDA, s. 63 (2); e.g., from the Law Society to the Court of Appeal: or from the General Medical Council to the Privy Council or from the licensing justices to the Crown Court.

TIME LIMIT

[100] An individual may complain to an industrial tribunal within three months of the date of the act complained of[1] but the tribunal may consider a complaint made out of time if it considers it just and equitable in all the circumstances to do so.[2]

Rules For Determination of When Time Runs

(a) Where the unlawful act is the inclusion of a term in a contract the act is treated as extending throughout the duration of the contract.[3]

(b) An act extending over a period is treated as being done at the end of that period.[4]

(c) A deliberate omission is treated as an act done at the time when the person in question decided upon it.[5] In the absence of evidence to the contrary, a person is taken to decide upon an omission *either* when he does an act inconsistent with the doing of the omitted act *or* at the end of the time when he might reasonably have been expected to do the omitted act if he was going to do it.[6]

NOTES

1. SDA, s. 76 (1). Months means calendar months: Interpretation Act 1889, s. 3. In *Radcliffe* v. *Bartholomew*, [1892] 1 Q.B. 161, a prosecution had to be launched within one calendar month "after the cause of complaint shall arise". The act complained of was committed on 30th May and information laid on 30th June. It was held to be in time. *Note* the application must be *received* within three months.

2. SDA, s. 76 (5); *cf. Dedman* v. *British Building and Engineering Application*, [1974] 1 All E.R. 520.

3. SDA, s. 76 (6) (*a*); e.g., a discriminatory clause in a contract of employment as to entitlement to holidays.

4. SDA, s. 76 (6) (*b*); e.g., all male employees are given the benefit of a special training course at some point during their first year, the year elapses and the female employee has not been given the chance of such a course: the 3 months would begin to run at the end of the year. See also *Flynn* v. *Co-op*, I.T. 5408/76.

5. SDA, s. 76 (6) (*c*).

6. SDA, s. 76 (5).

PROCEDURE FOR MAKING A COMPLAINT

[101] A complaint is made by submitting an originating application form in writing to an industrial tribunal.[1] The forms are available from the tribunal offices or any local employment office or job centre of the Employment Service Agency or unemployment benefit office of the Department of Employment.[2]

NOTES

1. I.e., in accordance with the Industrial Tribunals (Labour Relations) Regulations 1974, S.I. 1974 No. 1386. The application does not have to be in any form provided that it contains all the necessary information. *Smith* v. *Automobile Proprietary, Ltd.*, [1973] 2 All E.R. 1105.

2. G.9.2.

CONCILIATION

[102] Where a complaint has been made to an Industrial Tribunal under the SDA, it is the duty of the conciliation officer[1] on receipt of his copy of it to try to settle the dispute without its being determined by the tribunal *either* if he is requested to do so by both parties[2] *or* if he considers that he has a reasonable prospect of success in achieving such a settlement.[3] A conciliation officer can also act before any complaint has been made if he is asked to do so by a potential complainant or respondent.[4] In trying to settle or avoid a dispute a conciliation officer should where appropriate have regard to the desirability of encouraging the use of other procedures available for the settling of grievances.[5] Anything said to a conciliation officer in this context is privileged, unless the person choosing to make his statement chooses to waive the privilege.[6]

NOTES

1. A conciliation officer is a person appointed under para. 26 (1) of Sch. 1 of TULRA: SDA, s. 82 (1). But now see Employment Protection Act 1975, Sch. 18.

2. SDA, s. 64 (1) (*a*).

3. SDA, s. 64 (1) (*b*).

4. SDA, s. 64 (2).

5. SDA, s. 63 (3); e.g., the EOC has power to assist in the procurement of a settlement, SDA, s. 75 (2) (b). The Advisory, Conciliation and Arbitration Service, established under TULRA might also be able to assist.

6. SDA, s. 64 (4); *cf.* RRA 1968, s. 24; TULRA, Sch. 1, Part IV, para. 26 (5). This would not render inadmissible evidence which could have been given if there had been no communication to the officer: *N. & W. Grazebrook, Ltd.* v. *Walters*, [1973] 2 All E.R. 865. *Note* that under the general law relating to privilege in evidence, any document prepared solely for the purpose of communication to a conciliation officer *with a view to achieving a settlement of a dispute* is protected from disclosure. See *Cross on Evidence* (4th Edn.), pp. 261–4.

THE HEARING

[**103**] See S.I. 1974 No. 1386, r. 7 which describes the procedure at the hearing of an industrial tribunal. Such proceedings are relatively informal.

THE BURDEN OF PROOF

[**104**] In a *case of direct discrimination* a complainant must show less favourable treatment on the ground of sex (or marital status, as the case may be). In a *case of indirect discrimination* a complainant must show that the respondent applied a condition or requirement which would be applied equally to a person of the other sex (or an unmarried person of the same sex as the case may be) and which is to his or her detriment because he or she cannot comply with it. It is for the respondent to show that the condition is justifiable irrespective of sex (or marital status as the case may be). In a *case of victimisation* the complainant must show less favourable treatment for the prohibited reasons. It is for the respondent *in all cases* to raise any statutory defences or exceptions. The tribunal will decide all issues (and the case) on the civil test of the balance of probabilities.[1]

NOTE

1. Hewitt, p. 51 says that a complainant has to have enough evidence to "show a possibility [*sic*] of sex discrimination". This must be wrong.

EVIDENCE

[**105**] The ordinary rules of evidence in industrial tribunals apply.[1] *Note*, however, the question and answer procedure.[2]

NOTES

1. SDA, s. 74 (5).
2. See [**98**] above and S.I. 1975 No. 2048.

REMEDIES

[**106**] Where a tribunal finds in favour of a complaint it may award such of the following remedies as it considers just and equitable:

(a) an order declaring the rights of the parties;[1]

(b) an order requiring the respondent to pay to the complainant compensation;[2]

(c) a recommendation that the respondent take within a specified period action which appears to the tribunal to be practicable for the purpose of obviating or reducing the adverse effect on the complainant of the discrimination.[3]

NOTES

1. SDA, s. 65 (1) (a). Although the category of remedies is prefaced with the words "such of the following . . ." it is submitted that in all circumstances a Tribunal would make a declaratory order.

2. SDA, s. 65 (1) (b). The amount of compensation will correspond to the damages which a county or sheriff court could have awarded if the complaint had been one which could have been dealt with by a Court under the SDA: SDA, s. 65 (1) (b). Compensation will include all the ordinary heads of damage *including* compensation for injury to feelings: SDA, s. 66 (4)) *cf.* the position at common law for wrongful dismissal: *Addis* v. *Gramophone Co., Ltd.,* [1909] A.C. 488); £200 awarded for this: I.T. 4767/76/E. The maximum award cannot exceed the amount for the time being specified in para. 20 of Schedule 1 to TULRA 1974, which is at present £5,200: SDA, s. 65 (2). *Note* no compensation will be awarded in a case of indirect discrimination if the respondent proves that the indirect discrimination did not involve an intention to treat the complainant less favourably on the ground of sex or marital status: SDA, s. 66 (3). However, if the respondent did have such an intention, the case would be one of *direct* discrimination and the provision may therefore prove to be otiose.

3. SDA, s. 65 (1) (c); e.g., to give a job to a complainant whose application was rejected on grounds of sex, if the job is still available; or to consider the complainant for a further vacancy. If without reasonable justification the respondent fails to comply with a recommendation the tribunal may increase the compensation previously awarded or award compensation if none was previously awarded subject to the TULRA maximum (see above, n. 2; SDA, s. 65 (3)). It is submitted that the increase is subject to the limits referred to above; *contra,* Walker, p. 42. See now Employment Protection Act 1975, s. 75.

Note the Employment Protection Act 1975, s. 77, provides that if compensation is awarded by a tribunal both under the SDA and under TULRA then account shall be taken of compensation awarded under either, and the £5,200 limit is applied.

APPEALS

[**107**] There is right of appeal on a point of law against a decision of an industrial tribunal.[1]

NOTE

1. Employment Protection Act 1975, s. 88.

CHAPTER NINE

ENFORCEMENT: FIELD OF EDUCATION

INTRODUCTION

[**108**] Complaints about discrimination by responsible bodies for educational establishments are dealt with by a county court, or in Scotland, a sheriff court. The remedies are declarations, injunctions or damages. Complaints about discrimination in the public sector of education must first be referred to the appropriate Minister. The general duty in the public sector of education is enforceable by the appropriate Minister only. Complaints about employment in education are dealt with by an Industrial Tribunal.

TIME LIMIT

[**109**] Proceedings in respect of a claim by an individual that she has been discriminated against by a responsible body for an educational establishment in *the public sector*[1] or by a local education authority carrying out its functions under the Education Acts 1944–75 (or an education authority carrying out its functions under the Education (Scotland) Acts 1939–74)[2] are not to be instituted unless the claimant has given notice of the claim to the appropriate Minister[3] and *either* the Minister has by notice informed the claimant that he does not require further time to consider the matter *or* the period of two months has elapsed since the claimant gave notice to the Minister.[4] Proceedings must be instituted thereafter before the end of the period of six months beginning with the date when this restriction on their institution ceased to operate[5] subject to the court's discretion to consider a claim out of time if, in all the circumstances of the case, it considers it just and equitable to do so.[6]

NOTES
1. See asterisked establishments in [**71**].
2. See SDA, s. 22.
3. Complaints in respect of bodies in England should be sent to the Permanent Under-Secretary of State, Department of Education and Science, Elizabeth House, York Road, London, SE1 7PH. Complaints concerning bodies in Wales should be sent to The Secretary for Welsh Education, Welsh Education Office, 31 Cathedral Road, Cardiff, CF1 9UJ. Complaints concerning bodies in Scotland should be sent to The Secretary, Scottish Education Department, New St. Andrew's House, St. James Centre, Edinburgh, EH1 3SX; G.4.16.
4. SDA, s. 66 (5). If after two months the claimant has not heard from the Minister, he may issue proceedings in the normal way below. If the Minister has not reached a conclusion in the two months he will, without prejudice to the claimant's right to bring proceedings, continue his consideration of the claim and notify his decision as soon as possible: G.4.17.

5. SDA, s. 76 (2) (*b*). Unfortunately the SDA does not prescribe any time limit within which notice of the claim must be given to the Minister. Therefore a claimant might notify the Minister of a claim several years after the act of discrimination complained of took place, and time would only start to run against him from that date. This would seem to be a drafting error. However see para. 4 of Sch. 4 of RRB which proposes an amendment.

6. SDA, s. 76 (5).

PROCEDURE FOR MAKING A COMPLAINT

[110] See [120] below.

THE HEARING

[111] See [121] below.

THE BURDEN OF PROOF

[112] See [104] above.

EVIDENCE

[113] The ordinary rules of evidence in county and sheriff courts apply.[1] *Note* however the question and answer procedure.[2]

NOTES
1. SDA, s. 74 (5).
2. See [98] above and S.I. 1975 No. 2048.

REMEDIES

[114] See [124] below.

APPEALS

[115] See [125] below.

CONCURRENT JURISDICTION OF THE MINISTER

[116] Where there is a claim by an individual that she has been discriminated against by a responsible body for an educational establishment *in the public sector*[1] or by a local education authority carrying out its functions under the Education Acts 1944–75 (or an education authority carrying out its functions under the Education (Scotland) Acts 1939–74),[2] the appropriate Minister can exercise his appropriate powers under the Education Act 1944[3] (or the Education (Scotland) Act 1962 as the case may be).

NOTES
1. I.e., asterisked establishments under para. [71].
2. I.e., under SDA, s. 23.
3. SDA, s. 25 (2). If he is satisfied that such a body or authority has discriminated in the exercise of a power of the performance of a duty he may give such directions as to the

exercise of the power or the performance of the duty as appear to him to be expedient. Education Act 1944, s. 68. If he is satisfied that such a body or authority has failed to discharge a duty and thereby discriminated he may make an order declaring that the body or authority are in default in respect of that duty and give such directions to enforce its execution as appear to him to be expedient: Education Act 1944, s. 99. These directions are enforceable by mandamus, see Halsbury's Laws (3rd Edn.), Vol. 13, para. 1212. For like powers of the Secretary of State for Scotland, see Education (Scotland) Act 1962, s. 71: SDA, s. 25 (3). He also has power to cause a local enquiry to be held into the matter pursuant to his powers under the Education (Scotland) Act 1963, s. 68: SDA, s. 25 (5).

ENFORCEMENT OF THE GENERAL DUTY IN THE PUBLIC SECTOR OF EDUCATION

[117] The general duty in the public sector of education is enforceable by the appropriate Minister *only* in the exercise of his appropriate powers under the Education Act 1944 (or the Education (Scotland) Act 1962 as the case may be).[1]

NOTE
    1. SDA, s. 25 (2) see [116], n. 3 above.

CHAPTER TEN

ENFORCEMENT : THE PROVISION OF GOODS, FACILITIES AND SERVICES, THE DISPOSAL OR MANAGEMENT OF PREMISES

INTRODUCTION

[**118**] All complaints about discrimination in the field of provision of goods, facilities and services or the disposal or management of premises (including acts treated as being unlawful by virtue of the provisions dealing with aiding unlawful acts and vicarious liability) are dealt with by a county court, or, in Scotland, a sheriff court. The remedies are declarations, injunctions or damages.

TIME LIMIT

[**119**] An individual may complain to a county court or sheriff court within six months of the date of the Act complained of[1] but the court may consider a complaint made out of time if it considers it just and equitable in all the circumstances to do so.[2]

Rules for Determination of when Time Runs

See [**100**] above.

1. SDA, s. 76 (2).
2. SDA, s. 76(5); *cf. Dedman* v. *British Building and Engineering Appliances, Ltd.*, [1974] 1 All E.R. 520.

PROCEDURES FOR MAKING A CLAIM

[**120**] This is in accordance with the usual procedure in a county court[1] or sheriff court.

NOTE

1. See County Court Practice; County Courts Acts 1959, ss. 78 *et seq.*

THE HEARING

[**121**] This is in accordance with the usual procedure in a county court[1] or sheriff court.[2] *Note* that it is open to the judge in county court pro-

ceedings[3] or, in Scotland, the sheriff, on his own initiative *or* on the application of a party to the proceedings,[4] to appoint assessors to assist in the determination of a case.[5]

1. See County Court Practice. A county court or sheriff court has jurisdiction to entertain proceedings with respect to an act done on a ship, aircraft or hovercraft outside its district including such an act done outside Great Britain: SDA, s. 66 (8). Walker, p. 116, says, "This extension of the territorial jurisdiction of the county court is not limited to British ships, nor to the United Kingdom territorial waters, and must be by far the widest territorial jurisdiction the United Kingdom has ever claimed for any county court". This appears to ignore the restrictive effect of SDA, s. 36.

2. See Wallace, *Practice of the Sheriff Court of Scotland*.

3. SDA, s. 66 (6).

4. SDA, s. 66 (7).

5. E.g., to determine in a case of alleged indirect discrimination whether a particular requirement or condition is justifiable may require expert knowledge of the field in question; *cf.* RRA 1968, ss. 19 (7) and 20 (7), where a judge or sheriff must be assisted by two persons having "special knowledge and experience of problems connected with race and community relations". There is no equivalent provision in the SDA.

THE BURDEN OF PROOF

[**122**] See [**104**] above.

EVIDENCE

[**123**] See [**113**] above.

REMEDIES

[**124**] Where a county court or sheriff court finds in favour of a complainant it may award a declaration, an injunction (or order) or damages.[1] It also has power in appropriate cases to remove or modify a discriminatory term in a contract.[2]

NOTES

1. SDA, s. 66 (2). The actual statutory phrase is "all such remedies as . . . would be obtainable in the High Court or Court of Sessions". There is therefore no limit on the amount of damages recoverable which will apparently be quantified as in a case of tort or (in Scotland) reparation for breach of statutory duty: SDA, s. 66 (1). The reference to remedies "obtainable in the High Court", must, it is submitted, be construed as extending the county court jurisdiction in respect of the quantum of damages. Walker, p. 41, is doubtful. Damages will include damages for injury to feelings: SDA, s. 66 (4). Such damages are not recoverable under the RRA 1968; see Lester and Bindman, pp. 336–7. *Note* that no compensation will be awarded in a case of indirect discrimination if the defendant proves that the indirect discrimination did not involve an intention to treat the complainant less favourably on the ground of sex or marital status: SDA, s. 66 (3); see further [**106**], n. 2.

2. SDA, s. 77 (5).

APPEALS

[**125**] There is a right of appeal to the Court of Appeal against a decision of a county court, and to the Court of Session against a decision of a sheriff court. This is in accordance with the usual procedure in such courts.[1]

NOTE

1. See County Court Practice. County Courts Acts 1959, s. 108 *et seq.*

CHAPTER ELEVEN

THE EQUAL OPPORTUNITIES COMMISSION : GENERAL

INTRODUCTION

[**126**] The Commission is a public body established under the SDA with a general duty to promote equality of opportunity between the sexes, as well as its particular functions in enforcement.[1] It is also, in the language of the guide, "a principal source of information and advice for the general public about the Acts" (i.e. SDA and EPA).[2]

1. See [**97**] above. It must, in carrying out its duties which affect individual persons, act fairly: *Selvarajan* v. *R.R.B.*, [1976] 1 All E.R. 12.
2. G.1.2. The address of the Commission is: Equal Opportunities Commission, Overseas House, Quay Street, Manchester, M3 3HN.

STATUS

[**127**] The Equal Opportunities Commission[1] shall consist of at least eight but not more than fifteen individuals,[2] appointed by the Secretary of State on a full-time or part-time basis.[3] The Secretary of State shall appoint one of the Commissioners to be Chairman[4] of the Commission,[5] and either one or two of the Commissioners (as he thinks fit) to be deputy chairman or deputy chairmen of the Commission.[6]

NOTES
1. As to its incorporation and status see SDA, Schedule 3, paras. 1, 2. As to the tenure of office of the Commissioners see *ibid.*, para. 3. As to the tenure of office of the chairman and deputy chairman, see *ibid.*, para. 4 as to the remuneration of commissioners see *ibid.*, paras. 5, 6. As to application of certain of the foregoing provisions to additional commissioners see *ibid.*, para. 7. As to staff of the Commission, and the terms and conditions of their appointment see *ibid.*, paras. 8, 9 and 10. As to the proceedings and business of the Commission see *ibid.*, paras. 11, 12 and 13. *Note* especially that the validity of any proceedings of the Commission shall not be affected by any vacancy among the members of the Commission or by any defect in the appointment of any Commissioner or additional Commissioner, see *ibid.*, para. 12. As to the finances of the Commission, see *ibid.*, paras. 14 and 15. All Commissioners and Additional Commissioners are disqualified from membership of the House of Commons, see *ibid.*, para. 16.
2. The Secretary of State can amend this number by order.
3. SDA, s. 53 (1).
4. Not Chairperson!
5. SDA, s. 53 (2) (*a*). The first is Miss Betty Lockwood.
6. SDA, s. 53 (2) (*b*). The first is Lady Elspeth Howe.

THE DUTIES OF THE COMMISSION

[**128**] The duties of the Commission are to work towards the elimination

of discrimination;[1] to promote equality of opportunity between men and women generally;[2] and to keep under review the working of the SDA and the EPA and, when they are required by the Secretary of State or otherwise think it necessary, draw up and submit to the Secretary of State proposals for amending them.[3] In particular the Commission has the duty to keep under review those provisions in health and safety legislation[4] which require different treatment for men and women[5] *and*, if required by the Secretary of State, to make within the time specified by him a report to him[6] on a matter specified by him which is connected with their general duties[7] and concerns such provisions.[8] Further, whenever the Commission thinks it necessary, they shall draw up and submit to the Secretary of State proposals for amending such provisions.[9]

NOTES

1. SDA, s. 53 (1) (*a*).

2. SDA, s. 53 (1) (*b*).

3. SDA, s. 53 (1) (*c*). The Commission may undertake or assist (financially or otherwise) the undertaking by other persons of any research, and any educational activities, which appear to the Commission necessary or expedient in connection with their general duties, SDA, s. 54 (1). The Commission may also make charges for educational or other facilities or services made available by them: SDA, s. 54 (2).

4. SDA, s. 53 (4). The provisions are those defined as "relevant statutory provisions" by s. 53 of the Health and Safety at Work etc. Act 1974, Halsbury's Statutes, Vol. 44, p. 1139.

5. SDA, s. 55 (1) (*a*).

6. The Secretary of State shall cause the report to be published SDA, s. 55 (1).

7. I.e. the duties to work towards the elimination of discrimination and to promote equality of opportunity between men and women generally.

8. SDA, s. 55 (1) (*b*).

9. SDA, s. 55 (2). The Commission shall carry out their duties in relation to these provisions in consultation with the Health and Safety Commission: SDA, s. 55 (3).

The ambitions of the EOC have been extensively chronicled in public speeches by and interviews with its members. These include promoting a social climate where men work fewer hours at their job and share responsibilities in the home (*The Times*, 18th November, 1975); eliminating advertisements which stereotype women as e.g., users of detergents, *ibid.*, and school textbooks which stress differences between the roles of the sexes e.g., showing boys climbing trees and girls helping their mothers with the washing up as in the "Janet and John" series: *Daily Telegraph*, 21st January, 1976. It can also investigate areas of sex discrimination not covered by the Act, e.g., pensions, tax laws, the functions of the Supplementary Benefits Commission, the age of retirement and Factory Act prohibitions on women doing night work: *The Times*, 18th November, 1975, and the immigration rules made by the Secretary of State for Home Affairs under the Immigration Act 1971 in respect of which complaint has already been made to it by the United Kingdom Immigrant Service (UKIAS): *Daily Telegraph*, 23rd January, 1976. It will give advice generally, e.g., on how to word advertisements so that they may comply with the SDA: *Daily Telegraph*, 25th January, 1976. It will also monitor cases to discover where discriminatory practices are most apparent: *The Times*, 20th December, 1975.

In the first three weeks, the inquiries section dealt with more than 4,500 requests for information. But there were very few *actual* complaints. The Commission says people are still unsure about their rights under the new equality laws. It expects more calls for action after this information has become more widely known. Of the 4,559 inquiries, 1,972 were requests for information and 2,587 were requests for commission leaflets on how the equality laws affect housing, employment, education and other areas. A quarter of these inquiries concerned employment and the Equal Pay Act 1970 with both employers and employees asking for advice: *New Society*, 29th January, 1976.

ANNUAL REPORT OF THE COMMISSION

[129] As soon as practicable after the end of each calendar year the Commission shall make to the Secretary of State a report on their activities during the year.¹ This annual report shall include a general survey of developments, during the period to which it relates, in respect of matters falling within the scope of the Commission's duties.² The Secretary of State shall lay a copy of every annual report before each House of Parliament, and shall cause the report to be published.³

NOTES

1. SDA, s. 56 (1). A similar obligation was imposed on the Race Relations Board: RRA, s. 14 (7).
2 SDA, s. 56 (2).
3 SDA, s. 56 (3).

THE FUNCTIONS OF THE COMMISSION

[130] See [97] above.

FORMAL INVESTIGATIONS

[131] The Commission may, if they think fit, and shall if required by the Secretary of State, conduct a formal investigation for any purpose connected with the carrying out of their formal duties,¹ subject to compliance with the required procedure.² For the purposes of such an investigation the Commission may with the approval of the Secretary of State appoint, on a full-time or part-time basis, one or more individuals as additional Commissioners,³ and may nominate one or more Commissioners, with or without one or more additional commissioners to conduct such investigations on its behalf, and may delegate any of their functions in relation to the investigation to the persons so nominated.⁴

NOTES

1. The Commission's formal duties are set out in SDA, s. 53; i.e., to work towards the elimination of discrimination, to promote equality of opportunity between men and women and to keep under review the working of the SDA and the EPA.
2. SDA, s. 58 (1). The procedure is set out in SDA, s. 58 (2) and (3), namely that the terms of reference have been drawn up; and that the relevant notice has been given. And see the Sex Discrimination (Formal Investigations) Regulations 1975, S.I. 1975, No. 1993.
3. SDA, s. 57 (2).
4. SDA, s. 57 (3). It is not sufficient to nominate only additional commissioners. This restriction means that formal investigations will be carried out only infrequently.

TERMS OF REFERENCE AND NOTICE OF FORMAL INVESTIGATION

[132] Before the Commission embark on a formal investigation it must have terms of reference¹ to be drawn up by the Commission or, if the Commission is required by the Secretary of State to conduct the investigation, by the Secretary of State after consulting the Commission.² The Commission must give general notice³ of the holding of the investigation unless the terms of reference confine it to activities of persons named in them, in which case the Commission shall give such notice to those persons in the prescribed manner.⁴

The terms of reference may be revised from time to time by the Commission *or*, if the Commission is required by the Secretary of State to conduct the investigation, by the Secretary of State after consulting the Commission. In that case notice of the holding of the revised investigation must be given in the same way.[5]

NOTES
1. SDA, s. 58 (1) and (2). There is no guide in the SDA as to what matters should be included in the terms of reference.
2. SDA, s. 58 (2).
3. General notice means a notice published at a time and in a manner appearing to the publisher suitable for securing that the notice is seen within a reasonable time by persons likely to be affected by it: SDA, s. 82 (1).
4. SDA, s. 58 (3). Notice means notice in writing: SDA, s. 82 (1) and see S.I. 1975 No. 1993.
5. SDA, s. 58 (4).

POWER TO OBTAIN INFORMATION

[133] The Commission has power for the purpose of a formal investigation to require a person to furnish oral or written information or to produce documents.[1] The power is exercised by service of a notice;[2] but, with one exception, such a notice may be served only where *either* its service is authorised by the Secretary of State *or* the terms of reference of the investigation state that the Commission believe that a person named in them[3] may have broken, or be breaking, a provision of the SDA or EPA, and confine the investigation to such breaches.[4] *The exception* is where the terms of reference of the investigation state that the purpose is to monitor compliance with the requirements of a non-discrimination notice, and notice is given of the holding of the investigation within five years of the non-discrimination notice becoming final.[5] In this case the notice may be served without the consent of the Secretary of State;[6] but must be served within five years of the non-discrimination notice becoming final *or* within two years of notice being given of the holding of the investigation, whichever is the later.[7] In no circumstances can a notice require a person to give any information or produce any documents, which he could not be compelled to give or produce in civil proceedings before the High Court or Court of Session.[8] Furthermore a notice cannot require his attendance at any place unless the necessary expenses to and from that place have been paid or tendered to him.[9]

NOTES
1. SDA, s. 59 (1).
2. The notice must be in writing; SDA, s. 82 (1) and see S.I. 1975 No. 1993.
3. *Not* necessarily the person from whom information is required.
4. SDA, s. 59 (2).
5. SDA, s. 69 (1). For non-discrimination notices see [138].
6. *Ibid.*
7. SDA, s. 69 (2).
8. SDA, s. 59 (3) (*a*). See generally Cross on Evidence; 4th Edition, Ch. XI.
9. SDA, s. 59 (3) (*b*).

SANCTION FOR NON-COMPLIANCE WITH NOTICE REQUIRING INFORMATION
[134] If a person fails to comply with a notice requiring information which has been served on him, or the Commission has reasonable cause to believe that he intends not to comply with it, the Commission may apply

to a county court for an order requiring him to comply with it or with such directions for the like purposes as may be contained in the order.[1]

NOTE
1. SDA, s. 59 (4). The procedure is by originating application under C.C.R. 1936, O.6, r. 4 (1). The penalty for failure to comply with such an order without reasonable exercise is the same as that for neglecting a witness summons (£50: County Courts Act 1959, s. 84). For Scotland see SDA, s. 59 (5).

OFFENCE IN CONNECTION WITH NOTICE OR ORDER REQUIRING INFORMATION

[135] It is an offence punishable on summary conviction with a maximum fine of £400 *either* wilfully to alter, suppress, conceal or destroy a document which has been required by such a notice or order,[1] *or* in complying with such a notice or order, knowingly or recklessly to make any statement which is false in a material particular.[2]

NOTES
1. SDA, s. 59 (6) (*a*).
2. SDA, s. 59 (6) (*b*). Proceedings for such an offence may be instituted against any person at any place at which he has an office or other place of business *or* against an individual at any place where he resides, or at which he is for the time being as well as at any place permitted under the ordinary criminal jurisdiction; SDA, s. 59 (7).

REPORTS ON AND RECOMMENDATIONS PURSUANT TO FORMAL INVESTIGATION

[136] The Commission shall prepare a report of their findings in any formal investigation conducted by them.[1] If the formal investigation is one required by the Secretary of State the Commission shall deliver the report to the Secretary of State and the Secretary of State shall cause the report to be published, and, unless required by the Secretary of State, the Commission shall not publish the report.[2] If the formal investigation is not one required by the Secretary of State, the Commission shall either publish the report, or make it available for inspection.[3] In preparing any report for publication or for inspection the Commission shall exclude, so far as is consistent with their duties and the object of the report, any matter which relates to the private affairs of any individual or business interests of any person where the publication of that matter might, in the opinion of the Commission, prejudicially affect the individual or person.[4]

If in the light of any of their findings in a formal investigation, whether during the course or after its conclusion, it appears to the Commission necessary or expedient to do so they may *either* make recommendations to any person for changes in his or her policies or procedures, with a view to promoting equality or opportunity between men and women who are affected by any of that person's activities, *or* as to any other matters,[5] *or* make recommendations to the Secretary of State, whether for changes in the law[6] or otherwise.[7]

NOTES
1. SDA, s. 60 (2).
2. SDA, s. 60 (3).
3. SDA, s. 60 (4). Where a report is made available for inspection, anyone may, on

payment of a fee if necessary, inspect the report and/or a copy of it during ordinary office hours and/or take copies of all or any part of the report and/or to obtain from the Commission a certified copy of the report: SDA, s. 60 (5) (*b*). The Commission shall give general notice of the place or places where, and the times when, reports or copies may be so obtained: SDA, s. 60 (7). Copies will be available at the Commission's offices: G.11.8.

4. SDA, s. 61 (3); and see **[137]** below.

5. This gives the Commission the widest possible scope for making recommendations.

6. *Cf.* SDA, ss. 53 (1) (*c*) and 55 (2) for other powers of the Commission to recommend changes in the law.

7. SDA, s. 60 (1); and see n. 1 above.

RESTRICTIONS ON THE DISCLOSURE OF INFORMATION GIVEN IN CONNECTION WITH A FORMAL INVESTIGATION

[137] No information given to the Commission by any person ("the informant") in connection with a formal investigation shall be disclosed by the Commission, or by any person who is or has been a Commissioner, Additional Commissioner or employee of the Commission except on the order of any court,[1] *or* with the informant's consent[2] *or*, in the form of a summary or other general statement published by the Commission which does not identify the informant or any other person to whom the information relates[3] *or* in a report of the investigation published or made available for inspection by the Commission[4] *or* to the Commissioners, Additional Commissioners or employees of the Commission, *or*, so far as may be necessary for the proper performance of the functions of the Commission, to other persons[5] *or* for the purpose of any civil proceedings under the SDA to which the Commission are a party,[6] or any criminal proceedings.[7] It is an offence punishable on summary conviction with a maximum fine of £400 to disclose such information other than in the above circumstances.[8]

NOTES

1. SDA, s. 61 (1) (*a*).

2. SDA, s. 61 (1) (*b*).

3. SDA, s. 61 (1) (*c*).

4. SDA, s. 61 (1) (*d*). *Note:* a restriction on what may be included in this report is imposed by the SDA, s. 61 (3).

5. SDA, s. 61 (1) (*e*).

6. SDA, s. 61 (1) (*f*); i.e., where the Commission are entitled to bring proceedings under SDA, ss. 71, 72 and 73 in relation to an application for an injunction for enforcement of SDA, s. 38 (discriminatory advertisements), s. 39 (instructions to discriminate) or s. 40 (pressure to discriminate).

7. *Ibid.* For criminal proceedings under the SDA, see Appendix 2, *post.*

8. SDA, s. 61 (2).

NON-DISCRIMINATION NOTICES

[138] If, in the course of formal investigation,[1] the Commission becomes satisfied that a person is breaking or has broken the SDA or the EPA[2] the Commission may, subject to one precondition[3] and with one exception,[4] serve on him a non-discrimination notice.[5] The non-discrimination notice may require the person (i) not to commit any such breach of the SDA or of the EPA,[6] (ii) where compliance with this requirement involves changes in any of his practices or other arrangements, to inform the Commission that he has effected those changes and what those changes are,[7] (iii) to take such steps as may reasonably be required by the notice for the purpose of affording that information to other persons concerned,[8] (iv) to furnish the Commission with such other information as may reasonably be required by the notice in order to verify that the notice has been complied with.[9] The notice may specify the manner and form in which any information is to be furnished to the Commission, and the time at which it is to be so furnished, such time not being later than five years after the notice has become final.[10]

NOTES
1. See [131] above.
2. Whether or not proceedings have been brought in respect of the breach: SDA, s. 67 (1).
3. See [139] below.
4. See [139] below.
5. See S.I. 1975 No. 1993.
6. SDA, s. 67 (2) (a).
7. SDA, s. 67 (2) (b) (i).
8. SDA, s. 67 (2) (b) (ii).
9. SDA, s. 67 (3).
10. SDA, s. 67 (4). A non-discrimination notice becomes final when an appeal against the notice is dismissed, withdrawn or abandoned, or when the time for appealing expires without an appeal having been brought; for this purpose an appeal against a non-discrimination notice is to be taken as dismissed if the court or tribunal has submitted a new requirement in place of the one against which the appeal was made: SDA, s. 82 (4).

Precondition and Exception.

[139] The Commission shall not serve a non-discrimination notice on any person unless they have *first* given him notice that they are minded to do so with specific reasons[1] *and* have offered him an opportunity of making oral and/or written representations within a specified period of not less than 28 days;[2] *and* taken account of any representations so made by him.[3]

The Commission may not serve a non-discrimination notice in respect of any discrimination by responsible bodies for educational establishments and/or local education or education authorities (i.e. those acts of discrimination in respect of which the appropriate Minister has special statutory powers).[4] Instead, if the Commission become aware of any such discrimination, they must notify the Minister.[5]

NOTES
1. SDA, s. 67 (5) (a).
2. SDA, s. 67 (5) (b).
3. SDA, s. 67 (5) (c).
4. See Chapter 9, particularly [116], above.
5. SDA, s. 67 (6).

APPEALS AGAINST NON-DISCRIMINATION NOTICES

[140] A person may appeal against any requirement of a non-discrimination notice not later than six weeks after its service on him.[1] Where the requirement relates to the employment provisions of the SDA (or the

EPA) he must appeal to an Industrial Tribunal.[2] Otherwise he must appeal to the county or sheriff court.[3] Where the tribunal or court considers that a requirement appealed against is unreasonable *either* because it is based on an incorrect finding of fact or for any other reason[4] it shall quash the requirement[5] and may substitute an alternative requirement.[6] A non-discrimination notice becomes final when an appeal against it is dismissed, withdrawn or abandoned, or when the time for appealing expires without an appeal having been brought: and an appeal shall be treated as being dismissed if, notwithstanding that a requirement of the notice is quashed, an alternative requirement is substituted in its place.[7]

NOTES
1. SDA, s. 68 (1).
2. SDA, s. 68 (1) (a). For procedure on appeal see S.I. 1975 No. 2098.
3. SDA, s. 68 (1) (b). For jurisdiction see C.C.R. Ord. 46, r. 4 (a).
4. E.g. because it is oppressive.
5. SDA, s. 68 (2).
6. SDA, s. 68 (3). There is no right of appeal against a substituted requirement: SDA, s. 68 (4).
7. SDA, s. 82 (4).

INVESTIGATION INTO COMPLIANCE WITH NON-DISCRIMINATION NOTICE

[**141**] The formal investigations which the Commission is empowered to carry out include formal investigations into whether there has been compliance with the requirements of a non-discrimination notice.[1] If the terms of reference of the formal investigation state that this is its purpose[2] and notice is given of the holding of the investigation[3] within five years of the non-discrimination notice becoming final,[4] the Commission may service notices requiring information[5] without the consent of the Secretary of State.[6] The power to serve such notices lasts for two years after notice of the investigation is given *or* five years after the non-discrimination notice becomes final,[4] whichever is the later.[7]

NOTES
1. SDA, s. 57 (1).
2. SDA, s. 69 (1) (a) which continues ". . . but section 59 (2) (b) does not apply". It is not clear whether this means that, as a matter of law, s. 59 (2) (b) must not apply, or that the terms of reference must state that it does not apply. It would appear to mean the latter.
3. SDA, s. 58 (3); presumably the terms of reference will in this case confine the investigation to the activities of the person on whom the non-discrimination notice was served. Therefore such person only need be notified.
4. A non-discrimination notice becomes final when an appeal against the notice is dismissed, withdrawn or abandoned, *or* when the time for appealing expires without an appeal having been brought; and an appeal against a non-discrimination notice shall be taken to be dismissed if, notwithstanding, that a requirement of the notice is quashed on appeal, a direction is given in respect of it under SDA, s. 68 (3) (i.e. it is modified): SDA, s. 82 (4).
5. See SDA. s. 59 (1).
6. SDA, s. 69 (1). Such consent is normally required under SDA, s. 59 (1) (a).
7. SDA, s. 69 (2).

REGISTER OF NON-DISCRIMINATION NOTICES

[142] The Commission shall establish and maintain a register of non-discrimination notices[1] which have become final.[2] Anyone may, on payment of such fee as may be determined by the Commission (if necessary) inspect the register and/or a copy during ordinary office hours and/or take copies of any entry in the report and/or copy and/or obtain from the Commission a certified copy of any entry in it.[3] The Commission shall give general notice of the place or places where, and the times when, the register or a copy of it may be inspected.[4]

NOTES
  1. See [138].
  2. SDA, s. 70 (1). See [138], n. 10.
  3. SDA, s. 70 (2) and (3).
  4. SDA, s. 70 (4). The register is kept at the Commission's offices: G.11.15.

ROLE OF NON-DISCRIMINATION NOTICE

[143] When a non-discrimination notice is final, it renders the person on whom it is served liable for a period of five years to proceedings by the Commission for an injunction (or in Scotland an order) should the Commission consider that, unless restrained he is likely to commit certain breaches of the SDA[1] (or of the EPA).

NOTE
  1. This applies to all breaches including discriminatory practices *except* the provisions dealing with discriminatory advertisements and pressure and instructions to discriminate.

ENFORCEMENT: PERSISTENT DISCRIMINATION

[144] Where it appears to the Commission that a person on whom *either* a non-discrimination notice has been served *or* a court *or* tribunal finding has been made (and the notice or finding became final within the previous five years[1]) is likely unless restrained to commit certain breaches of the SDA[2] (or of the EPA), the Commission *may* seek an injunction (or in Scotland an order) from the county (or sheriff) court, and the court, if satisfied that the application is well founded, *may* grant the injunction or order in the terms applied for or more limited terms.[3]

NOTES
  1. A non-discrimination notice or a finding by a court or tribunal becomes final when an appeal against the notice or finding is dismissed, withdrawn or abandoned or the time for appealing expires without an appeal having been brought; and an appeal against a non-discrimination notice shall be taken to be dismissed if, notwithstanding that a requirement of the notice is quashed on appeal, a direction is given in respect of it under SDA, s. 68 (3): SDA, s. 82 (4).
  2. This applies to all breaches including discriminatory practices *except* of the provisions dealing with discriminatory advertisements and pressure and instructions to discriminate.
  3. SDA, s. 71 (1). The Commission have a discretion whether to seek, and the court whether to grant an injunction or order. Note also that an injunction or order cannot be granted against the Crown: SDA, s. 85 (8), (9).
  Note Where the Commission institutes proceedings in respect of persistent discrimination, it may not allege in those proceedings that the person sued has been in breach of any of the *employment* provisions of the SDA (or of the EPA) unless there is a finding by an industrial tribunal to this effect, and the finding has become final: SDA, s. 71 (2). There

is thus provision made for obtaining such a finding *before* the application is made to the court: SDA, s. 73 (1) and see [145]. Such a finding by an Industrial Tribunal must be treated as conclusive by the court: SDA, s. 73 (3). There is no need for similar preliminary action when the discrimination is in a *non-employment field*.

PRELIMINARY ACTION IN EMPLOYMENT CASES

[145] The Commission has power (with a view to instituting proceedings for persistent discrimination)[1] to make a complaint to an Industrial Tribunal[2] that a person has been in breach of the employment provision of the SDA (or of the EPA), and the Tribunal may make a finding to that effect, and, if they think it just and equitable to do so, a declaratory order[3] *or* a recommendation[4] *but not* an order for compensation.[5]

NOTES
    1. See above, [144].
    2. There is a time limit of six months: SDA, s. 76 (4); and see SDA, ss. 76 (5) and [100].
    3. See [106], n. 1 above.
    4. See [106], n. 3 above.
    5. SDA, s. 73 (1). See *note* to [144], n. 3 above. Walker p. 187 says "a complaint under section 73 is specifically envisaged by the section to be a prelude to . . . an application to an industrial tribunal for a declaratory order or recommendation". It is submitted that this is not so. It is itself such an application; and is a prelude to an application for an injunction under SDA, s. 71 (1) or SDA, s. 72 (4) only.

ENFORCEMENT: DISCRIMINATORY PRACTICES

[146] The Commission has exclusive power to deal with discriminatory practices. Subject to the usual procedures: (*a*) it can carry out formal investigations;[1] (*b*) it can issue non-discrimination notices;[2] (*c*) it can apply for an injunction or order for persistent discrimination.[3]

NOTES
    1. See [131].
    2. See [138].
    3. See [144].

Discriminatory Advertisements, Pressures and Instructions to Discriminate

[147] The Commission has exclusive power to deal with discriminatory advertisements, and pressure and instructions to discriminate. Subject to the usual procedures: (*a*) it can carry out formal investigations;[1] (*b*) it can issue non-discrimination notices;[2] (*c*) it can institute legal proceedings[3] for a decision whether an alleged breach has occurred[4] (to an industrial tribunal where the breach relates to the employment provisions,[5] to a county or Sheriff court in any other case[6])[7] *or* (if it appears to the Commission that the person will be in breach again[8]) for an injunction (or in Scotland, an order) from the county (or, in Scotland, sheriff) court; and the court, if satisfied that the application is well founded *may* grant the injunction or order in the terms applied for *or* more limited terms.[9]

NOTES
    1. See [131].
    2. See [138].

3. There is a time limit of six months beginning when the act to which the proceedings relate was done: SDA, s. 76 (3). See SDA, s. 76 (5) and [**100**].
4. SDA, s. 72 (2) (*a*).
5. SDA, s. 72 (3) (*a*).
6. SDA, s. 72 (3) (*b*).
7. SDA, s. 72 (4). Since an Industrial Tribunal cannot grant an injunction, the Commission cannot apply for *both* when the breach relates to employment.
8. SDA, s. 72 (4). There is no need to show that the person concerned was originally the subject of a non-discrimination notice or a court or Tribunal finding; *cf.* SDA, s. 71 (1), [**144**] above but see n. 9.
9. SDA, s. 72 (4). The provisions described in [**145**] apply to applications for an injunction or order in respect of discriminatory advertisements, and pressure and instructions to discriminate: SDA, s. 73 (1). *Note* when the Commission institutes such proceedings it may not allege in them that the person concerned has already broken any of the employment provisions of the SDA (or the EPA) unless there is, or the Commission has obtained a finding to that effect (see [**145**]) and the finding has become final: SDA, s. 72 (5). In some cases therefore, the Commission will have to seek a finding from an Industrial Tribunal that a person has broken one of the employment provisions of the SDA, wait for that finding to become final, and then institute proceedings for an injunction, all within six months! Now, however, see RRB, Sch. 4, where this is remedied.

ASSISTANCE BY THE COMMISSION

[**148**] The Commission has power to assist an individual who is an actual or prospective complainant.[1] However, the Commission may assist an individual only where the case raises a question of principle[2] or where it is unreasonable, having regard to the complexity of the case or the position of the individual *vis à vis* the other party, to expect the individual to deal with the case unaided,[3] or where some other special consideration applies.[4] In such cases, the assistance which the Commission may give includes giving advice,[5] seeking a settlement,[6] and arranging for legal advice[7] or assistance or representation at any stage in any proceedings.[8] Legal costs incurred by the Commission will be charged to any costs payable to the complainant.[9]

NOTES

1. The Commission must act fairly in considering an application for assistance: *Selvajaran v. Race Relations Board*, [1976] 1 All E.R. 12.
2. SDA, s. 75 (1) (*c*).
3. SDA, s. 75 (1) (*b*). The legal advice and assistance scheme under the Legal Aid Act 1974 is available to assist persons who consider they have been discriminated against under the SDA; but the legal aid scheme will only be available for proceedings in county or Sheriff courts (and *not* in Industrial Tribunals).
4. SDA, s. 74 (1). *Quaere* whether the fact that a claim has attracted public attention may be such a special consideration.
5. SDA, s. 75 (2) (*a*).
6. SDA, s. 75 (2) (*b*).
7. SDA, s. 75 (2) (*c*). Presumably counsel will still have to be instructed by a solicitor.
8. SDA, s. 75 (2) (*d*), subject to the proviso that the assistance should not affect the law and practice regulating who may appear in, conduct, defend and address the court in any proceedings: *ibid*. It does not appear that the Commission is entitled to pay a successful respondent's costs.
9. SDA, s. 75 (3); but not to damages. The charge is subject to any charge under the Legal Aid Act 1974 and is subject to any provision in that Act for payment of any sum into the legal aid fund: SDA, s. 75 (4).

CHAPTER TWELVE

COMMENCEMENT AND EXTENT

[**149**] The SDA, Part I (discrimination to which the Act applies) and Part VIII (supplemental) came into force on the passing of the Act on 12th November, 1975. The SDA, Part II (discrimination in the employment field), Part III (discrimination in other fields), Part IV (other unlawful acts), Part V (general exceptions from Parts II to IV), Part VI (Equal Opportunities Commission) and Part VII (enforcement) came into force on 29th December, 1975[1] with exceptions relating to ss. 8 (6),[2] 22,[3] 25,[3] 38 (1),[4] 53,[5] 56,[6] 83 (1)[2] and 86.[7] The SDA is not retrospective.[8] The SDA applies to Great Britain but does not extend to Northern Ireland.[9]

NOTES

1. SDA, s. 83 (2), S.I. 1975 No. 1845, art. 3.
2. *Ibid.*, art. 4. Amendments to EPA relating to terms of an occupational pension scheme are not to come into force until 6th April, 1978.
3. *Ibid.*, art. 5. It is not unlawful to discriminate in respect of offers of or applications for admission to the relevant educational establishments made before 1st September, 1976.
4. S.I. 1975 No. 2112. It was not unlawful to publish or cause to be published an advertisement which would otherwise be in breach of s. 38 before 1st April, 1976 if the advertisement was printed for publication or made up for such printing before 15th April, 1975.
5. S.I. 1975 No. 1845, art. 6, SDA, s. 53 (establishment and duties of EOC) came into force on 12th November, 1975.
6. *Ibid.*, art. 7. SDA, s. 56 (annual reports of the EOC) came into force on 1st January, 1976.
7. *Ibid.*, art. 8. This relates to SDA, s. 86 (government appointments outside s. 6).
8. *Amies* v. *I.L.E.A.*, I.T. 1637/76/D; *Flynn* v. *Co-op*, I.T. 5408/76.
9. SDA, s. 87 (2), save that members of the EOC are disqualified from membership of the Northern Ireland Assembly: Sch. 3, para. 16.

APPENDIX I

THE RELATIONSHIP OF THE SEX DISCRIMINATION ACT AND THE EQUAL PAY ACT

1. The EPA is in part amended by the SDA (SDA, s. 8 (1)) and set out as amended in Schedule 1 of the SDA (SDA, s. 8 (6)). It provides for a person of one sex, employed by the same employer as a person of another sex (or by an associated employer), to be treated not less favourably than that other person in respect of pay *and* other terms of his or her contract of employment, where he or she is employed on work which is of the same or a broadly similar nature *or* on work which has been given an equal value to that other person's work under a job evaluation scheme. The main device used is an equality clause. If a woman is employed on such work on terms less favourable than those accorded to men on such work, her contract of employment is deemed to be modified by an equality clause so as to be no longer less favourable, e.g. so that she is given the right to the same pay as such men. Breaches of her contract as modified give rise, *inter alia*, to remedies by way of arrears of remuneration or damages, and, in appropriate cases, to an injunction. (The EPA also has provisions dealing with the removal of discrimination from collective agreements, employers' pay structures and statutory wages orders.) It is therefore much narrower in scope than the SDA as (the ancillary provisions apart): (i) it is concerned only with the field of employment; whereas the SDA is concerned, in addition, with the fields of education, and of the provision of goods, facilities and services and the disposal or management of premises; (ii) it is concerned only with discrimination on grounds of sex, whereas the SDA (in the field of employment) is concerned with discrimination on grounds of marital status and (generally) with discrimination by way of victimisation; (iii) it is concerned only with contractual terms and conditions of employment: whereas the SDA is concerned with discrimination outside as well as inside the ambit of the contract of employment; (iv) it is concerned only with comparisons between persons of different sexes where the employer employs persons of both sexes

Note: By reason of para. 4 of the Sex Discrimination Act 1975 (Commencement) Order 1975 (S.I. 1845) s. 8 (6) SDA, in so far as it amends s. 6 of the EPA to provide that an equality clause shall operate in relation to terms relating to membership of an occupational pension scheme, it shall not come into force until 6th April, 1978. The appendix to S.I. 1845 makes a transitional amendment to EPA, s. 6, until that date.

on work which is the same or of a broadly similar nature *or* on work which has been given an equal value under a job evaluation scheme: whereas the SDA invites a comparison between the treatment accorded to a person of one sex with the treatment accorded (*or* that *would* be accorded) to a person of another sex.

2. The provisions of the SDA ensure that there is no overlap between a person's rights under the SDA and a person's rights under the EPA in the field of employment—the only area of potential overlap. Complaints about discrimination covered by the EPA are dealt with under the EPA; complaints about discrimination outside the scope of the EPA and within the scope of the SDA are dealt with under the SDA. However, while a respondent cannot as a matter of law be liable under both acts, as a matter of procedure an applicant does not have to elect under which act to proceed. In the field of employment jurisdiction to give relief for discrimination is vested in Industrial Tribunals. An applicant can make a complaint in the alternative under the SDA and under the EPA when it is not clear which is appropriate, just as an applicant can make a complaint in the alternative under TULRA 1974 and the RPA 1965 when it is not clear whether a dismissal was unfair and/or by reason of redundancy. The Industrial Tribunal, seized of the complaint, can make the appropriate determination under the provisions of the appropriate Act when the evidence is complete.

3. The division of scope of the SDA and the EPA results in the following situation. As regards sex discrimination:

(i) if the less favourable treatment relates to the terms on which an employer offers employment, other than those consisting of the payment of money and the terms would *not* be incorporated in the contract of employment, the SDA (SDA, s. 6 (1) (*b*)) applies; e.g. an employer offers a woman a job but tells her that she will not go on the annual staff outing, although male staff do;

(ii) if the less favourable treatment relates to the terms on which an employer offers employment, consisting of the payment of money, and the terms would *not* be incorporated in the contract of employment, the SDA applies (SDA, s. 6 (1) (*b*)); e.g. an employer offers a woman a job but tells her that she will not get the discretionary Christmas bonus, although male employees do;

(iii) if the less favourable treatment relates to the terms on which an employer offers employment, other than those consisting of the payment of money, and the terms *would* be incorporated in the contract of employment, but would *not* fall to be modified by virtue of an equality clause, the SDA (SDA, s. 6 (1) (*b*)) applies; e.g. an employer offers a woman a job but tells her that she will only have three weeks' annual holiday. The employer employs no men in the same job at the time (so that the EPA cannot apply), but in the past has given men in the same job four weeks' annual holiday;

(iv) if the less favourable treatment relates to the terms on which an employer offers employment other than those consisting of the payment of money, and the terms *would* be incorporated in the contract of employment, and *would* fall to be modified by virtue of an equality clause, the EPA applies (SDA, s. 6 (1) (*b*); EPA, s. 8 (3)); e.g. an employer offers a woman a job but tells her that she will only have three weeks annual holiday. The employer employs men in the same job who have four weeks' annual holiday; accordingly, if the woman accepted the offer, her contract of employment would fall to be modified by virtue of an equality clause to provide for four weeks' annual holiday;

(v) if the less favourable treatment relates to the terms on which an employer offers employment, consisting of the payment of money, and the terms *would* be incorporated in the contract of employment, but would *not* fall to be modified by virtue of an equality clause, there is no remedy (SDA, ss. 6 (1) (*b*) and 6 (5)); e.g. an employer offers a woman a job at £30 per week; the employer employs no men in the same job at the time (so that the EPA cannot apply) but in the past has paid men in the same job £40 per week;

(vi) if the less favourable treatment relates to the terms on which an employer offers employment, consisting of the payment of money, and the terms *would* be incorporated in the contract of employment, and *would* fall to be modified by virtue of an equality clause, the SDA applies (SDA, ss. 6 (1) (*b*), 6 (5) and 8 (3)); e.g. an employer offers a woman a job at £30 per week; the employer employs men in the same job at £40 per week; accordingly, if the woman accepted the offer, her contract of employment would fall to be modified by virtue of an equality clause to provide for payment of £40 per week;

(vii) if the less favourable treatment relates to the provision of benefits, other than those consisting of the payment of money, and the provision of the benefits is *not* regulated by the contract of employment, the SDA (SDA, s. 6 (2) (*a*)) applies; e.g. an employer does not take a woman on the annual staff outing, although all male staff are taken;

(viii) if the less favourable treatment relates to the provision of benefits, consisting of the payment of money, and the provision of the benefits is *not* regulated by the contract of employment, the SDA (SDA, s. 6 (2) (*a*)) applies; e.g. an employer does not pay a woman a discretionary Christmas bonus, although he pays one to all male staff;

(ix) if the less favourable treatment relates to the provision of benefits regulated by the contract of employment other than those consisting of money, but does *not* involve contravention of a term modified by virtue of an equality clause, the SDA (SDA, s. 6 (2) (*a*)) applies; e.g. an employer gives a woman three weeks annual holiday in accordance with the terms of her contract of employment; he employs no men in the same job at the time, but in the past has given men in the same job four week's annual holiday;

(x) if the less favourable treatment consists of the contravention of a term in the contract of employment, concerned with the provision of benefits other than those consisting of money, which *has been* modified by virtue of an equality clause, the EPA applies (SDA, ss. 6 (2) (*a*) and 8 (5)); e.g. the contract of employment given to a woman by an employer provides for three weeks' annual holiday. The employer employs men in the same job who have four weeks' annual holiday; accordingly, the women's contract of employment is modified by virtue of the equality clause to provide for four weeks' annual holiday; nonetheless the employer only allows her three;

(xi) if the less favourable treatment relates to the provision of benefits regulated by the contract of employment consisting of the payment of money, but does *not* involve contravention of a term modified by virtue of an equality clause, there is no remedy (SDA, ss. 6 (2) (a) and 6 (6)); e.g. an employer pays a woman £30 per week in accordance with the terms of her contract of employment; he employs no men in the same job, but in the past has paid men in the same job £40 per week;

(xii) if the less favourable treatment consists of the contravention of a term in the contract of employment, concerned with the provision of benefits consisting of the payment of money, which has been modified by virtue of an equality clause, the EPA applies (SDA, ss. 6 (2) (a) and 8 (5)); e.g. the contract of employment given to a woman by an employer provides for payment of £30 per week; the employer employs men in the same job at £40 per week; accordingly, the woman's contract of employment is modified by virtue of the equality clause to provide for payment of £40 per week; nonetheless the employer pays her only £30 per week;

(xiii) if the less favourable treatment consists of any other form of discrimination against an employee, the SDA (SDA, ss. 6 (1) (a) (c) and 6 (2) (a), (b)) applies.

4. In addition there is *no remedy* for a married person discriminated against on grounds of marital status by an employer as regards *either* the terms on which he *offers* employment, where the terms relate to money (SDA, ss. 6 (1) (b) and 6 (5)) *or* the terms in the contract of employment, where they relate to the payment of money (SDA, ss. 6 (2) (a) and 6 (6)).

APPENDIX II

CRIMINAL LIABILITY UNDER THE SEX DISCRIMINATION ACT

The SDA creates five criminal offences:

(1) It is an offence for an employer knowingly or recklessly to make a statement to an employment agency or a local education authority (or, in Scotland, an education authority) to the effect that it could lawfully discriminate in relation to the provision of its services because the services concerned employment which the employer could lawfully refuse to offer the woman. The offender will be liable on summary conviction to a maximum fine of £400 (SDA, s. 15 (6)).

(2) It is an offence for a person who causes an advertisement to be published knowingly or recklessly to make a statement, which is in a material respect false or misleading, to the publisher of the advertisement to the effect that the publisher could lawfully publish a discriminatory advertisement because the act, which the advertisement might be taken to indicate an intention to do, would not itself be unlawful. The offender will be liable on summary conviction to a maximum fine of £400 (SDA, s. 38 (5)).

(3) It is an offence for a person, who is aided by another person, knowingly or recklessly to make a statement, which is in a material respect false or misleading, to the person by whom he is aided, that the act which he aids would not be unlawful. The offender will be liable on summary conviction to a maximum fine of £400 (SDA, s. 42 (4)).

(4) It is an offence for a person wilfully to alter, suppress, conceal or destroy a document which he has been required by a notice or order to produce for the purposes of a formal investigation by the Commission *or* in complying with such notice or order, knowingly or recklessly to make any statement which is false in a material particular. The offender will be liable on summary conviction to a maximum fine of £400 (SDA, s. 59 (7)).

(5) It is an offence for any Commissioner, additional Commissioner, or employee of the Commission, past or present, to disclose information given to the Commission in connection with a formal investigation, otherwise than in accordance with the provisions of the SDA. The offender will be liable on summary conviction to a maximum fine of £400 (SDA, s. 61 (2)).

APPENDIX III

SOME THOUGHTS ON STATUTORY INTERPRETATION

The approach adopted by the House of Lords to the problems of statutory interpretation of the RRA 1968 suggest that there is no method of statutory interpretation peculiar to the new genus of statutes concerned with discrimination. But it may be of assistance to practitioners concerned with construing ambiguous passages in the SDA to bear in mind the way in which the House of Lords dealt with its direct ancestor.

In *Ealing London Borough Council* v. *Race Relations Board*, [1972] A.C. 342, Lord Simon said (at p. 361): "The courts have five principal avenues of approach to the ascertainment of the legislative intention: (1) examination of the social background, as specifically proved if not within common knowledge, in order to identify the social or juristic defect which is the likely subject of remedy; (2) a conspectus of the entire relevant body of the law for the same purpose; (3) particular regard to the long title of the statute to be interpreted (and, where available, the preamble), in which the general legislative objectives will be stated; (4) scrutiny of the actual words to be interpreted, in the light of the established canons of interpretation; (5) examination of the other provisions of the statute in question (or of other statutes in *pari materia*) for the illumination which they throw on the particular words which are the subject of interpretation." He added that "difficult questions can arise when these various avenues lead in different directions".

The House of Lords in different cases have laid stress on different aspects of this general scheme. In *Charter* v. *Race Relations Board*, [1973] 1 All E.R. 512 (issue: was a political club within the scope of the RRA 1968?) emphasis was placed on the need to derive the policy of the Act from its provisions as a whole. Lord Reid said (at p. 516): "In determining the precise scope of [s. 2] we must read the Act as a whole in the light of any general policy which its terms disclose." (And see Lord Hodson at p. 525e, Lord Simon at p. 527e, Lord Cross at p. 530d.) In *Applin* v. *Race Relations Board*, [1974] 2 All E.R. 73 (issue: was fostering a service within the meaning of the RRA 1968?) Lord Reid said at p. 77 that "the proper approach is to see whether, taking the natural meaning of the words . . ." the foster-parents came within the scope of the provision. Lord Simon, by contrast, laid emphasis on the "mischief rule" (p. 89) and said (at p. 90): "Where the paramount statutory purpose is palpable, the fact that it has not been carried through into every conceivable situation does not, in my view, mean that 'the mischief rule' ceases to have any value. At the very least it should operate, where Parliament has stipulated express exemptions in derogation of its paramount statutory purpose, to cause the courts to hesitate in going on to imply further exemptions in added derogation". He did add, however (*ibid.*): "a linguistic examination is in any event called for as a check against interpretation in the light of statutory purpose", and (which is relevant to an act like the SDA) "in examining the language of a statute which affects people in their ordinary unspecialised lives, there is a 'golden' rule that the words are presumptively intended in their natural, ordinary and grammatical meaning", subject to glosses added by the Interpretation Act 1889 (p. 91) —and, presumably, by the interpretation section of the Act itself.

This traditional priority accorded to language above social purpose was, at least, a shift away from the rigorous views expressed by the House of Lords in the first case which came before them, *Ealing London Borough Council* v. *Race Relations Board*, [1972] A.C. 342 (issue: was it unlawful to discriminate on grounds of nationality under the RRA 1968?). In that case their Lordships treated the RRA as a quasi-penal statute. Lord Donovan said (at p. 355): "If the council is to be stigmatised as being guilty of an unlawful act under the 1968 Act I think that that conclusion ought to be reached with reasonable confidence". Viscount Dilhorne required (at p. 360) "a clear indication" that the RRA was concerned with discrimination on grounds of nationality. Lord Simon said that in a statute "involving penal provisions" (which the SDA does*) "the courts will look for unambiguous expression, and, in the event of ambiguity, will prefer the narrower construction" (p. 363). Only Lord Kilbrandon represented a more literal view, when he said (at p. 363): "I would not accept the view that there is some presumption here in favour of freedom from liability; the race relations code does, of course, contain some criminal sanctions, and it restricts liberty, but, on the other hand, it is conceived as a measure of social reform and relief of distress. Not much help is to be got from presumptions either for freedom or in favour of benevolent interpretation."

In sum there is no truly consistent approach to be discerned in the approach of their Lordships; and, in at least one recent case in a different field, the House of Lords have held that reports of Committees presented to Parliament containing proposals for legislation may be looked at in order to resolve an ambiguity by reference to the mischief which the statute was intended to remedy. But it is still not permissible to study such a report for a direct statement of what the proposed legislation means, still less to read reports of Parliamentary debates (*Black-Clawson International, Ltd.* v. *Papierwerke Waldhof-Aschaffenberg A.G.*, [1975] 1 All E.R. 810).

*See Appendix II.

APPENDIX IV

SCHEDULE OF COMPARATIVE PROVISIONS OF THE SEX DISCRIMINATION ACT, RACE RELATIONS BILL AND RACE RELATIONS ACT

SDA	RRB	RRA	SDA	RRB	RRA
1	1	1	51	41	3(2)
4	2		52 (1)	42	10
5	3		53	43	
6	4	8	54	45	
7	5	3	56	54	
9	7		57	47	
10	8	8	58	48	
11	10		59	49	
12	11	4	60	50	
13	12		61	51	
14	13		63	53	
15	14		64	54	
16	15		65	55	
17	16		66	56	22
22	17		67	57	
23	18		68	58	
25	19		69	59	
29	20	2	70	60	
30	21	5/7	71	61	21
32	22	7	72	62	
35 (3)	23		73	63	
31	24		74	64	
36	27	11	75	65	
37	28		76	67	
38	29	6	77	70	23
39	30		80	71	
40	31	12	81	72	
41	32	13	85	73	27
42	33	12	86	74	
43	34	9	82	76	
48	38		Sch. 3	Sch. 1	
50	40				

BODY IN CHARGE OF EDUCATIONAL INSTITUTION	DISCRIMINATION MADE UNLAWFUL	Sex discrimination when carrying out functions under the Education Acts 1944–75 or the Education (Scotland) Acts 1939–74 (SDA, s.23)
1. Local Education Authority (E, W)		*
2. Local Education Authority or Manager or Governor in respect of an educational establishment maintained by L.E.A. (E, W)		
3. (a) Proprietor of an Independent School (not being a special school) (b) Proprietor of a special school not maintained by L.E.A. (E, W)		
4. Governing body of a University (E, W, S)		
5. Governing body of a designated establishment providing full or part-time education not falling within 2–4 above, within the categories: (a) recognised Polytechnic (b) establishment in respect of which grants are payable (i) under s.100, Education Act 1944 (ii) otherwise out of money provided by Parliament (c) Assisted by L.E.A. under s.42 Education Act 1944 (d) providing full-time education to persons over compulsory school age but under 19 (E, W)		
6. Education authority (S)		*
7. Education authority in respect of educational establishment managed by it (S)		
8. Managers receiving grants under s.75(c) or (d) of Education (Scotland) Act 1962 in respect of educational establishment (S)		
9. Proprietor of an Independent School (S)		
10. Managers of an educational establishment not falling within 7–9 above providing full- or part-time school or further education (S)		

E, W = England and Wales; S = Scotland

Note: In Great Britain, the following forms of discrimination are made unlawful for all other educational institutions, e.g. Inns of Court, commercial language schools, etc.: refusing or deliberately omitting to provide facilities for education; refusing or deliberately omitting to provide facilities of the like quality, in the like manner and on the like terms as are normal in

DISCRIMINATION IN EDUCATION

Sex discrimination in providing facilities for education, and any ancillary benefits or services (SDA, s.25 (1))	Sex discrimination in the terms on which admittance is offered to a pupil; by refusing an application for admission; in affording access to benefits, facilities or services; by excluding pupil or subjecting pupil to other detriment (SDA, s.22)
*	
*	*
(b) *	*
	*
(a) * (b) (i) * (c) *	(a) * (b) (i) * (b) (ii) * (c) * (d) *
*	*
	*
*	*
	*
	*

relation to members of the public of the other sex or, where the victim of discrimination belongs to a section of the public, to members of the other sex of that section (SDA, s.29 (1), (2) (d)).

THE SEX DISCRIMINATION ACT 1975
(1975 c. 65)

ARRANGEMENT OF SECTIONS

PART I
DISCRIMINATION TO WHICH ACT APPLIES

PART II
DISCRIMINATION IN THE EMPLOYMENT FIELD
Discrimination by employers

Discrimination by other bodies

Special cases

PART III
DISCRIMINATION IN OTHER FIELDS
Education

Sex Discrimination Act 1975

Goods, facilities, services and premises

Arrangement of sections

Enforcement in employment field

Enforcement of Part III

Non-discrimination notices

Other enforcement by Commission

Help for persons suffering discrimination

Period within which proceedings to be brought

Part VIII

Supplemental

An Act to render unlawful certain kinds of sex discrimination and discrimination on the ground of marriage, and establish a Commission with the function of working towards the elimination of such discrimination and promoting equality of opportunity between men and women generally; and for related purposes.
[12th November 1975]

Northern Ireland. This Act, except Sch. 3, para. 16, *post*, does not apply; see s. 87 (2), *post*.

93

PART I

DISCRIMINATION TO WHICH ACT APPLIES

1. Sex discrimination against women

(1) A person discriminates against a woman in any circumstances relevant for the purposes of any provision of this Act if—

    (*a*) on the ground of her sex he treats her less favourably than he treats or would treat a man, or

    (*b*) he applies to her a requirement or condition which applies or would apply equally to a man but—

        (i) which is such that the proportion of women who can comply with it is considerably smaller than the proportion of men who can comply with it, and

        (ii) which he cannot show to be justifiable irrespective of the sex of the person to whom it is applied, and

        (iii) which is to her detriment because she cannot comply with it.

(2) If a person treats or would treat a man differently according to the man's marital status, his treatment of a woman is for the purposes of subsection (1) (*a*) to be compared to his treatment of a man having the like marital status.

COMMENCEMENT
    See s. 83 (3) and (4), *post.*

DISCRIMINATE
    S. 82 (1). Discrimination and related terms shall be construed in accordance with s. 5 (1).

WOMAN
    S. 82 (1). See also s. 5 (2).

MAN
    S. 82 (1). See also s. 5 (2).

CIRCUMSTANCES RELEVANT
    Discrimination in the employment field is dealt with in Part II (ss. 6–21) of this Act, and discrimination in other fields (in particular, education, goods, facilities, services and premises) is dealt with in Part III (ss. 22–36), *post.* See also Part IV for other unlawful acts.

THE ACT
    S. 82 (7) (*d*): includes Schedules to the Act.

TRANSITIONAL PROVISIONS
    See s. 83 (5), *post.*

PERSON
    S. 19, Interpretation Act 1889: the expression "person" shall, unless the contrary intention appears, include any body of persons corporate or unincorporate.

HE
    S. 1 (1) (*a*) and (*b*), Interpretation Act 1889: words in the masculine gender shall include the feminine.
    S. 2 (2): cf. Employment Protection Act 1975, ss. 34–52.

COMMENTARY
    See para. [2], *ante.*

---

2. Sex discrimination against men

(1) Section 1, and the provisions of Parts II and III relating to sex discrimination against women, are to be read as applying equally to the treatment of men, and for that purpose shall have effect with such modifications as are requisite.

(2) In the application of subsection (1) no account shall be taken of special treatment afforded to women in connection with pregnancy or childbirth.

PART
See s. 82 (7) (*a*).

PART II
Discrimination in the employment field: ss. 6–21.

PART III
Discrimination in other fields: ss. 22–36.

DISCRIMINATION
Defined in s. 82 (1), to be read with s. 5 (1).

WOMAN
S. 82 (1) and s. 5 (2).

MAN
S. 82 (1) and s. 5 (2).

COMMENTARY
See paras. [3] and [4], *ante*.

3. Discrimination against married persons in employment field

(1) A person discriminates against a married person of either sex in any circumstances relevant for the purposes of any provision of Part II if—

> (*a*) on the ground of his or her marital status he treats that person less favourably than he treats or would treat an unmarried person of the same sex, or
> (*b*) he applies to that person a requirement or condition which he applies or would apply equally to an unmarried person but—
>> (i) which is such that the proportion of married persons who can comply with it is considerably smaller than the proportion of unmarried persons of the same sex who can comply with it, and
>> (ii) which he cannot show to be justifiable irrespective of the marital status of the person to whom it is applied, and
>> (iii) which is to that person's detriment because he cannot comply with it.

(2) For the purposes of subsection (1), a provision of Part II framed with reference to discrimination against women shall be treated as applying equally to the treatment of men, and for that purpose shall have effect with such modifications as are requisite.

DISCRIMINATES
S. 82 (1): to be construed in accordance with s. 5 (1).

CIRCUMSTANCES RELEVANT
See notes to s. 1, *ante*.

PART II
Ss. 6–21, *post*.

PART
S. 82 (7) (*a*).

WOMAN
S. 82 (1), to be read with s. 5 (2).

MAN
S. 82 (1), to be read with s. 5 (2).

PERSON
>S. 19, Interpretation Act 1889: includes any body of persons, corporate or unincorporate.

HE
>S. 1 (1) (*a*) and (*b*) Interpretation Act 1889: masculine includes the feminine.

COMMENTARY
>See para. [5], *ante*.

---

4. Discrimination by way of victimisation

(1) A person ("the discriminator") discriminates against another person ("the person victimised") in any circumstances relevant for the purposes of any provision of this Act if he treats the person victimised less favourably than in those circumstances he treats or would treat other persons, and does so by reason that the person victimised has—

>(*a*) brought proceedings against the discriminator or any other person under this Act or the Equal Pay Act 1970, or
>
>(*b*) given evidence or information in connection with proceedings brought by any person against the discriminator or any other person under this Act or the Equal Pay Act 1970, or
>
>(*c*) otherwise done anything under or by reference to this Act or the Equal Pay Act 1970 in relation to the discriminator or any other person, or
>
>(*d*) alleged that the discriminator or any other person has committed an act which (whether or not the allegation so states) would amount to a contravention of this Act or give rise to a claim under the Equal Pay Act 1970,

or by reason that the discriminator knows the person victimised intends to do any of those things, or suspects the person victimised has done, or intends to do, any of them.

(2) Subsection (1) does not apply to treatment of a person by reason of any allegation made by him if the allegation was false and not made in good faith.

(3) For the purposes of subsection (1), a provision of Part II or III framed with reference to discrimination against women shall be treated as applying equally to the treatment of men and for that purpose shall have effect with such modifications as are requisite.

EQUAL PAY ACT 1970
>See 40 Halsbury's Statutes (3rd Edn.), p. 561. The Act is amended by s. 8 and Sch. 1, Part I, *post*. The amended Act is set out in Sch. 1, Part II, *post*.

PART
>S. 82 (7) (*a*).

PART II
>Ss. 6–21.

PART III
>Ss. 22–36.

CONTRAVENTION OF THIS ACT
>I.e. a contravention of any of the provisions of Parts II, III or IV.

PROCEEDINGS UNDER THIS ACT
>Proceedings taken under Part VII of the Act.

CIRCUMSTANCES RELEVANT
>See notes to s. 1, *ante*.

PERSON
PERSON
  S. 19, Interpretation Act 1889, includes a body corporate or unincorporate.

HE
  S. 1 (1) (*a*) and (*b*), Interpretation Act 1889: masculine includes the feminine.

COMMENTARY
  See para. [**6**], *ante*.

---

5. Interpretation

(1) In this Act—

  (*a*) references to discrimination refer to any discrimination falling within sections 1 to 4; and
  (*b*) references to sex discrimination refer to any discrimination falling within section 1 or 2,

and related expressions shall be construed accordingly.

  (2) In this Act—

  "woman" includes a female of any age, and
  "man" includes a male of any age.

  (3) A comparison of the cases of persons of different sex or marital status under section 1 (1) or 3 (1) must be such that the relevant circumstances in the one case are the same, or not materially different, in the other.

WOMAN AND MAN
  S. 82 (1) defines man and woman "unless the context otherwise requires".

PART II

DISCRIMINATION IN THE EMPLOYMENT FIELD

Discrimination by employers

6. Discrimination against applicants and employees

(1) It is unlawful for a person, in relation to employment by him at an establishment in Great Britain, to discriminate against a woman—

  (*a*) in the arrangements he makes for the purpose of determining who should be offered that employment, or
  (*b*) in the terms on which he offers her that employment, or
  (*c*) by refusing or deliberately omitting to offer her that employment.

  (2) It is unlawful for a person, in the case of a woman employed by him at an establishment in Great Britain, to discriminate against her—

  (*a*) in the way he affords her access to opportunities for promotion, transfer or training, or to any other benefits, facilities or services, or by refusing or deliberately omitting to afford her access to them, or
  (*b*) by dismissing her, or subjecting her to any other detriment.

  (3) Except in relation to discrimination falling within section 4, subsections (1) and (2) do not apply to employment—

  (*a*) for the purposes of a private household, or

(*b*) where the number of persons employed by the employer, added to the number employed by any associated employers of his, does not exceed five (disregarding any persons employed for the purposes of a private household).

(4) Subsections (1) (*b*) and (2) do not apply to provision in relation to death or retirement.

(5) Subject to section 8 (3), subsection (1) (*b*) does not apply to any provision for the payment of money which, if the woman in question were given the employment, would be included (directly or by reference to a collective agreement or otherwise) in the contract under which she was employed.

(6) Subsection (2) does not apply to benefits consisting of the payment of money when the provision of those benefits is regulated by the woman's contract of employment.

(7) Subsection (2) does not apply to benefits, facilities or services of any description if the employer is concerned with the provision (for payment or not) of benefits, facilities or services of that description to the public, or to a section of the public comprising the woman in question, unless—

(*a*) that provision differs in a material respect from the provision of the benefits, facilities or services by the employer to his employees, or
(*b*) the provision of the benefits, facilities or services to the woman in question is regulated by her contract of employment, or
(*c*) the benefits, facilities or services relate to training.

COMMENCEMENT
See s. 83 (2), *post*, and the note "orders under this section" thereto.

EMPLOYMENT
Defined in s. 82 (1).

EMPLOYMENT AT AN ESTABLISHMENT IN GREAT BRITAIN
This is to be construed in accordance with s. 10, *post*. "Great Britain" means England, Scotland and Wales by virtue of the Union with Scotland Act 1706, preamble, art. 1 (6 Halsbury's Statutes (3rd Edn.), p. 502) and the Wales and Berwick Act 1746, s. 3 (32 Halsbury's Statutes (3rd Edn.), p. 412) and it includes territorial waters by virtue of s. 82 (1), *post*.

ENFORCEMENT
See ss. 62–65, 67–71 and 73–76, *post*.

COLLECTIVE AGREEMENT
This expression is not defined, but *cf.* the definition in the Trade Union and Labour Relations Act 1974, s. 30 (1) (44 Halsbury's Statutes (3rd Edn.), p. 1781).

DISCRIMINATE
S. 82, to be construed in accordance with s. 5 (1) as any discrimination falling within ss. 1–4.

DISCRIMINATION AGAINST A WOMAN
See s. 1. By s. 2 this section has to be read as applying also to the treatment of men. By s. 3 this section has to be read as applying also to the treatment of married persons. By s. 4 this section refers also to discrimination by way of victimisation.

GREAT BRITAIN
Defined in s. 82 (1).

PERSON
For application to the Crown: s. 85.
S. 19, Interpretation Act 1889: person shall include a body corporate or unincorporate.

ACCESS
S. 82 (1), to be construed in accordance with s. 50.

TRAINING
S. 82 (1) includes any form of education or instruction. N.B. exception, s. 48.

WOMAN
Defined in s. 82 (1) and in s. 5 (2).

MAN
Defined in s. 82 (1) and in s. 5 (2).

GENERAL EXCEPTIONS
Ss. 43–52, *post.*

SECTION 6
Sub-s. (1): exception of midwife, s. 20 (1).
Sub-s. (1) (*a*): exception in s. 7 (1) (*a*).
Sub-s. (1) (*b*). See ss. 6 (5) and 8 (3) for acts contravening this subsection.
Sub-s. (1) (*c*): exception in s. 7 (1) (*a*).
Sub-s. (2): exceptions in ss. 6 (6), (7) and 8 (5).
Sub-s. (2) (*a*): exceptions in s. 7 (1) (*b*) and 20 (2).
Sub-s. (3). Power to amend in s. 80 (1) (*a*).

HE
Masculine includes feminine and plural: s. 1 (1) (*a*) and (*b*), Interpretation Act 1889.

COMMENTARY
See paras. [**38**], [**39**], [**41**] and Appendix I, *ante.*

---

7. Exception where sex is a genuine occupational qualification

(1) In relation to sex discrimination—

    (*a*) section 6 (1) (*a*) or (*c*) does not apply to any employment where being a man is a genuine occupational qualification for the job, and

    (*b*) section 6 (2) (*a*) does not apply to opportunities for promotion or transfer to, or training for, such employment.

(2) Being a man is a genuine occupational qualification for a job only where—

    (*a*) the essential nature of the job calls for a man for reasons of physiology (excluding physical strength or stamina) or, in dramatic performances or other entertainment, for reasons of authenticity, so that the essential nature of the job would be materially different if carried out by a woman; or

    (*b*) the job needs to be held by a man to preserve decency or privacy because—

        (i) it is likely to involve physical contact with men in circumstances where they might reasonably object to its being carried out by a woman, or

        (ii) the holder of the job is likely to do his work in circumstances where men might reasonably object to the presence of a woman because they are in a state of undress or are using sanitary facilities; or

    (*c*) the nature or location of the establishment makes it impracticable for the holder of the job to live elsewhere than in premises provided by the employer, and—

     (i) the only such premises which are available for persons holding that kind of job are lived in, or normally lived in, by men and are not equipped with separate sleeping accommodation for women and sanitary facilities which could be used by women in privacy from men, and

     (ii) it is not reasonable to expect the employer either to equip those premises with such accommodation and facilities or to provide other premises for women; or

(d) the nature of the establishment, or of the part of it within which the work is done, requires the job to be held by a man because—

     (i) it is, or is part of, a hospital, prison or other establishment for persons requiring special care, supervision or attention, and

     (ii) those persons are all men (disregarding any woman whose presence is exceptional), and

     (iii) it is reasonable, having regard to the essential character of the establishment or that part, that the job should not be held by a woman; or

(e) the holder of the job provides individuals with personal services promoting their welfare or education, or similar personal services, and those services can most effectively be provided by a man, or

(f) the job needs to be held by a man because of restrictions imposed by the laws regulating the employment of women, or

(g) the job needs to be held by a man because it is likely to involve the performance of duties outside the United Kingdom in a country whose laws or customs are such that the duties could not, or could not effectively, be performed by a woman, or

(h) the job is one of two to be held by a married couple.

(3) Subsection (2) applies where some only of the duties of the job fall within paragraphs (a) to (g) as well as where all of them do.

(4) Paragraph (a), (b), (c), (d), (e), (f) or (g) of subsection (2) does not apply in relation to the filling of a vacancy at a time when the employer already has male employees—

(a) who are capable of carrying out the duties falling within that paragraph, and

(b) whom it would be reasonable to employ on those duties and

(c) whose numbers are sufficient to meet the employer's likely requirements in respect of those duties without undue inconvenience.

COMMENCEMENT
    See s. 83 (2), *post*, and the note "orders under this section" thereto.

BEING A MAN IS A GENUINE OCCUPATIONAL QUALIFICATION FOR THE JOB
    This is to be construed in accordance with sub-ss. (2)–(4) above.

POWER TO AMEND THIS SECTION
    S. 80 (1) (a).

SEX DISCRIMINATION
    By s. 5 the reference is to any discrimination falling within s. 1 and s. 2.

DISCRIMINATION
    By s. 82 (1) discrimination to be interpreted by reference to s. 5 (1).

EMPLOYMENT
> See s. 82 (1) definition.

ESTABLISHMENT
> S. 10 for place of establishment.

EDUCATION
> Defined in s. 82 (1); note exception in s. 7 (2) (*e*).

MAN
> Defined in s. 82 (1) and s. 5 (2). S. 1 (1) (*a*) and (*b*), Interpretation Act 1889: masculine includes feminine and plural.

WOMAN
> S. 82 (1) and s. 5 (2). By s. 2 the reference to women is to be read also as applying to men for the purposes of s. 2. By s. 3 this section has to be read as applying also to the treatment of married persons for the purposes of s. 3. By s. 4 this section refers also to discrimination by way of victimisation.

GENUINE OCCUPATIONAL QUALIFICATION
> By s. 82 (1) the meaning given to this phrase in s. 7 (2) is to apply generally for the purposes of the act.

PERSON
> S. 19, Interpretation Act 1889 includes a body corporate or unincorporate. For application to the Crown, see s. 85.

INDIVIDUALS
> This word is doubtless used instead of the word "persons" in order to exclude corporations; cf. *Whitney v. Inland Revenue Commrs.*, [1926] A.C. 37 at p. 43.

UNITED KINGDOM
> Great Britain and Northern Ireland: Royal and Parliamentary Titles Act 1927, s. 2 (2); Northern Ireland Constitution Act 1973, s. 1; exclusive of the Channel Islands and the Isle of Man. For extension of English law to these places see 6 Halsbury's Laws of England (4th Edn.), paras. 1203–1206. Acts may be extended by Orders in Council. As to "Great Britain", see the note "Employment . . . at an establishment in Great Britain" to s. 6, *ante*.

RESTRICTIONS REGULATING THE EMPLOYMENT OF WOMEN
> For the relevant enactments, see the preliminary note to the title Employment, 12 Halsbury's Statutes (3rd Edn.), p. 6 (and note the amendment made by s. 21 (1), *post*).

COMMENTARY
> See paras. [**42**] and [**43**], *ante*.

---

8. Equal Pay Act 1970

(1) In section 1 of the Equal Pay Act 1970, the following are substituted for subsections (1) to (3)—

> "(1) If the terms of a contract under which a woman is employed at an establishment in Great Britain do not include (directly or by reference to a collective agreement of otherwise) an equality clause they shall be deemed to include one.
>
> (2) An equality clause is a provision which relates to terms (whether concerned with pay or not) of a contract under which a woman is employed (the "woman's contract"), and has the effect that—
>
>> (*a*) where the woman is employed on like work with a man in the same employment—

    (i) if (apart from the equality clause) any term of the woman's contract is or becomes less favourable to the woman than a term of a similar kind in the contract under which that man is employed, that term of the woman's contract shall be treated as so modified as not to be less favourable, and

    (ii) if (apart from the equality clause) at any time the woman's contract does not include a term corresponding to a term benefiting that man included in the contract under which he is employed, the woman's contract shall be treated as including such a term;

(b) where the woman is employed on work rated as equivalent with that of a man in the same employment—

    (i) if (apart from the equality clause) any term of the woman's contract determined by the rating of the work is or becomes less favourable to the woman than a term of a similar kind in the contract under which that man is employed, that term of the woman's contract shall be treated as so modified as not to be less favourable, and

    (ii) if (apart from the equality clause) at any time the woman's contract does not include a term corresponding to a term benefiting that man included in the contract under which he is employed and determined by the rating of the work, the woman's contract shall be treated as including such a term.

(3) An equality clause shall not operate in relation to a variation between the woman's contract and the man's contract if the employer proves that the variation is genuinely due to a material difference (other than the difference of sex) between her case and his."

(2) Section 1 (1) of the Equal Pay Act 1970 (as set out in subsection (1) above) does not apply in determining for the purposes of section 6 (1) (b) of this Act the terms on which employment is offered.

(3) Where a person offers a woman employment on certain terms, and if she accepted the offer then, by virtue of an equality clause, any of those terms would fall to be modified, or any additional term would fall to be included, the offer shall be taken to contravene section 6 (1) (b).

(4) Where a person offers a woman employment on certain terms, and subsection (3) would apply but for the fact that, on her acceptance of the offer, section 1 (3) of the Equal Pay Act 1970 (as set out in subsection (1) above) would prevent the equality clause from operating, the offer shall be taken not to contravene section 6 (1) (b).

(5) An act does not contravene section 6 (2) if—

(a) it contravenes a term modified or included by virtue of an equality clause, or

(b) it would contravene such a term but for the fact that the equality clause is prevented from operating by section 1 (3) of the Equal Pay Act 1970.

(6) The Equal Pay Act 1970 is further amended as specified in Part I of Schedule 1, and accordingly has effect as set out in Part II of Schedule 1.

COMMENCEMENT
    See s. 83 (2), *post*, and the note "orders under this section" thereto, where a particular reference is made to the amendment of the EPA.

EQUAL PAY ACT 1970
    Amended act set out in Schedule 1; see 40 Halsbury's Statutes (3rd Edn.), p. 561; for s. 1 see p. 562.

WOMAN
    Ss. 82 (1) and 5 (2).
    By s. 2 the reference to woman is to be read as applying also to men. By s. 3 this section has to be read as applying also to the treatment of married persons. By s. 4 this section also applies to discrimination by way of victimisation. By the Equal Pay Act 1970, s. 1 (13), as inserted by sub-s. (6) above and Sch. 1, Part II, para. 1 (4), *post*, provisions of that section framed with reference to women and their treatment relative to men are to be read as applying equally in a converse case to men and their treatment relative to women.

WOMAN IS EMPLOYED ON LIKE WORK WITH A MAN
    Like work defined in s. 1 (4) of the Equal Pay Act 1970. See Sch. 1, Part II.

WOMAN IS EMPLOYED ON WORK RATED AS EQUIVALENT WITH THAT OF A MAN
    Rated as equivalent defined in s. 1 (5) of the Equal Pay Act 1970. See Sch. 1, Part II.

ESTABLISHMENT IN GREAT BRITAIN
    To be construed in accordance with s. 10.

EMPLOYED
    S. 82 (1). S. 1 (6) (*a*) EPA.

EQUALITY CLAUSE
    By s. 82 (1) the meaning given in this section is to apply throughout the Act.

MAN
    Ss. 82 (1) and 5 (2).

SUBSECTION (1)
    See Equal Pay Act, s. 1. A less favourable term may also be unlawful discrimination: s. 6 (1) (*b*); s. 8 (3).

ACT
    S. 82 (1) includes a deliberate omission.

PERSON
    Interpretation Act 1889, s. 19: person includes a body corporate or unincorporate. Application to Crown: s. 85. N.B. special provision in s. 85 (6).

MAN IN THE SAME EMPLOYMENT
    Defined in s. 1 (6) of the Equal Pay Act as amended by Sch. 1, Part I of this Act.

COMMENTARY
    See Appendix I, *ante*.

---

9. Discrimination against contract workers

(1) This section applies to any work for a person ("the principal") which is available for doing by individuals ("contract workers") who are employed not by the principal himself but by another person, who supplies them under a contract made with the principal.

(2) It is unlawful for the principal, in relation to work to which this section applies, to discriminate against a woman who is a contract worker—

    (*a*) in the terms on which he allows her to do that work, or

    (*b*) by not allowing her to do it or continue to do it, or
    (*c*) in the way he affords her access to any benefits, facilities or services or by refusing or deliberately omitting to afford her access to them, or
    (*d*) by subjecting her to any other detriment.

(3) The principal does not contravene subsection (2) (*b*) by doing any act in relation to a woman at a time when if the work were to be done by a person taken into his employment being a man would be a genuine occupational qualification for the job.

(4) Subsection (2) (*c*) does not apply to benefits, facilities or services of any description if the principal is concerned with the provision (for payment or not) of benefits, facilities or services of that description to the public, or to a section of the public to which the woman belongs, unless that provision differs in a material respect from the provision of the benefits, facilities or services by the principal to his contract workers.

COMMENCEMENT
    See s. 83 (2), *post*, and the note "orders under this section" thereto.

DISCRIMINATION
    S. 82 (1) to be construed in accordance with s. 5 (1).

WOMAN
    Ss. 82 (1) and 5 (2). By s. 2 a reference to a woman is to be read as applying also to men. By s. 3 this section has to be read as applying also to the treatment of married persons for the purposes of s. 3. By s. 4 this section has to be read as applying to discrimination by way of victimisation for the purposes of s. 4.

ACT
    S. 82 (1).

EMPLOYED
    S. 82 (1).

GENUINE OCCUPATIONAL QUALIFICATION
    S. 82 (1) and s. 7 (2). See also s. 7 (3) and (4), *ante*, and note, as to discrimination against men, s. 2, *ante*.

PERSON
    Includes a body corporate and unincorporate: s. 19, Interpretation Act 1889; application to the Crown: s. 85.

INDIVIDUALS
    See note to s. 7, *ante*.

HE
    Interpretation Act 1889, s. 1 (1) (*a*) and (*b*): masculine includes feminine and plural.

IT IS UNLAWFUL, ETC.
    Sub-s. (2) above must be read subject to the exceptions in sub-ss. (3) and (4) above; and for general exceptions, see Part V (ss. 43–52), *post*.

ACCESS TO BENEFITS
    See s. 50, *post*.

ENFORCEMENT
    For relevant provisions relating to enforcement, see ss. 62–65, 67–71 and 73–76, *post*.

COMMENTARY
    See para. [**45**], *ante*.

---

10. Meaning of employment at establishment in Great Britain

(1) For the purposes of this Part and section 1 of the Equal Pay Act 1970 ("the relevant purposes"), employment is to be regarded as being at an establishment in Great Britain unless the employee does his work wholly or mainly outside Great Britain.

(2) Subsection (1) does not apply to—

(a) employment on board a ship registered at a port of registry in Great Britain, or

(b) employment on aircraft or hovercraft registered in the United Kingdom and operated by a person who has his principal place of business, or is ordinarily resident, in Great Britain;

but for the relevant purposes such employment is to be regarded as being at an establishment in Great Britain unless the employee does his work wholly outside Great Britain.

(3) In the case of employment on board a ship registered at a port of registry in Great Britain (except where the employee does his work wholly outside Great Britain, and outside any area added under subsection (5)) the ship shall for the relevant purposes be deemed to be the establishment.

(4) Where work is not done at an establishment it shall be treated for the relevant purposes as done at the establishment from which it is done or (where it is not done from any establishment) at the establishment with which it has the closest connection.

(5) In relation to employment concerned with exploration of the sea bed or subsoil or the exploitation of their natural resources, Her Majesty may by Order in Council provide that subsections (1) and (2) shall each have effect as if the last reference to Great Britain included any area for the time being designated under section 1 (7) of the Continental Shelf Act 1964, except an area or part of an area in which the law of Northern Ireland applies.

(6) An Order in Council under subsection (5) may provide that, in relation to employment to which the Order applies, this Part and section 1 of the Equal Pay Act 1970 are to have effect with such modifications as are specified in the Order.

(7) An Order in Council under subsection (5) shall be of no effect unless a draft of the Order was laid before and approved by each House of Parliament.

COMMENCEMENT
See s. 83 (2), *post*, and the note "orders under this section" thereto.

EQUAL PAY ACT 1970
Set out in Sch. 1; see also s. 8. S. 1, EPA is amended by s. 8 (1) (b), *ante*, and Sch. 1, Part I, para. 1. Amended text set out in Sch. 1, Part II, *post*.

GREAT BRITAIN
S. 82 (1). See s. 6, *ante*.

UNITED KINGDOM
Great Britain and Northern Ireland: Royal and Parliamentary Titles Act 1927, s. 2 (2); Northern Ireland Constitution Act 1973, s. 1. Exclusive of the Channel Islands and the Isle of Man; for extension of English law to these places see 6 Halsbury's Laws (4th Edn.), paras. 1203–1206; Acts may be extended by Orders in Council.

EMPLOYMENT
S. 82 (1).

THIS PART
I.e. Part II, ss. 6–21 of the Act.

PART
S. 82 (7) (*a*).

PERSON
S. 19, Interpretation Act 1889 includes a body corporate or unincorporate; for application to the Crown: s. 85. N.B. s. 85 (7).

POWER TO MAKE ORDERS
S. 81. Exercisable by Statutory Instrument. See the Statutory Instruments Act 1946, s. 1 (1), 32 Halsbury's Statutes (3rd Edn.), p. 668. No orders yet made under sub-s. (5) above.

CONTINENTAL SHELF ACT 1964
22 Halsbury's Statutes (3rd Edn.), p. 587.

ORDERS IN COUNCIL MADE UNDER S. 1 (7)
C.S. (Designation of Areas) Order 1964, S.I. 1964 No. 697.
C.S. (Designation of Additional Areas) Order 1965, S.I. 1965 No. 1531.
C.S. (Designation of Additional Areas) Order 1968, S.I. 1968 No. 891.
C.S. (Designation of Additional Areas) Order 1971, S.I. 1971 No. 594.
C.S. (Designation of Additional Areas) Order 1974, S.I. 1974 No. 1489.

HE
S. 1 (1) (*a*) and (*b*), Interpretation Act 1889: masculine includes feminine and plural.

WHOLLY OR MAINLY
The expression "wholly or mainly" (or "exclusively" or "mainly") has been judicially considered at various times; see in particular, *Re Hatschek's Patents, Ex parte Zerenner*, [1909] 2 Ch. 68; *Miller* v. *Owners of Ottilie*, [1944] K.B. 188; [1944] 1 All E.R. 277; *Berthelemy* v. *Neale*, [1952] 1 All E.R. 437; also *Franklin* v. *Gramophone Co., Ltd.*, [1948] 1 K.B. 542; [1948] 1 All E.R. 353 at pp. 555 and 358 respectively, *per* Somervell, L.J.

REGISTRATION OF SHIPS
Merchant Shipping Act 1894, ss. 2 *et seq.*, 31 Halsbury's Statutes (3rd Edn.), pp. 75 *et seq.*

AIRCRAFT
Air Navigation Order 1974, S.I. 1974 No. 1114, arts. 3 and 4.

HOVERCRAFT
Hovercraft (General) Order 1972, S.I. 1972 No. 674, arts. 4 and 5. For the meaning of "hovercraft"; cf. the definition in the Hovercraft Act 1968, s. 4 (1), 31 Halsbury's Statutes (3rd Edn.), p. 729.

ORDINARILY RESIDENT
"Ordinarily" means here according to the way in which one's life is usually ordered; see *Levene* v. *Inland Revenue Comrs.*, [1928] A.C. 217; [1928] All E.R. Rep. 746, at p. 232 and p. 754, respectively, *per* Lord Warrington of Clyffe. "I think the converse of 'ordinarily' is 'extraordinarily' and that part of the regular order of a man's life, adopted voluntarily and for settled purposes, is not 'extraordinary'"; see *Inland Revenue Comrs.* v. *Lysaght*, [1928] A.C. 234; [1928] All E.R. 575 at p. 243 and p. 580, respectively, *per* Viscount Sumner.
A temporary sojourn may become ordinary residence owing to circumstances beyond the control of the person concerned; see *Re Mackenzie*, [1941] Ch. 69; [1940] 4 All E.R. 310; and cf. *Re Bright, Ex parte Bright* (1903), 51 W.R. 342, C.A.; *R.* v. *Denman, Ex parte Staal* (1917), 86 L.J.K.B. 1328; and *Pittar* v. *Richardson* (1918), 87 L.J.K.B. 59. However, ordinary residence can be changed in a day; see, in particular, *Macrae* v. *Macrae*, [1949] P. 397; [1949] 2 All E.R. 34, C.A. See also *Hopkins* v. *Hopkins*, [1951] P. 116; [1950] 2 All E.R. 1035; *Stransky* v. *Stransky*, [1954] P. 428; [1954] 2 All E.R. 536; and *Lewis* v. *Lewis*, [1956] 1 All E.R. 375; and cf. *Lowry* v. *Lowry*, [1952] P. 252; [1952] 2 All E.R. 61.
See also the note "Resides" to s. 32, *post*.

COMMENTARY
See para. [**36**], *ante*.

Discrimination by other bodies

11. Partnerships

(1) It is unlawful for a firm consisting of six or more partners, in relation to a position as partner in the firm, to discriminate against a woman—

    (*a*) in the arrangements they make for the purpose of determining who should be offered that position, or

    (*b*) in the terms on which they offer her that position, or

    (*c*) by refusing or deliberately omitting to offer her that position, or

    (*d*) in a case where the woman already holds that position—

        (i) in the way they afford her access to any benefits, facilities or services, or by refusing or deliberately omitting to afford her access to them, or

        (ii) by expelling her from that position, or subjecting her to any other detriment.

(2) Subsection (1) shall apply in relation to persons proposing to form themselves into a partnership as it applies in relation to a firm.

(3) Subsection (1) (*a*) and (*c*) do not apply to a position as partner where, if it were employment, being a man would be a genuine occupational qualification for the job.

(4) Subsection (1) (*b*) and (*d*) do not apply to provision made in relation to death or retirement.

(5) In the case of a limited partnership references in subsection (1) to a partner shall be construed as references to a general partner as defined in section 3 of the Limited Partnerships Act 1907.

COMMENCEMENT
    See s. 83 (2), *post* and the note "orders under this section" thereto.

DISCRIMINATION
    S. 82 (1) to be construed in accordance with s. 5 (1).

WOMAN
    Ss. 82 (1), 5 (2). By s. 2 a reference to a woman is to be read as applying also to a man. By s. 3 this section has to be read as applying also to the treatment of married persons for the purposes of s. 3. By s. 4 this section has to be read as applying also to discrimination by way of victimisation.

EMPLOYMENT
    S. 82 (1).

FIRM
    S. 82 (1).

GENUINE OCCUPATIONAL QUALIFICATION
    Construed in accordance with s. 7 (2) by reason of s. 82 (1).

LIMITED PARTNERSHIPS ACT 1907
    See 24 Halsbury's Statutes (3rd Edn.), p. 526.

SUBSECTION (4)
    Power to amend or repeal this sub-section: s. 80 (1) (*b*).

SUBSECTION (1)
    Power to amend or to alter the number of partners specified: s. 80 (1) (*d*).

Sub-s. (1) above must be read subject to the exceptions in sub-ss. (3) and (4) above; and for general exceptions, see Part V (ss. 43–52), *post.*

ENFORCEMENT
For relevant provisions relating to enforcement, see ss. 62–65, 67–71 and 73–76, *post.*

AFFORDING ACCESS TO BENEFITS ETC.
See s. 50, *post.*

COMMENTARY
See para. [**46**], *ante.*

---

12. Trade unions etc.

(1) This section applies to an organisation of workers, an organisation of employers, or any other organisation whose members carry on a particular profession or trade for the purposes of which the organisation exists.

(2) It is unlawful for an organisation to which this section applies, in the case of a woman who is not a member of the organisation, to discriminate against her—

(*a*) in the terms on which it is prepared to admit her to membership, or
(*b*) by refusing, or deliberately omitting to accept, her application for membership.

(3) It is unlawful for an organisation to which this section applies, in the case of a woman who is a member of the organisation, to discriminate against her—

(*a*) in the way it affords her access to any benefits, facilities or services, or by refusing or deliberately omitting to afford her access to them, or
(*b*) by depriving her of membership, or varying the terms on which she is a member, or
(*c*) by subjecting her to any other detriment.

(4) This section does not apply to provision made in relation to the death or retirement from work of a member.

COMMENCEMENT
See s. 83 (2), *post*, and the note "orders under this section" thereto.

SUBSECTION (4)
Power to amend this sub-section: s. 80 (1) (*b*).

TRANSITIONAL PROVISIONS
See Schedule 4.

PROFESSION
See s. 82 (1).

TRADE
See s. 82 (1).

WOMAN
Ss. 82 (1), 5 (2). By s. 2 a reference to a woman is to be read as applying also to a man. By s. 3 this section has to be read as applying also to the treatment of married persons for the purposes of s. 3. By s. 4 this section has to be read as applying also to discrimination by way of victimisation.

DISCRIMINATION
S. 82 (1) to be construed in accordance with s. 5 (1).

EXEMPTION
There are specific exemptions to this section in s. 48 and s. 49.

GENERAL EXCEPTIONS
See Part V (ss. 43–52).

ORGANISATION OF WORKERS/ORGANISATION OF EMPLOYERS
These expressions are not defined, but cf. the definitions in the Industrial Relations Act 1971, ss. 61 (1) and 62 (1), 41 Halsbury's Statutes (3rd Edn.), pp. 2219, 2220 (repealed).

ENFORCEMENT
For relevant provisions, see ss. 62–65, 67–71 and 73–76, *post*.

COMMENTARY
See para. [**47**], *ante*.

---

13. Qualifying bodies

(1) It is unlawful for an authority or body which can confer an authorisation or qualification which is needed for, or facilitates, engagement in a particular profession or trade to discriminate against a woman—

    (*a*) in the terms on which it is prepared to confer on her that authorisation or qualification, or

    (*b*) by refusing or deliberately omitting to grant her application for it, or

    (*c*) by withdrawing it from her or varying the terms on which she holds it.

(2) Where an authority or body is required by law to satisfy itself as to his good character before conferring on a person an authorisation or qualification which is needed for, or facilitates, his engagement in any profession or trade then, without prejudice to any other duty to which it is subject, that requirement shall be taken to impose on the authority or body a duty to have regard to any evidence tending to show that he, or any of his employees, or agents (whether past or present), has practised unlawful discrimination in, or in connection with, the carrying on of any profession or trade.

(3) In this section—

    (*a*) "authorisation or qualification" includes recognition, registration, enrolment, approval and certification,

    (*b*) "confer" includes renew or extend.

(4) Subsection (1) does not apply to discrimination which is rendered unlawful by section 22 or 23.

COMMENCEMENT
See s. 83 (2), *post*, and the note "orders under this section" thereto.

DISCRIMINATION
S. 82 (1) to be construed in accordance with s. 5 (1).

WOMAN
S. 82 (1) and s. 5 (2). By s. 2 a reference to a woman is to be read as applying also to a man. By s. 3 this section has to be read as applying also to the treatment of married persons for the purposes of s. 3. By s. 4 this section has to be read as applying also to discrimination by way of victimisation.

PROFESSION
S. 82 (1).

TRADE
S. 82 (1).

EXCEPTION
On the grounds of religion: s. 19 (2).

GENERAL EXCEPTIONS
Part V (ss. 43–52).

HIS
Interpretation Act 1889, s. 1 (1) (*a*) and (*b*): masculine includes feminine and plural.

PERSON
Interpretation Act 1889: includes a body corporate or unincorporate.

ENFORCEMENT
Proceedings under Part II are normally brought in the Industrial Tribunal, but by s. 63 (2) a complaint under s. 13 (1) should not be brought before the tribunal if another enactment provides for an appeal or proceedings in the nature of an appeal.

UNLAWFUL DISCRIMINATION
This expression, as such, is not defined but it is submitted that the discrimination referred to is any discrimination falling within ss. 1–4, *ante* (see s. 5 (1), *ante*), and that "unlawful" discrimination is discrimination which is made unlawful by any of the provisions of this Part (ss. 6–21) or Part III (ss. 22–36) of the Act or those provisions taken together with ss. 41 and 42, *post*. Note, however, that for the purposes of sub-s. (2) above only unlawful discrimination in, or in connection with, the carrying on of any profession or trade is relevant.

COMMENTARY
See para. [**51**] and [**52**], *ante*.

---

14. Vocational training bodies

(1) It is unlawful for a person to whom this subsection applies, in the case of a woman seeking or undergoing training which would help to fit her for any employment, to discriminate against her—

(*a*) in the terms on which that person affords her access to any training courses or other facilities, or

(*b*) by refusing or deliberately omitting to afford her such access, or

(*c*) by terminating her training.

(2) Subsection (1) applies to—

(*a*) industrial training boards established under section 1 of the Industrial Training Act 1964;

(*b*) the Manpower Services Commission, the Employment Service Agency, and the Training Services Agency;

(*c*) any association which comprises employers and has as its principal object, or one **of** its principal objects, affording their employees access to training facilities;

(*d*) any other person providing facilities for training for employment, being a person designated for the purposes of this paragraph in an order made by or on behalf of the Secretary of State.

(3) Subsection (1) does not apply to discrimination which is rendered unlawful by section 22 or 23.

COMMENCEMENT
See s. 83 (2), *post*, and the note "orders under this section" thereto.

DISCRIMINATE
  S. 82 (1) to be construed in accordance with s. 5 (1).

WOMAN
  S. 82 (1) and s. 5 (2). By s. 2 a reference to a woman is to be read as applying also to a man. By s. 3 this section has to be read as applying also to the treatment of married persons for the purposes of s. 3. By s. 4 this section has to be read as applying also to discrimination by way of victimisation.

TRAINING
  S. 82 (1).

EMPLOYMENT
  S. 82 (1).

DESIGNATE
  S. 82 (3).

PERSON
  S. 19, Interpretation Act 1889: includes a body corporate or unincorporate. For application to the Crown: s. 85.

SUBSECTION (2) (*d*)
  There is an express exception of this subsection in s. 81 (1) and (2) regarding the making of orders.

EXCEPTIONS
  S. 20 (3) for training as a midwife. See also s. 47.

GENERAL EXCEPTIONS
  See Part V (ss. 43–52).

SECRETARY OF STATE
  S. 12, Interpretation Act 1889: one of Her Majesty's principal Secretaries of State for the time being.

INDUSTRIAL TRAINING ACT 1964
  See 12 Halsbury's Statutes (3rd Edn.), p. 219, and for the amended text of s. 1 see vol. 43, *ibid.*, pp. 468, 481.

SECTION 16
  This section takes precedence over s. 16.

ENFORCEMENT
  For relevant provisions see ss. 62–65, 67–71 and 73–76, *post.*

MANPOWER SERVICES COMMISSION
  Employment Service Agency, Training Services.

AGENCY
  These bodies are established by the Employment and Training Act 1973, s. 1, Sch. 1, 43 Halsbury's Statutes (3rd Edn.), pp. 436, 455.

COMMENTARY
  See para. [54], *ante.*

---

15. Employment agencies

(1) It is unlawful for an employment agency to discriminate against a woman—
  (*a*) in the terms on which the agency offers to provide any of its services, or
  (*b*) by refusing or deliberately omitting to provide any of its services, or
  (*c*) in the way it provides any of its services.

(2) It is unlawful for a local education authority or an education authority to do any act in the performance of its functions under section 8 of the Employment and Training Act 1973 which constitutes discrimination.

(3) References in subsection (1) to the services of an employment agency include guidance on careers and any other services related to employment.

(4) This section does not apply if the discrimination only concerns employment which the employer could lawfully refuse to offer the woman.

(5) An employment agency or local education authority or an education authority shall not be subject to any liability under this section if it proves—

> (a) that it acted in reliance on a statement made to it by the employer to the effect that, by reason of the operation of subsection (4), its action would not be unlawful, and
>
> (b) that it was reasonable for it to rely on the statement.

(6) A person who knowingly or recklessly makes a statement such as is referred to in subsection (5) (a) which in a material respect is false or misleading commits an offence, and shall be liable on summary conviction to a fine not exceeding £400.

COMMENCEMENT
> See s. 83 (2), *post*, and the note "orders under this section" thereto.

DISCRIMINATE
> S. 82 (1) construed in accordance with s. 5 (1).

WOMAN
> S. 82 (1) and s. 5 (2). By s. 2 a reference to a woman is to be read as applying also to a man. By s. 3 this section has to be read as applying also to the treatment of married persons for the purposes of s. 3. By s. 4 this section has to be read as applying also to discrimination by way of victimisation.

EMPLOYMENT AGENCY
> S. 82 (1).

LOCAL EDUCATION AUTHORITY
> Defined by the Education Act 1944, s. 6 (1), Sch. 1, Part I, 11 Halsbury's Statutes (3rd Edn.), pp. 189, 265, together with the Local Government Act 1972, ss. 1 (10), 20 (6), 192 (1), vol. 42, *ibid.*, pp. 854, 868, 1020, and the London Government Act 1963, s. 30, vol. 20, *ibid.*, p. 482.

EDUCATION AUTHORITY
> S. 82 (1).

EMPLOYMENT
> S. 82 (1).

LAWFULLY REFUSE TO OFFER
> S. 7, genuine occupational qualification; exceptions listed in Part V, ss. 43–52. Also s. 51, an act done under a statutory authority.

EMPLOYMENT AND TRAINING ACT 1973
> 43 Halsbury's Statutes (3rd Edn.), p. 434, s. 8 at p. 445.

PERSON
> S. 19, Interpretation Act 1889: includes a body corporate or unincorporate. See also s. 2, Interpretation Act 1889 for definition of person in connection with an offence liable to summary conviction.

EXCEPTIONS
> Sub-ss. (1) an (2) must be read subject to the general exceptions in Part V (ss. 43–52), *post*. Note also sub-ss. (4) and (5), above.

SUMMARY CONVICTION

Summary jurisdiction and procedure in England and Wales are mainly governed by the Magistrates' Courts Act 1952, 21 Halsbury's Statutes (3rd Edn.), p. 316, and certain provisions of the Criminal Justice Act 1967, vol. 21, *ibid.*, p. 363.

KNOWINGLY

There is authority for saying that, where a person deliberately refrains from making inquiries the results of which he might not care to have, this constitutes in law actual knowledge of the facts in question; see *Knox* v. *Boyd*, 1941 S.C. (J.) 82, at p. 86, and *Taylor's Central Garages (Exeter), Ltd.* v. *Roper* (1951), 115 J.P. 445, at pp. 449, 450, *per* Devlin, J.; and see also, in particular, *Mallon* v. *Allon*, [1964] 1 Q.B. 385; [1963] 3 All E.R. 843, at pp. 394 and 847, respectively. Yet, mere neglect to ascertain what would have been found out by making reasonable inquiries is not tantamount to knowledge; see *Taylor's Central Garages (Exeter), Ltd.* v. *Roper, ubi supra, per* Devlin, J.; and cf. *London Computator Ltd.* v. *Seymour*, [1944] 2 All E.R. 11; but see *Mallon* v. *Allon, ubi supra.*

RECKLESSLY

On the meaning of this expression, see, in particular, *Derry* v. *Peek* (1889), 14 App. Cas. 337; [1886–90] All E.R. Rep. 1; *Williams Brothers Direct Supply Stores, Ltd.* v. *Cloote* (1944), 60 T.L.R. 270; *R.* v. *Bates*, [1952] 2 All E.R. 842 (on appeal *sub nom. R.* v. *Russell*, [1953] 1 W.L.R. 77; 97 Sol. Jo. 12); *R.* v. *Mackinnon*, [1959] 1 Q.B. 150; [1958] 3 All E.R. 657; *R.* v. *Grunwald*, [1963] 1 Q.B. 935; [1960] 3 All E.R. 380; *Shawinigan Ltd.* v. *Vokins & Co., Ltd.*, [1961] 3 All E.R. 396; and *M.F.I. Warehouses, Ltd.* v. *Nattrass*, [1973] 1 All E.R. 762.

MATERIAL RESPECT

Cf. the note "Material particular" to s. 59, *post.*

FALSE

A statement may be false on account of what it omits even though it is literally true; see *R.* v. *Lord Kylsant*, [1932] 1 K.B. 442; [1931] All E.R. Rep. 179, and *R.* v. *Bishirgian*, [1936] 1 All E.R. 586; and cf. *Curtis* v. *Chemical Cleaning and Dyeing Co. Ltd.*, [1951] 1 K.B. 805; [1951] 1 All E.R. 631, C.A., at pp. 808, 809 and p. 634, respectively.

COMMENTARY

See para. [**55**], *ante.*

---

16. Manpower Services Commission, etc.

(1) It is unlawful for any of the following bodies to discriminate in the provision of facilities or services under section 2 of the Employment and Training Act 1973—

    (*a*) the Manpower Services Commission;
    (*b*) the Employment Service Agency;
    (*c*) the Training Services Agency.

(2) This section does not apply in a case where—

    (*a*) section 14 applies, or
    (*b*) the body is acting as an employment agency.

COMMENCEMENT

See s. 83 (2), *post*, and the note "orders under this section" thereto.

DISCRIMINATE

S. 82 (1) to be construed in accordance with s. 5 (1).

EMPLOYMENT AGENCY

S. 15.

EMPLOYMENT AND TRAINING ACT 1973, S. 2
See 43 Halsbury's Statutes (3rd Edn.), p. 437.

EXCEPTIONS
General exceptions in Part V (ss. 43–57), *post.*

MANPOWER SERVICES COMMISSION: EMPLOYMENT SERVICE AGENCY:
TRAINING SERVICES AGENCY
These bodies are established by the Employment and Training Act 1973, s. 1, Sch. 1,
43 Halsbury's Statutes (3rd Edn.), pp. 436, 455.

ENFORCEMENT
For relevant provisions see ss. 62–65, 67–71 and 73–76, *post.*

COMMENTARY
See para. [**59**], *ante.*

Special cases

17. Police

(1) For the purposes of this Part, the holding of the office of constable shall be treated as employment—

> (*a*) by the chief officer of police as respects any act done by him in relation to a constable or that office;
>
> (*b*) by the police authority as respects any act done by them in relation to a constable or that office.

(2) Regulations made under section 33, 34 or 35 of the Police Act 1964 shall not treat men and women differently except—

> (*a*) as to requirements relating to height, uniform or equipment, or allowances in lieu of uniform or equipment, or
>
> (*b*) so far as special treatment is accorded to women in connection with pregnancy or childbirth, or
>
> (*c*) in relation to pensions to or in respect of special constables or police cadets.

(3) Nothing in this Part renders unlawful any discrimination between male and female constables as to matters such as are mentioned in subsection (2) (*a*).

(4) There shall be paid out of the police fund—

> (*a*) any compensation, costs or expenses awarded against a chief officer of police in any proceedings brought against him under this Act, and any costs or expenses incurred by him in any such proceedings so far as not recovered by him in the proceedings; and
>
> (*b*) any sum required by a chief officer of police for the settlement of any claim made against him under this Act if the settlement is approved by the police authority.

(5) Any proceedings under this Act which, by virtue of subsection (1), would lie against a chief officer of police shall be brought against the chief officer of police for the time being or, in the case of a vacancy in that office, against the person for the time being performing the functions of that office; and references in subsection (4) to the chief officer of police shall be construed accordingly.

(6) Subsections (1) and (3) apply to a police cadet and appointment as a police cadet as they apply to a constable and the office of constable.

(7) In this section—

"chief officer of police"—

    (*a*) in relation to a person appointed, or an appointment falling to be made, under a specified Act, has the same meaning as in the Police Act 1964,

    (*b*) in relation to any other person or appointment means the officer who has the direction and control of the body of constables or cadets in question;

"police authority"—

    (*a*) in relation to a person appointed, or an appointment falling to be made, under a specified Act, has the same meaning as in the Police Act 1964,

    (*b*) in relation to any other person or appointment, means the authority by whom the person in question is or on appointment would be paid;

"police cadet" means any person appointed to undergo training with a view to becoming a constable;

"police fund" in relation to a chief officer of police within paragraph (*a*) of the above definition of that term has the same meaning as in the Police Act 1964, and in any other case means money provided by the police authority;

"specified Act" means the Metropolitan Police Act 1829, the City of London Police Act 1839 or the Police Act 1964.

(8) (*Applies to Scotland.*)

COMMENCEMENT
    See s. 83 (2), *post*, and the note "orders under this section" thereto.

DISCRIMINATE
    S. 82 (1) to be construed in accordance with s. 5 (1).

PART
    S. 82 (7) (*a*).

THIS PART
    I.e. Part II.

EMPLOYMENT
    S. 82 (1).

MEN
    S. 82 (1) and s. 5 (2).

WOMEN
    S. 82 (1) and s. 5 (2).

PROCEEDINGS
    S. 63 in the Industrial Tribunal. See Part VII.

APPLICATION TO THE CROWN
    See s. 85 (3).

POLICE ACT 1964
    25 Halsbury's Statutes (3rd Edn.), p. 330.

METROPOLITAN POLICE ACT 1829
    25 Halsbury's Statutes (3rd Edn.), p. 239.

POLICE (SCOTLAND) ACT 1967
    25 Halsbury's Statutes (3rd Edn.), p. 396.

PERSON
    S. 19, Interpretation Act: includes a body corporate or unincorporate.

OFFICE OF CONSTABLE
    Note the word "office": sub-s. (1) is not concerned with the holding of the rank of constable. As to the office of constable, see 30 Halsbury's Laws (3rd Edn.), pp. 43 *et seq.*

REGULATIONS . . . SHALL NOT TREAT MEN AND WOMEN DIFFERENTLY
    This section supersedes s. 8 of the Equal Pay Act 1970, now repealed by s. 8 (6) of this Act. See Sch. 1, Part I, *post.*

CHIEF OFFICER OF POLICE, POLICE AUTHORITY AND POLICE FUND
    Defined in s. 62 of the Police Act 1964 (see above) and Sch. 8 on that Act. The definitions in Sch. 8 are to the following effect:

Police Area	*Police Authority*	*Chief Officer of Police*	*Police Fund*
City of London	The Common Council	Commissioner of City of London Police	The fund out of which the expenses of the city police are paid
Metropolitan police district	Secretary of State	Commissioner of Police of the Metropolis	Metropolitan police fund
A county	Police committee	Chief Constable	County fund
A combined area	Combined police authority	Chief Constable	Combined police fund

COMMENTARY
    See paras. [63] and [64], *ante.*

18. Prison officers

(1) Nothing in this Part renders unlawful any discrimination between male and female prison officers as to requirements relating to height.

(2) In section 7 (2) of the Prison Act 1952 the words "and if women only are received in a prison the Governor shall be a woman" are repealed.

COMMENCEMENT
    See s. 83 (2), *post*, and the note "orders under this section" thereto.

DISCRIMINATION
    S. 82 (1) to be construed in accordance with s. 5 (2).

PART
    S. 82 (7) (*a*).

THIS PART
    I.e. Part II.

PRISON ACT 1952
    S. 7 (2). See 25 Halsbury's Statutes (3rd Edn.), p. 832.

COMMENTARY
    See para. [65], *ante.*

19. Ministers of religion, etc.

(1) Nothing in this Part applies to employment for purposes of an organised religion where the employment is limited to one sex so as to comply with the

doctrines of the religion or avoid offending the religious susceptibilities of a significant number of its followers.

(2) Nothing in section 13 applies to an authorisation or qualification (as defined in that section) for purposes of an organised religion where the authorisation or qualification is limited to one sex so as to comply with the doctrines of the religion or avoid offending the religious susceptibilities of a significant number of its followers.

COMMENCEMENT
See s. 83 (2), *post* and the note "orders under this section" thereto.

POWER TO AMEND THIS SECTION
S. 80 (1) (*a*).

PART
S. 82 (7) (*a*).

THIS PART
I.e. Part II.

EMPLOYMENT
S. 82 (1).

COMMENTARY
See para. [**66**], *ante*.

---

20. Midwives

(1) Section 6 (1) does not apply to employment as a midwife.

(2) Section 6 (2) (*a*) does not apply to promotion, transfer or training as a midwife.

(3) Section 14 does not apply to training as a midwife.

(4) In the Midwives Act 1951 the following section is inserted after section 35—

"35A. Extension of Act to men

From 1st January 1976 references in this Act to women (except to a woman in childbirth) apply equally to men."

(5) (*Applies to Scotland.*)

COMMENCEMENT
See s. 83 (2), *post*, and the note "orders under this section" thereto.

POWER TO AMEND THESE SUBSECTIONS
S. 80 (1) (*a*), *post*.

MIDWIVES ACT 1951
21 Halsbury's Statutes (3rd Edn.), p. 599.

EMPLOYMENT
S. 82 (1).

CONSEQUENTIAL REPEAL AND TRANSITIONAL PROVISIONS
For a repeal in the Midwives Act 1951 (21 Halsbury's Statutes (3rd Edn.), p. 509 consequential on this Act, see s. 83 (3), (4) and Sch. 6, *post*; and for a transitional provision, see s. 83 (1) and Sch. 4, para. 3, *post*.

COMMENTARY
See para. [**67**], *ante*.

21. Mineworkers

(1) The following shall be substituted for section 124 (1) of the Mines and Quarries Act 1954 (which provides that no female shall be employed below ground at a mine)—

"(1) No female shall be employed in a job the duties of which ordinarily require the employee to spend a significant proportion of his time below ground at a mine which is being worked".

(2) Throughout the Coal Mines Regulation Act 1908, for "workman" or "man" there is substituted "worker", and for "workmen" or "men" there is substituted "workers".

COMMENCEMENT
See s. 83 (2), *post*, and the note "orders under this section" thereto.

EMPLOYMENT
S. 82 (1).

MINE
See s. 180, Mines and Quarries Act, below.

MINES AND QUARRIES ACT 1954
22 Halsbury's Statutes (3rd Edn.), p. 279.

COAL MINES REGULATION ACT 1908
22 Halsbury's Statutes (3rd Edn.), p. 70.

COMMENTARY
See para. [**68**], *ante*.

PART III

DISCRIMINATION IN OTHER FIELDS

Education

22. Discrimination by bodies in charge of educational establishments

It is unlawful, in relation to an educational establishment falling within column 1 of the following table, for a person indicated in relation to the establishment in column 2 (the "responsible body") to discriminate against a woman—

(a) in the terms on which it offers to admit her to the establishment as a pupil, or

(b) by refusing or deliberately omitting to accept an application for her admission to the establishment as a pupil, or

(c) where she is a pupil of the establishment—

(i) in the way it affords her access to any benefits, facilities or services, or by refusing or deliberately omitting to afford her access to them, or

(ii) by excluding her from the establishment or subjecting her to any other detriment.

TABLE

Establishment	*Responsible body*
ENGLAND AND WALES	
1. Educational establishment maintained by a local education authority.	Local education authority or managers or governors, according to which of them has the function in question.
2. Independent school not being a special school.	Proprietor.
3. Special school not maintained by a local education authority.	Proprietor.
4. University.	Governing body.
5. Establishment (not falling within paragraphs 1 to 4) providing full-time or part-time education, being an establishment designated under section 24 (1).	Governing body.

. . . . . .

COMMENCEMENT

See s. 83 (2), *post*, and the note "orders under this section" thereto. N.B. under that section the transitional provisions made relating to admission of pupils to educational establishments.

DISCRIMINATE

S. 82 (1) to be construed in accordance with s. 5 (1).

WOMAN

S. 82 (1) and s. 5 (2).

By s. 2 a reference to a woman is to be read as applying also to a man. By s. 4 this section has to be read as applying also to discrimination by way of victimisation.

LOCAL EDUCATION AUTHORITY

See note to s. 15, *ante*.

EDUCATION

S. 82 (1): any form of training or instruction.

EDUCATION ESTABLISHMENT

S. 82 (1). For definition for Scotland see s. 145 (17) of the Education (Scotland) Act 1962.

PUPIL

S. 82 (1).

ACCESS

S. 82 (1). Defined in s. 50 as including a person indirectly providing access.

SCHOOL

S. 82 (1): has the meaning given by s. 114 (1) of Education Act 1944, in Scotland given by s. 145 (42) of the Education (Scotland) Act 1962.

SPECIAL SCHOOL

See definition in Education Act 1944, s. 9 (5), 11 Halsbury's Statutes (3rd Edn.), p. 164.

UNIVERSITY

S. 82 (1): includes a university college and the college, school or hall of a university.

INDEPENDENT SCHOOL
Has the meaning given by s. 114 (1) of Education Act 1944 (Scotland), s. 145 (23), Education (Scotland) Act 1962.

GENERAL EXCEPTIONS
See Part V (ss. 43–52, *post*).

EXCEPTIONS
S. 22 (*a*) and (*b*): see s. 26, single sex establishments. S. 22 (*c*): see s. 26 (2) boarding facilities; s. 26 (3) particular courses of instruction. S. 28: exception for courses in physical training or for teachers of physical training. S. 36 (5) for benefits facilities and services outside Great Britain.

PROPRIETOR
S. 82 (1); s. 114 (1), Education Act 1944; for Scotland: s. 145 (37), Education (Scotland) Act 1962.

PROCEDURE
For bringing a claim under this section against a body to which s. 25 (1) applies, see s. 66 (5) concerning notice to Secretary of State.

SECTION 78
For rules concerning property applicable for the provision of education in an establishment in paras. 1–5 of the Table.

SECTIONS 78 AND 79
For powers of the Secretary of State in relation to educational charities and endowments.

EMPLOYERS
See s. 82 (2) for associated employers.

TRANSITIONAL PROVISIONS
Sch. 2, ss. 5, 6, 7, 8, 9; Sch. 4, para. 4.

PERSON
S. 19, Interpretation Act 1889: includes a body corporate or unincorporate.

ENFORCEMENT
For relevant provisions see ss. 62, 66–71 and 74–76, *post*.

COMMENTARY
See para. [**71**], *ante*.

---

23. Other discrimination by local education authorities

(1) It is unlawful for a local education authority, in carrying out such of its functions under the Education Acts 1944 to 1975 as do not fall under section 22, to do any act which constitutes sex discrimination.

(2) (*Applies to Scotland.*)

COMMENCEMENT
See s. 83 (2), *post*, and the note "orders under this section" thereto.

SEX DISCRIMINATION
S. 82 (1): discrimination and related terms construed in accordance with s. 5 (1) which refers to ss. 1 and 2.

LOCAL EDUCATION AUTHORITY
See the note to s. 15, *ante*.

EDUCATION AUTHORITY
In relation to Scotland has the same meaning as in s. 145 (16) of the Education (Scotland) Act 1962.

ACT
  S. 82 (1) includes a deliberate omission.

UPPER LIMIT OF COMPULSORY SCHOOL AGE
  S. 82 (1).

GENERAL EXCEPTIONS
  See Part V (ss. 43–52), *post*.

EXCEPTIONS
  S. 28: further education courses in physical training or for teachers of physical training.
  S. 36 (5): for benefits facilities and services outside G.B.

BRINGING CLAIMS
  For bringing claims under this section against a body to which s. 25 (1) applies, see
  s. 66 (5) concerning notice to Secretary of State.

ENFORCEMENT GENERALLY
  See ss. 62, 66–71 and 74–76, *post*.

EDUCATION ACTS 1944 TO 1975
  Education Act 1944, 11 Halsbury's Statutes (3rd Edn.), p. 153.
  Education Act 1946, *ibid.*, p. 282.
  Education Act 1959, *ibid.*, p. 313.
  Education Act 1962, *ibid.*, p. 314.
  Education Act 1964, *ibid.*, p. 323.
  Education Act 1967, *ibid.*, p. 333.
  Education Act 1968, *ibid.*, p. 337.
  Education (Miscellaneous Provisions) Act 1948, *ibid.*, p. 294.
  Education (Miscellaneous Provisions) Act 1953, *ibid.*, p. 303.
  Education (No. 2) Act 1968, *ibid.*, p. 342.
  Education (Handicapped Children) Act 1970, 40 Halsbury's Statutes (3rd Edn.),
  p. 541.
  Education Act 1973, 43 Halsbury's Statutes (3rd Edn.), p. 404.
  Education Act 1975, 45 Halsbury's Statutes (3rd Edn.), p. 311.

COMMENTARY
  See para. [**72**], *ante*.

---

24. Designated establishments

(1) The Secretary of State may by order designate for the purposes of paragraph 5 of the table in section 22 such establishments of the description mentioned in that paragraph as he thinks fit.

(2) An establishment shall not be designated under subsection (1) unless—

   (a) it is recognised by the Secretary of State as a polytechnic, or

   (b) it is an establishment in respect of which grants are payable out of money provided by Parliament, or

   (c) it is assisted by a local education authority in accordance with a scheme approved under section 42 of the Education Act 1944, or

   (d) it provides full-time education for persons who have attained the upper limit of compulsory school age but not the age of nineteen.

(3) A designation under subsection (1) shall remain in force until revoked notwithstanding that the establishment ceases to be within subsection (2).

COMMENCEMENT
  See s. 83 (2), *post*, and the note "orders under this section" thereto.

BY ORDER
S. 81 (1): powers exercisable by statutory instrument; see also s. 81 (4) and (5).

PARA. 5 OF S. 22
Establishments providing full-time or part-time education not mentioned in paras. 1–4.

EDUCATION
S. 82 (1) any form of training or instruction.

LOCAL EDUCATION AUTHORITY
See note to s. 15, *ante.*

DESIGNATED ESTABLISHMENTS
S. 82 (3).
Certain establishments have already been designated by: The Sex Discrimination (Designated Educational Establishments) Order 1975, S.I. 1975 No. 1902; the Sex Discrimination (Designated Educational Establishments) (Wales) Order 1975, S.I. 1975 No. 2113.

TRANSITIONAL EXEMPTION ORDERS
For an establishment designated under s. 24 (1); Sch. 2, para. 3.

EDUCATION ACT 1944
11 Halsbury's Statutes (3rd Edn.), p. 153.

SECRETARY OF STATE
S. 12, Interpretation Act 1889: one of her Majesty's Principal Secretaries of State for the time being.

UPPER LIMIT OF COMPULSORY SCHOOL AGE
For meaning see s. 82 (1), *post.*

ATTAINED . . . THE AGE OF 19
A person attains a given age at the commencement of the relevant anniversary of the date of his birth; see the Family Law Reform Act 1969, s. 9, 17 Halsbury's Statutes (3rd Edn.), p. 798.

ORDERS UNDER THIS SECTION
The Sex Discrimination (Designated Educational Establishments) Order 1975, S.I. 1975 No. 1902. The Sex Discrimination (Designated Educational Establishments) (Wales) Order 1975, S.I. 1975 No. 2113.

COMMENTARY
See para. [**70**], *ante.*

---

25. General duty in public sector of education

(1) Without prejudice to its obligation to comply with any other provision of this Act, a body to which this subsection applies shall be under a general duty to secure that facilities for education provided by it, and any ancillary benefits or services, are provided without sex discrimination.

(2) The following provisions of the Education Act 1944, namely—
    (*a*) section 68 (power of Secretary of State to require duties under that Act to be exercised reasonably), and
    (*b*) section 99 (powers of Secretary of State where local education authorities etc. are in default),

shall apply to the performance by a body to which subsection (1) applies of the duties imposed by sections 22 and 23 and shall also apply to the performance of the general duty imposed by subsection (1), as they apply to the performance by a local education authority of a duty imposed by that Act.

(3) (*Applies to Scotland.*)

(4) The sanctions in subsections (2) and (3) shall be the only sanctions for breach of the general duty in subsection (1), but without prejudice to the enforcement of sections 22 and 23 under section 66 or otherwise (where the breach is also a contravention of either of those sections).

(5) (*Applies to Scotland.*)

(6) Subsection (1) applies to—

(a) local education authorities in England and Wales;
(b) (*applies to Scotland*)
(c) any other body which is a responsible body in relation to—

    (i) an establishment falling within paragraph 1, 3 or 7 of the table in section 22;

    (ii) an establishment designated under section 24 (1) as falling within paragraph (a) or (c) or section 24 (2);

    (iii) an establishment designated under section 24 (1) as falling within paragraph (b) of section 24 (2) where the grants in question are payable under section 100 of the Education Act 1944.

COMMENCEMENT
See s. 83 (2), *post*, and the note "orders under this section" thereto. N.B. under that section the transitional provisions made relating to admission of pupils to educational establishments.

SEX DISCRIMINATION
S. 82 (1): discrimination and related terms to be construed in accordance with s. 5 (1), referring to ss. 1 and 2.

EDUCATION AUTHORITY
In relation to Scotland has the meaning in s. 145 (16), Education (Scotland) Act 1962.

LOCAL EDUCATION AUTHORITY
See note to s. 15, *ante*.

EDUCATION
Includes any form of training or instruction.

RESPONSIBLE BODY
S. 22.

EXCEPTIONS
S. 26: single sex establishments. S. 28: physical training or courses for teachers of physical training. S. 36 (5): benefits, facilities and services outside G.B. S. 46: communal accommodation.

EDUCATION ACT 1944
11 Halsbury's Statutes (3rd Edn.), p. 153.

ENFORCEMENT
The EOC cannot serve a non-discrimination notice in respect of acts over which the Secretary of State has powers under s. 25 (2) and (3); see s. 67.

SECRETARY OF STATE
S. 12, Interpretation Act 1889: one of Her Majesty's Principal Secretary's of State for the time being.

TRANSITIONAL PROVISIONS
Sch. 4, para. 4.

COMMENTARY
See para. [73], *ante*.

26. Exception for single-sex establishments

(1) Sections 22 (*a*) and (*b*) and 25 do not apply to the admission of pupils to any establishment (a "single-sex establishment") which admits pupils of one sex only, or which would be taken to admit pupils of one sex only if there were disregarded pupils of the opposite sex—

(*a*) whose admission is exceptional, or

(*b*) whose numbers are comparatively small and whose admission is confined to particular courses of instruction or teaching classes.

(2) Where a school which is not a single-sex establishment has some pupils as boarders and others as non-boarders, and admits as boarders pupils of one sex only (or would be taken to admit as boarders pupils of one sex only if there were disregarded boarders of the opposite sex whose numbers are comparatively small), sections 22 (*a*) and (*b*) and 25 do not apply to the admission of boarders and sections 22 (*c*) (i) and 25 do not apply to boarding facilities.

(3) Where an establishment is a single-sex establishment by reason of its inclusion in subsection (1) (*b*), the fact that pupils of one sex are confined to particular courses of instruction or teaching classes shall not be taken to contravene section 22 (*c*) (i) or the duty in section 25.

COMMENCEMENT
See s. 83 (2), *post*, and the note "orders under this section" thereto.

PUPIL
In Scotland includes student of any age.

SCHOOL
S. 82 (1); interpretation: s. 114 (1), Education Act 1944; in Scotland, s. 145 (42), Education (Scotland) Act 1962.

EDUCATION ACT 1944
11 Halsbury's Statutes (3rd Edn.) p. 153.

COMMENTARY
See paras. [**74**] and [**77**], *ante*.

27. Exception for single-sex establishments turning co-educational

(1) Where at any time—

(*a*) the responsible body for a single-sex establishment falling within column 1 of the table in section 22 determines to alter its admissions arrangements so that the establishment will cease to be a single-sex establishment, or

(*b*) section 26 (2) applies to the admission of boarders to a school falling within column 1 of that table but the responsible body determines to alter its admissions arrangements so that section 26 (2) will cease so to apply,

the responsible body may apply in accordance with Schedule 2 for an order (a "transitional exemption order") authorising discriminatory admissions during the transitional period specified in the order.

(2) Where during the transitional period specified in a transitional exemption order applying to an establishment the responsible body refuses or deliberately omits to accept an application for the admission of a person to the

establishment as a pupil the refusal or omission shall not be taken to contravene any provision of this Act.

(3) Subsection (2) does not apply if the refusal or omission contravenes any condition of the transitional exemption order.

(4) Except as mentioned in subsection (2), a transitional exemption order shall not afford any exemption from liability under this Act.

(5) Where, during the period between the making of an application for a transitional exemption order in relation to an establishment and the determination of the application, the responsible body refuses or deliberately omits to accept an application for the admission of a person to the establishment as a pupil the refusal or omission shall not be taken to contravene any provision of this Act.

COMMENCEMENT
    See s. 83 (2), *post*, and the note "orders under this section" thereto.

RESPONSIBLE BODY
    S. 22.

SINGLE SEX ESTABLISHMENTS
    S. 26.

DISCRIMINATION
    S. 82 (1) to be construed in accordance with s. 5 (1).

PUPIL
    In Scotland includes a student of any age.

ORDERS
    S. 81: usual power to make orders expressly excepts this section.

TRANSITIONAL ORDERS
    See Sch. 2 and Sch. 4, para. 4.

SHALL NOT BE TAKEN TO CONTRAVENE ANY PROVISION OF THIS ACT
    The provision which is particularly relevant is s. 22 (6), *ante* (as read with s. 2, *ante*).

COMMENTARY
    See paras. [**74**] and [**75**], *ante*.

28. Exception for physical training

Sections 22, 23 and 25 do not apply to any further education course being—

    (*a*) a course in physical training, or

    (*b*) a course designed for teachers of physical training.

COMMENCEMENT
    S. 83 (2), *post*, and the note "orders under this section" thereto.

FURTHER EDUCATION
    S. 82 (1): defined as having the meaning given by s. 41 (*a*) of the Education Act 1944 and in Scotland has the meaning given by s. 145 (21) of the Education (Scotland) Act 1962.

TRAINING
    S. 82 (1): includes any form of education or instruction.

COMMENTARY
    See para. [**75**], *ante*.

Goods, facilities, services and premises

29. Discrimination in provision of goods, facilities or services

(1) It is unlawful for any person concerned with the provision (for payment or not) of goods, facilities or services to the public or a section of the public to discriminate against a woman who seeks to obtain or use those goods, facilities or services—

> (*a*) by refusing or deliberately omitting to provide her with any of them, or
>
> (*b*) by refusing or deliberately omitting to provide her with goods, facilities or services of the like quality, in the like manner and on the like terms as are normal in his case in relation to male members of the public or (where she belongs to a section of the public) to male members of that section.

(2) The following are examples of the facilities and services mentioned in subsection (1)—

> (*a*) access to and use of any place which members of the public or a section of the public are permitted to enter;
>
> (*b*) accommodation in a hotel, boarding house or other similar establishment;
>
> (*c*) facilities by way of banking or insurance or for grants, loans, credit or finance;
>
> (*d*) facilities for education;
>
> (*e*) facilities for entertainment, recreation or refreshment;
>
> (*f*) facilities for transport or travel;
>
> (*g*) the services of any profession or trade, or any local or other public authority.

(3) For the avoidance of doubt it is hereby declared that where a particular skill is commonly exercised in a different way for men and for women it does not contravene subsection (1) for a person who does not normally exercise it for women to insist on exercising it for a woman only in accordance with his normal practice or, if he reasonably considers it impracticable to do that in her case, to refuse or deliberately omit to exercise it.

COMMENCEMENT
> See s. 83 (2), *post*, and the note "orders under this section" thereto.

POWER TO AMEND
> S. 80: this gives the Secretary of State power to amend Parts II, III or IV to render lawful an act otherwise unlawful under s. 29 (1).

DISCRIMINATE
> S. 82 (1) construed in accordance with s. 5 (1).

WOMAN
> S. 82 (1) and s. 5 (2). By s. 2 a reference to a woman is to be read as applying also to a man. By s. 4 this section has to be read as applying also to discrimination by way of victimisation for the purposes of s. 4.

ACCESS
> S. 82 (1) construed in accordance with s. 50 as including persons indirectly concerned with access to benefits.

EDUCATION
> Includes any form of training or instruction: s. 82 (1).

MEN
S. 82 (1) and s. 5 (2).

TRADE
Includes any business: s. 82 (1).

EDUCATION
S. 82 (1) includes any form of training or instruction.

EXCEPTIONS
S. 32: exceptions to s. 29 (1). S. 33: exceptions to s. 29 (1) in the case of the constitution, organisation or administration of political parties. S. 34: exceptions to s. 29 (1) in the case of voluntary bodies. Further exceptions listed in s. 35 and s. 44. Exception in s. 45 to s. 29 (2) (c). S. 46: regarding communal accommodation.

GENERAL EXCEPTIONS
See Part V (ss. 43–52), *post*.

PERSON
S. 19, Interpretation Act 1889: includes a body corporate or unincorporate.

ENFORCEMENT
For relevant provisions, see ss. 62, 66–71 and 74–76, *post*.

COMMENTARY
See paras. [**79**] and [**80**], *ante*.

30. Discrimination in disposal or management of premises

(1) It is unlawful for a person, in relation to premises in Great Britain of which he has power to dispose, to discriminate against a woman—

(a) in the terms on which he offers her those premises, or

(b) by refusing her application for those premises, or

(c) in his treatment of her in relation to any list of persons in need of premises of that description.

(2) It is unlawful for a person, in relation to premises managed by him, to discriminate against a woman occupying the premises—

(a) in the way he affords her access to any benefits or facilities, or by refusing or deliberately omitting to afford her access to them, or

(b) by evicting her, or subjecting her to any other detriment.

(3) Subsection (1) does not apply to a person who owns an estate or interest in the premises and wholly occupies them unless he uses the services of an estate agent for the purposes of the disposal of the premises, or publishes or causes to be published an advertisement in connection with the disposal.

COMMENCEMENT
See s. 83 (2), *post*, and the note "orders under this section" thereto.

POWER TO AMEND
Power to amend Parts II, III and IV to render lawful an act which, without the amendment, would be unlawful under this section: s. 80.

DISCRIMINATE
S. 82 (1) to be construed in accordance with s. 5 (1).

WOMAN
S. 82 (1) and s. 5 (2). By s. 2 a reference to a woman is to be read as applying also to a man. By s. 4 this section has to be read as applying also to discrimination by way of victimisation.

DISPOSE
S. 82 (1) in relation to premises includes granting a right to occupy the premises and any reference to acquiring the premises shall be construed accordingly.

ACCESS
S. 82 (1) construed in accordance with s. 50 including persons indirectly concerned with the access to benefits.

ESTATE AGENT
S. 82 (1) defines estate agent.

ADVERTISEMENT
S. 82 (1); s. 38: rules as to discriminatory advertising.

PERSON
S. 19, Interpretation Act 1889: includes a body corporate or unincorporate.

HE
S. 1 (1) (a) and (b), Interpretation Act 1889: included in the masculine are feminine and plural.

EXCEPTIONS
S. 32. Small dwellings: s. 34. Voluntary bodies: s. 35.

GENERAL EXCEPTIONS
Part V (ss. 43–52), *post.*

ENFORCEMENT
See ss. 62, 66–71 and 74–76, *post.*

GREAT BRITAIN
I.e., England, Scotland and Wales; see the Union with Scotland Act 1706, preamble, art. 1, 6 Halsbury's Statutes (3rd Edn.), 502, and the Wales and Berwick Act 1746, s. 3, 32 Halsbury's Statutes (3rd Edn.), 412.

COMMENTARY
See paras. [**86**], [**87**] and [**88**], *ante.*

---

31. Discrimination: consent for assignment or sub-letting

(1) Where the licence or consent of the landlord or of any other person is required for the disposal to any person of premises in Great Britain comprised in a tenancy, it is unlawful for the landlord or other person to discriminate against a woman by withholding the licence or consent for disposal of the premises to her.

(2) Subsection (1) does not apply if—

    (a) the person withholding a licence or consent, or a near relative of his ("the relevant occupier") resides, and intends to continue to reside, on the premises, and

    (b) there is on the premises, in addition to the accommodation occupied by the relevant occupier, accommodation (not being storage accommodation or means of access) shared by the relevant occupier with other persons residing on the premises who are not members of his household, and

    (c) the premises are small premises as defined in section 32 (2).

(3) In this section "tenancy" means a tenancy created by a lease or sub-lease, by an agreement for a lease or sub-lease or by a tenancy agreement or in

pursuance of any enactment; and "disposal", in relation to premises comprised in a tenancy, includes assignment or assignation of the tenancy and sub-letting or parting with possession of the premises or any part of the premises.

(4) This section applies to tenancies created before the passing of this Act as well as to others.

COMMENCEMENT
See s. 83 (2), *post*, and the note "orders under this section" thereto.

POWER TO AMEND
Power to amend Parts II, III and IV, to render lawful an act which without the amendment would be unlawful under this section: s. 80.

SUBSECTION (2)
The Secretary of State is empowered to amend this section by order: s. 80 (1).

DISPOSE
S. 82 (1): in relation to premises, includes granting a right to occupy the premises and any reference to acquiring the premises shall be construed accordingly.

DISCRIMINATE
S. 82 (1) construed in accordance with s. 5 (1).

WOMAN
S. 82 (1) and s. 5 (2). By s. 2 a reference to a woman is to be read as applying also to a man. By s. 4 this section has to be read as applying also to discrimination by way of victimisation.

NEAR RELATIVE
Defined in s. 82 (5).

PERSON
S. 19, Interpretation Act 1889: includes a body corporate or unincorporate.

GREAT BRITAIN
See the note to s. 30, *ante*.

EXCEPTIONS
For general exceptions, see Part V (ss. 43–52), *post*.

ENFORCEMENT
For relevant provisions, see ss. 62, 66–71 and 74–76, *post*.

PASSING OF THIS ACT
This Act received Royal Assent on 12th November, 1975.

RESIDES
A person resides where in common parlance he lives, and a temporary absence is immaterial providing there is an intention to return and a house or lodging to which to return: see *R. v. St. Leonard's, Shoreditch (Inhabitants)*, [1865] 1 Q.B. 21; *R. v. Glossop Union*, [1866] 1 Q.B. 227. There is authority for saying that a person may be resident in more than one place at the same time: see *Levene v. Inland Revenue Comrs.*, [1928] A.C. 217; [1928] All E.R. Rep. 746, H.L., *per* Viscount Cave, L.C., at pp. 223 and 749 respectively, and *Langford Property Co., Ltd. v. Tureman*, [1949] 1 K.B. 29; *sub nom. Langford Property Co., Ltd. v. Athanassoglou*, [1948] 2 All E.R. 722, C.A., and see also *Fox v. Stirk*, [1970] 2 Q.B. 463; [1970] 3 All E.R. 7, C.A.

COMMENTARY
See para. [**93**], *ante*.

32. Exception for small dwellings

(1) Sections 29 (1) and 30 do not apply to the provision by a person of accommodation in any premises, or the disposal of premises by him, if—

- (a) that person or a near relative of his ("the relevant occupier") resides, and intends to continue to reside, on the premises, and
- (b) there is on the premises, in addition to the accommodation occupied by the relevant occupier, accommodation (not being storage accommodation or means of access) shared by the relevant occupier with other persons residing on the premises who are not members of his household, and
- (c) the premises are small premises.

(2) Premises shall be treated for the purposes of subsection (1) as small premises if—

- (a) in the case of premises comprising residential accommodation for one or more households (under separate letting or similar agreements) in addition to the accommodation occupied by the relevant occupier, there is not normally residential accommodation for more than two such households and only the relevant occupier and any member of his household reside in the accommodation occupied by him;
- (b) in the case of premises not falling within paragraph (a), there is not normally residential accommodation on the premises for more than six persons in addition to the relevant occupier and any members of his household.

COMMENCEMENT
See s. 83 (2), *post*, and the note "orders under this section" thereto.

POWER TO AMEND
The Secretary of State is empowered to amend this section by order: s. 80 (1).

DISPOSE
S. 82 (1): in relation to premises, includes granting a right to occupy the premises and any reference to acquiring the premises shall be construed accordingly.

NEAR RELATIVE
S. 82 (5).

RESIDES
See note to s. 31.

PERSON
S. 19, Interpretation Act 1889: includes a body corporate or unincorporate.

COMMENTARY
See paras. [89] and [90], *ante*.

---

33. Exception for political parties

(1) This section applies to a political party if—

- (a) it has as its main object, or one of its main objects, the promotion of parliamentary candidatures for the Parliament of the United Kingdom, or
- (b) it is an affiliate of, or has as an affiliate, or has similar formal links with, a political party within paragraph (a).

(2) Nothing in section 29 (1) shall be construed as affecting any special provision for persons of one sex only in the constitution, organisation or administration of the political party.

(3) Nothing in section 29 (1) shall render unlawful an act done in order to give effect to such a special provision.

COMMENCEMENT
See s. 83 (2), *post*, and the note "orders under this section" thereto.

AMENDMENT
The Secretary of State is empowered to amend this section by order: s. 80 (1).

ACT
S. 82 (1), *post*, includes a deliberate omission.

COMMENTARY
See para. [85], *ante*.

34. Exception for voluntary bodies

(1) This section applies to a body—
- (*a*) the activities of which are carried on otherwise than for profit, and
- (*b*) which was not set up by any enactment.

(2) Sections 29 (1) and 30 shall not be construed as rendering unlawful—
- (*a*) the restriction of membership of any such body to persons of one sex (disregarding any minor exceptions), or
- (*b*) the provision of benefits, facilities or services to members of any such body where the membership is so restricted,

even though membership of the body is open to the public, or to a section of the public.

(3) Nothing in section 29 or 30 shall—
- (*a*) be construed as affecting a provision to which this subsection applies, or
- (*b*) render unlawful an act which is done in order to give effect to such a provision.

(4) Subsection (3) applies to a provision for conferring benefits on persons of one sex only (disregarding any benefits to persons to the opposite sex which are exceptional or are relatively insignificant), being a provision which constitutes the main object of a body within subsection (1).

COMMENCEMENT
See s. 83 (2), *post*, and the note "orders under this section" thereto.

POWER TO AMEND
The Secretary of State is empowered to amend this section by order: s. 80 (1).

FACILITIES AND SERVICES
Examples are given in s. 29 (2).

ACT
This includes a deliberate omission: see s. 82 (1).

COMMENTARY
See para. [91], *ante*.

35. Further exceptions from ss. 29 (1) and 30

(1) A person who provides at any place facilities or services restricted to men does not for that reason contravene section 29 (1) if—

> (*a*) the place is, or is part of, a hospital, reception centre provided by the Supplementary Benefits Commission or other establishment for persons requiring special care, supervision or attention, or
>
> (*b*) the place is (permanently or for the time being) occupied or used for the purposes of an organised religion, and the facilities or service are restricted to men so as to comply with the doctrines of that religion or avoid offending the religious susceptibilities of a significant number of its followers, or
>
> (*c*) the facilities or services are provided for, or are likely to be used by, two or more persons at the same time, and
>
>> (i) the facilities or services are such, or those persons are such, that male users are likely to suffer serious embarrassment at the presence of a woman, or
>>
>> (ii) the facilities or service are such that a user is likely to be in a state of undress and a male user might reasonably object to the presence of a female user.

(2) A person who provides facilities or services restricted to men does not for that reason contravene section 29 (1) if the services or facilities are such that physical contact between the user and any other person is likely, and that other person might reasonably object if the user were a woman.

(3) Sections 29 (1) and 30 do not apply—

> (*a*) to discrimination which is rendered unlawful by any provision in column 1 of the table below, or
>
> (*b*) to discrimination which would be so unlawful but for any provision in column 2 of that table, or
>
> (*c*) to discrimination which contravenes a term modified or included by virtue of an equality clause.

TABLE

Provision creating illegality	*Exception*
Part II	Sections 6 (3), 7 (1) (*b*), 15 (4), 19 and 20.
	Schedule 4 paragraphs 1 and 2.
Section 22 or 23	Sections 26, 27 and 28.
	Schedule 4 paragraph 4.

COMMENCEMENT
   See s. 83 (2), *post*, and the note "orders under this section" thereto.

POWER TO AMEND
   The Secretary of State is empowered to amend this section by order: s. 80 (1).

FACILITIES AND SERVICES
   Examples given in s. 29 (2).

MEN
   S. 82 (1) and s. 5 (2).

WOMEN
   S. 82 (1) and s. 5 (2).

EQUALITY CLAUSE
    S. 82 (1).

COMMUNAL ACCOMMODATION
    See s. 46 (8), *post.*

PERSON
    S. 19, Interpretation Act 1889: includes a body corporate or unincorporate. S. 1 (1) (*a*) and (*b*), Interpretation Act 1889: masculine includes feminine and plural.

RESTRICTED TO MEN
    This section applies with the necessary modifications to discrimination against men: see ss. 2 and 4 (3), *ante.*

SUPPLEMENTARY BENEFITS COMMISSION
    This body was established by the Supplementary Benefit Act 1966, s. 3, Sch. 1, 23 Halsbury's Statutes (3rd Edn.), pp. 697, 720.

PART
    See s. 82 (7), *post.*

COMMENTARY
    See para. [**84**], *ante.*

Extent

36. Extent of Part III

(1) Section 29 (1)—

   (*a*) does not apply to goods, facilities or services outside Great Britain except as provided in subsections (2) and (3), and
   (*b*) does not apply to facilities by way of banking or insurance or for grants, loans, credit or finance, where the facilities are for a purpose to be carried out, or in connection with risks wholly or mainly arising, outside Great Britain.

(2) Section 29 (1) applies to the provision of facilities for travel outside Great Britain where the refusal or omission occurs in Great Britain or on a ship, aircraft or hovercraft within subsection (3).

(3) Section 29 (1) applies on and in relation to—

   (*a*) any ship registered at a port of registry in Great Britain, and
   (*b*) any aircraft or hovercraft registered in the United Kingdom and operated by a person who has his principal place of business, or is ordinarily resident, in Great Britain,
   (*c*) any ship, aircraft or hovercraft belonging to or possessed by Her Majesty in right of the Government of the United Kingdom.

even if the ship, aircraft or hovercraft is outside Great Britain.

(4) This section shall not render unlawful an act done in or over a country outside the United Kingdom, or in or over that country's territorial waters, for the purpose of complying with the laws of that country.

(5) Sections 22, 23 and 25 do not apply to benefits, facilities or services outside Great Britain except—

   (*a*) travel on a ship registered at a port of registry in Great Britain, and
   (*b*) benefits, facilities or services provided on a ship so registered.

COMMENCEMENT
See s. 83 (2), *post*, and the note "orders under this section" thereto.

GOODS, FACILITIES AND SERVICES
Examples given in s. 29 (2).

GREAT BRITAIN
S. 82 (1): includes such of the territorial waters of the U.K. as are adjacent to G.B. See also note to s. 30, *ante*.

UNITED KINGDOM
Great Britain and Northern Ireland: Royal and Parliamentary Titles Act 1927, s. 2 (2). Northern Ireland Constitution Act 1973, s. 1. The Channel Islands and the Isle of Man are excluded though: see 6 Halsbury's Laws (4th Edn.), paras. 1203–1206.

ACT
S. 82 (1): includes a deliberate omission.

HER MAJESTY
S. 30, Interpretation Act 1889: reference to the Crown shall be construed as a reference to the Sovereign for the time being. For application to the Crown, see s. 85.

REGISTRATION OF SHIPS, ETC.
See s. 10, *ante*.

TERRITORIAL WATERS
See note to s. 82, *post*.

COMMENTARY
See para. [**81**], *ante*.

PART IV
OTHER UNLAWFUL ACTS

37. Discriminatory practices

(1) In this section "discriminatory practice" means the application of a requirement or condition which results in an act of discrimination which is unlawful by
virtue of any provision of Part II or III taken with section 1 (1) (*b*) or 3 (1) (*b*)
or which would be likely to result in such an act of discrimination if the persons
to whom it is applied were not all of one sex.

(2) A person acts in contravention of this section if and so long as—

    (*a*) he applies a discriminatory practice, or

    (*b*) he operates practices or other arrangements which in any circum-
stances would call for the application by him of a discriminatory
practice.

(3) Proceedings in respect of a contravention of this section shall be brought
only by the Commission in accordance with sections 67 to 71 of this Act.

COMMENCEMENT
See s. 83 (2), *post*, and the note "orders under this section" thereto.

DISCRIMINATE
S. 82 (1) construed in accordance with s. 5 (1), as limited by sub-s. (1) above.

ACT
S. 82 (1): includes a deliberate omission.

INFORMATION
Power to obtain information in relation to this section: s. 59 (2).

NON-DISCRIMINATION NOTICE
Power to serve a non-discrimination notice in relation to a breach of this section: s. 67 (1) (*b*).

INJUNCTION
Powers of the EOC to act where there has been a breach of this section by obtaining an injunction: s. 71.

THE COMMISSION
S. 82 (1), *post*.

PERSON
S. 19, Interpretation Act 1889: includes a body corporate or unincorporate. S. 1 (1) (*a*) and (*b*), Interpretation Act 1889: masculine includes feminine and plural.

PART II
Ss. 6–21.

PART III
Ss. 22–36.

GENERAL EXCEPTIONS
See Part V, *post*.

ENFORCEMENT
See relevant provisions of ss. 62, 67–71, *post*.

COMMENTARY
See para. **[8]**, *ante*.

---

38. Discriminatory advertisements

(1) It is unlawful to publish or cause to be published an advertisement which indicates, or might reasonably be understood as indicating, an intention by a person to do any act which is or might be unlawul by virtue of Part II or III.

(2) Subsection (1) does not apply to an advertisement if the intended act would not in fact be unlawful.

(3) For the purposes of subsection (1), use of a job description with a sexual connotation (such as "waiter", "salesgirl", "postman" or "stewardess") shall be taken to indicate an intention to discriminate, unless the advertisement contains an indication to the contrary.

(4) The publisher of an advertisement made unlawful by subsection (1) shall not be subject to any liability under that subsection in respect of the publication of the advertisement if he proves—

(*a*) that the advertisement was published in reliance on a statement made to him by the person who caused it to be published to the effect that, by reason of the operation of subsection (2), the publication would not be unlawful, and

(*b*) that it was reasonable for him to rely on the statement.

(5) A person who knowingly or recklessly makes a statement such as is referred to in subsection (4) which in a material respect is false or misleading commits an offence, and shall be liable on summary conviction to a fine not exceeding £400.

COMMENCEMENT
See s. 83 (2), *post*, and the note "orders under this section" thereto. Note under that section the transitional provision relating to discriminatory advertisements printed before 1st April, 1976.

ACT
S. 82 (1) includes a deliberate omission.

PART
S. 82 (7) (*a*): reference to a Part is a reference to the Part of the Act so numbered.

PART II
Ss. 6–21.

PART III
Ss. 22–36.

DISCRIMINATE
S. 82 (1) construed in accordance with s. 5 (1).

INFORMATION
Power to obtain information under this section: s. 59 (2).

NON-DISCRIMINATION NOTICE
Power to serve a non-discrimination notice in relation to a breach of this section: s. 67 (1).

INJUNCTION
Power of the EOC to act where there has been a breach of this section by obtaining an injunction: s. 72.

PERSON
S. 19, Interpretation Act 1889: includes a body corporate or unincorporate. See s. 2, Interpretation Act for meaning of person in connection with a summary offence. Application to the crown: see s. 85, *post*. S. 1 (1) (*a*) and (*b*), Interpretation Act 1889: masculine includes feminine and plural.

ADVERTISEMENT
See s. 82 (1).

COMMENTARY
See paras. [9], [10] and [11], *ante*.

39. Instructions to discriminate

It is unlawful for a person—

    (*a*) who has authority over another person, or

    (*b*) in accordance with whose wishes that other person is accustomed to act,

to instruct him to do any act which is unlawful by virtue of Part II or III, or procure or attempt to procure the doing by him of any such act.

COMMENCEMENT
See s. 83 (2), *post*, and the note "orders under this section" thereto.

ACT
S. 82 (1): includes a deliberate omission.

PART
S. 82 (7) (*a*): reference to a Part is a reference to the Part of this Act so numbered.

INFORMATION
Power to obtain information under this section: s. 59 (2).

NON-DISCRIMINATION NOTICE
Power to serve a non-discrimination notice in relation to a breach of this section: s. 67 (1).

INJUNCTION
Power to seek an injunction for breach of this section: s. 72.

PERSON
S. 19, Interpretation Act 1889: includes a body corporate or unincorporate. S. 1 (1) (*a*)
and (*b*), *ibid*.: masculine includes feminine and plural.

COMMENTARY
See para. [**12**], *ante*.

40. Pressure to discriminate

(1) It is unlawful to induce, or attempt to induce, a person to do any act which
contravenes Part II or III by—

(*a*) providing or offering to provide him with any benefit, or
(*b*) subjecting or threatening to subject him to any detriment.

(2) An offer or threat is not prevented from falling within subsection (1)
because it is not made directly to the person in question, if it is made in such a
way that he is likely to hear of it.

COMMENCEMENT
See s. 83 (2), *post*, and the note "orders under this section" thereto.

PART
S. 82 (7): reference to a Part is a reference to the part of the Act so numbered.

INFORMATION
Power to obtain information under this section: s. 59 (2).

NON-DISCRIMINATION NOTICE
Power to serve a non-discrimination notice in relation to a breach of this section:
s. 67 (1).

INJUNCTION
Power of the EOC to act where there has been a breach of this section by obtaining an injunction: s. 72.

PERSON
S. 19, Interpretation Act 1889: includes a body corporate or unincorporate. S. 1 (1) (*a*)
and (*b*), Interpretation Act 1889, masculine includes feminine and plural.

ACT
Includes a deliberate omission: s. 82 (1).

COMMENTARY
See para. [**13**], *ante*.

41. Liability of employers and principals

(1) Anything done by a person in the course of his employment shall be treated
for the purposes of this Act as done by his employer as well as by him, whether
or not it was done with the employer's knowledge or approval.

(2) Anything done by a person as agent for another person with the authority
(whether express or implied, and whether precedent or subsequent) of that other
person shall be treated for the purposes of this Act as done by that other person
as well as by him.

(3) In proceedings brought under this Act against any person in respect of an act alleged to have been done by an employee of his it shall be a defence for that person to prove that he took such steps as were reasonably practicable to prevent the employee from doing that act, or from doing in the course of his employment acts of that description.

COMMENCEMENT
See s. 83 (2), *post*, and the note "orders under this section" thereto.

EMPLOYMENT
S. 82 (1): means employment under a contract of service or apprenticeship or a contract personally to execute any work or labour, and related expressions shall be construed accordingly.

ACT
S. 82 (1) includes a deliberate omission.

A PERSON IN COURSE OF EMPLOYMENT/A PERSON AS AGENT
For personal liability see s. 42 (2).

PROCEEDINGS
A complaint under this section in relation to employment may be presented to the Industrial Tribunal: s. 63. A claim in relation to a breach of Part III is the subject of civil proceedings under s. 66. Note in particular ss. 63 (1) (*b*) and 66 (1) (*b*).

PERSON
S. 19, Interpretation Act 1889: means a body corporate or unincorporate.

REASONABLY PRACTICABLE
This is a narrower term than "physically possible" and involves a weighing of the risk against the measures necessary to eliminate the risk; see, in particular, *Edwards* v. *National Coal Board*, [1949] 1 K.B. 704; [1949] 1 All E.R. 743, C.A.; *McCarthy* v. *Coldair, Ltd.*, [1951] 2 T.L.R. 1226; and *Marshall* v. *Gotham Co., Ltd.*, [1954] A.C. 360; [1954] 1 All E.R. 937, H.L., at pp. 369, 370 and p. 939, respectively, *per* Lord Oaksey, and at pp. 372, 373 and p. 942, respectively, *per* Lord Reid. See also *Braham* v. *J. Lyons & Co., Ltd.*, [1962] 3 All E.R. 281, C.A.; *Dorman Long (Steel), Ltd.* v. *Bell*, [1964] 1 All E.R. 617, H.L.; and *Nimmo* v. *Alexander Cowan and Sons, Ltd.*, [1968] A.C. 107; [1967] 3 All E.R. 187, H.L.

COMMENTARY
See paras. [16] and [17], *ante*.

42. Aiding unlawful Acts

(1) A person who knowingly aids another person to do an act made unlawful by this Act shall be treated for the purpose of this Act as himself doing an unlawful act of the like description.

(2) For the purposes of subsection (1) an employee or agent for whose act the employer or principal is liable under section 41 (or would be so liable but for section 41 (3)) shall be deemed to aid the doing of the act by the employer or principal.

(3) A person does not under this section knowingly aid another to do an unlawful act if—

(*a*) he acts in reliance on a statement made to him by that other person that, by reason of any provision of this Act, the act which he aids would not be unlawful, and

(*b*) it is reasonable for him to rely on the statement.

(4) A person who knowingly or recklessly makes a statement such as is referred to in subsection (3) (*a*) which in a material respect is false or misleading commits an offence, and shall be liable on summary conviction to a fine not exceeding £400.

COMMENCEMENT
See s. 83 (2), *post*, and the note "orders under this section" thereto.

ACT
S. 82 (1) includes a deliberate omission.

PROCEEDINGS
A complaint under this section in relation to employment should be presented to the Industrial Tribunal: s. 63. A claim in relation to a breach of Part III may be the subject of civil proceedings: s. 66.

PERSON
S. 19, Interpretation Act 1889: includes a body corporate or unincorporate. S. 2, Interpretation Act for person in connection with summary proceedings. S. 1 (1) (*a*) and (*b*), Interpretation Act: masculine includes feminine and plural.

KNOWINGLY
See the note to s. 15, *ante*.

RECKLESSLY
See the note to s. 15, *ante*.

FALSE
See the note to s. 15, *ante*.

SUMMARY CONVICTION
See the note to s. 15, *ante*.

MADE UNLAWFUL
I.e. any act unlawful by any provision of Part II, Part III or Part IV of the Act.

COMMENTARY
See para. [**14**], *ante*.

PART V

GENERAL EXCEPTIONS FROM PARTS II TO IV

43. Charities

(1) Nothing in Parts II to IV shall—
(*a*) be construed as affecting a provision to which this subsection applies, or
(*b*) render unlawful an act which is done in order to give effect to such a provision.

(2) Subsection (1) applies to a provision for conferring benefits on persons of one sex only (disregarding any benefits to persons of the opposite sex which are exceptional or are relatively insignificant), being a provision which is contained in a charitable instrument.

(3) In the application of this section in England and Wales—
(*a*) "charitable instrument" means an enactment or other instrument

passed or made for charitable purposes, or an enactment or other instrument so far as it relates to charitable purposes;

(b) "charitable purposes" means purposes which are exclusively charitable according to the law of England and Wales.

(4) (*Applies to Scotland.*)

COMMENCEMENT
   S. 83 (2), *post*, and the note "orders under this section" thereto.

POWER TO AMEND
   Secretary of State has power to amend this section by order: s. 80 (1).

PART
   S. 82 (7) (*a*): reference to a Part is a reference to the Part of the Act so numbered.

PARTS II TO IV
   I.e. ss. 6–41 of this Act.

CHARITABLE PURPOSES
   See 5 Halsbury's Laws (4th Edn.), paras. 501 *et seq.*

COMMENTARY
   See para. [20], *ante.*

44. Sport, etc.

Nothing in Parts II to IV shall, in relation to any sport, game or other activity of a competitive nature where the physical strength, stamina or physique of the average woman puts her at a disadvantage to the average man, render unlawful any act related to the participation of a person as a competitor in events involving that activity which are confined to competitors of one sex.

COMMENCEMENT
   S. 83 (2), *post*, and the note "orders under this section" thereto.

PART
   S. 82 (7) (*a*): reference to a Part is a reference to the Part of the Act so numbered.

PARTS II TO IV
   I.e. ss. 6–42 of this Act.

WOMAN
   S. 82 (1) and s. 5 (2).

MAN
   S. 82 (1) and s. 5 (2).

ACT
   S. 82 (1) includes a deliberate omission.

POWER TO AMEND
   The Secretary of State has power to amend this section by order. See s. 80 (1) (*a*).

COMMENTARY
   See para. [21], *ante.*

45. Insurance, etc.

Nothing in Parts II to IV shall render unlawful the treatment of a person in relation to an annuity, life assurance policy, accident insurance policy, or similar matter involving the assessment of risk, where the treatment—

(*a*) was effected by reference to actuarial or other data from a source on which it was reasonable to rely, and

(*b*) was reasonable having regard to the data and any other relevant factors.

COMMENCEMENT

See s. 83 (2), *post*, and the note "orders under this section" thereto.

PART

S. 82 (7) (*a*): reference to a Part is reference to the Part of the Act so numbered.

PARTS II TO IV

I.e. ss. 6–42 of the Act.

SECTION 29 (2) (*c*)

This section is an exception to the rule set out in s. 29 (2) (*c*).

POWER TO AMEND

The Secretary of State has power to amend this section by order: s. 80 (1) (*a*).

COMMENTARY

See para. [**27**], *ante*.

---

46. Communal accommodation

(1) In this section "communal accommodation" means residential accommodation which includes dormitories or other shared sleeping accommodation which for reasons of privacy or decency should be used by men only, or by women only (but which may include some shared sleeping accommodation for men, and some for women, or some ordinary sleeping accommodation).

(2) In this section "communal accommodation" also includes residential accommodation all or part of which should be used by men only, or by women only, because of the nature of the sanitary facilities serving the accommodation.

(3) Nothing in Part II or III shall render unlawful sex discrimination in the admission of persons to communal accommodation if the accommodation is managed in a way which, given the exigencies of the situation, comes as near as may be to fair and equitable treatment of men and women.

(4) In applying subsection (3) account shall be taken of—

(*a*) whether and how far it is reasonable to expect that the accommodation should be altered or extended, or that further alternative accommodation should be provided and

(*b*) the frequency of the demand or need for use of the accommodation by men as compared with women.

(5) Nothing in Part II or III shall render unlawful sex discrimination against a woman, or against a man, as respects the provision of any benefit, facility or service if—

(*a*) the benefit, facility or service cannot properly and effectively be provided except for those using communal accommodation, and

(*b*) in the relevant circumstances the woman or, as the case may be, the man could lawfully be refused the use of the accommodation by virtue of subsection (3).

(6) Neither subsection (3) nor subsection (5) is a defence to an act of sex discrimination under Part II unless such arrangements as are reasonably

practicable are made to compensate for the detriment caused by the discrimination; but in considering under subsection (5) (*b*) whether the use of communal accommodation could lawfully be refused (in a case based on Part II), it shall be assumed that the requirements of this subsection have been complied with as respects subsection (3).

(7) Section 25 shall not apply to sex discrimination within subsection (3) or (5).

(8) This section is without prejudice to the generality of section 35 (1) (*c*).

COMMENCEMENT
See s. 83 (2), *post*, and the note "orders under this section" thereto.

MEN
S. 82 (1) and s. 5 (2).

WOMEN
S. 82 (1) and s. 5 (2).

DISCRIMINATION
S. 82 (1) to be construed in accordance with s. 5 (1).

BENEFIT FACILITY AND SERVICE
Examples given in s. 29 (2).

REASONABLY PRACTICABLE
See the note to s. 41, *ante*.

ACT
S. 82 (1) includes a deliberate omission.

POWER TO AMEND
The Secretary of State has power to amend this section by order: s. 80 (1) (*a*).

COMMENTARY
See paras. [22], [23], [24], [25] and [26], *ante*.

---

47. Discriminatory training by certain bodies

(1) Nothing in Parts II to IV shall render unlawful any act done in relation to particular work by a training body in, or in connection with—

(*a*) affording women only, or men only, access to facilities for training which would help to fit them for that work, or

(*b*) encouraging women only, or men only, to take advantage of opportunities for doing that work,

where it appears to the training body that at any time within the 12 months immediately preceding the doing of the act there were no persons of the sex in question doing that work in Great Britain, or the number of persons of that sex doing the work in Great Britain was comparatively small.

(2) Where in relation to particular work it appears to a training body that although the condition for the operation of subsection (1) is not met for the whole of Great Britain it is met for an area within Great Britain, nothing in Parts II to IV shall render unlawful any act done by the training body in, or in connection with—

(*a*) affording persons who are of the sex in question, and who appear likely to take up that work in that area, access to facilities for training which would help to fit them for that work, or (*b*) encouraging persons of that sex to take advantage of opportunities in the area for doing that work.

(3) Nothing in Parts II to IV shall render unlawful any act done by a training body in, or in connection with, affording persons access to facilities for training which would help to fit them for employment, where it appears to the training body that those persons are in special need of training by reason of the period for which they have been discharging domestic or family responsibilities to the exclusion of regular full time employment.

The discrimination in relation to which this subsection applies may result from confining the training to persons who have been discharging domestic or family responsibilities, or from the way persons are selected for training, or both.

(4) In this section "training body" means—

(*a*) a person mentioned in section 14 (2) (*a*) or (*b*), or
(*b*) any other person being a person designated for the purposes of this section in an order made by or on behalf of the Secretary of State,

and a person may be designated under paragraph (*b*) for the purposes of subsections (1) and (2) only, or of subsection (3) only, or for all those subsections.

COMMENCEMENT

See s. 83 (2), *post*, and the note "orders under this section" thereto.

ACT

S. 82 (1) includes a deliberate omission.

WOMAN

S. 82 (1) and s. 5 (2).

MAN

S. 82 (1) and s. 5 (2).

MONTHS

I.e. calendar months: Interpretation Act 1889, s. 3, 32 Halsbury's Statutes (3rd Edn.), p. 436.

ACCESS

S. 82 (1) construed in connection with s. 50 includes indirect provision of access.

TRAINING

S. 82 (1) includes any form of education or instruction.

GREAT BRITAIN

S. 82 (1) includes territorial waters of the United Kingdom adjacent to Great Britain; and see the note to s. 30, *ante*.

PART

S. 82 (7) (*a*): reference to a Part is a reference to the Part of the Act so numbered.

EMPLOYMENT

S. 82 (1): means employment under a contract of service or of apprenticeship or a contract personally to execute any work and labour, and related expressions shall be construed accordingly.

DISCRIMINATION

S. 82 (1): to be construed in accordance with s. 5 (1).

DESIGNATE

S. 82 (1) construed in accordance with s. 82 (3).

ORDER
S. 81; Orders are generally made under this section but s. 47 (4) (*b*) is expressly excluded.

COMMENTARY
See para. [**47**], *ante*.

---

48. Other discriminatory training etc.

(1) Nothing in Parts II to IV shall render unlawful any act done by an employer in relation to particular work in his employment, being an act done in, or in connection with,—

    (*a*) affording his female employees only, or his male employees only, access to facilities for training which would help to fit them for that work, or

    (*b*) encouraging women only, or men only, to take advantage of opportunities for doing that work,

where at any time within the twelve months immediately preceding the doing of the act there were no persons of the sex in question among those doing that work or the number of persons of that sex doing the work was comparatively small.

(2) Nothing in section 12 shall render unlawful any act done by an organisation to which that section applies in, or in connection with—

    (*a*) affording female members of the organisation only, or male members of the organisation only, access to facilities for training which would help to fit them for holding a post of any kind in the organisation, or

    (*b*) encouraging female members only, or male members only, to take advantage of opportunities for holding such posts in the organisation,

where at any time within the twelve months immediately preceding the doing of the act there were no persons of the sex in question among persons holding such posts in the organisation or the number of persons of that sex holding such posts was comparatively small.

(3) Nothing in Parts II to IV shall render unlawful any act done by an organisation to which section 12 applies in, or in connection with, encouraging women only, or men only, to become members of the organisation where at any time within the twelve months immediately preceding the doing of the act there were no persons of the sex in question among those members or the number of persons of that sex among the members was comparatively small.

COMMENCEMENT
See s. 83 (2), *post*, and the note "orders under this section" thereto.

PART
S. 82 (7) (*a*): reference to a Part is a reference to the Part of the Act so numbered.

PARTS II TO IV
I.e. ss. 6–42 of the Act.

ACT
S. 82 (1) includes a deliberate omission.

EMPLOYMENT
Defined in s. 82 (1).

TRAINING
S. 82 (1) includes any form of education and instruction.

WOMEN
    S. 82 (1) and s. 5 (2).

MEN
    S. 82 (1) and s. 5 (2).

ACCESS
    S. 82 (1), construed in connection with s. 50, includes indirect provision of access.

MONTHS
    I.e. calendar months; see Interpretation Act 1889, s. 3, 32 Halsbury's Statutes (3rd Edn.), p. 436.

POWER TO AMEND
    The Secretary of State has power to amend this section by order: s. 80 (1) (a), *post*.

COMMENTARY
    See para. [**31**], *ante*.

---

49. Trade union etc.: elective bodies

(1) If an organisation to which section 12 applies comprises a body the membership of which is wholly or mainly elected, nothing in section 12 shall render unlawful provision which ensures that a minimum number of persons of one sex are members of the body—

(a) by reserving seats on the body for persons of that sex, or
(b) by making extra seats on the body available (by election or co-option or otherwise) for persons of that sex on occasions when the number of persons of that sex in the other seats is below the minimum,

where in the opinion of the organisation the provision is in the circumstances needed to secure a reasonable lower limit to the number of members of that sex serving on the body; and nothing in Parts II to IV shall render unlawful any act done in order to give effect to such a provision.

(2) This section shall not be taken as making lawful—

(a) discrimination in the arrangements for determining the persons entitled to vote in an election of members of the body, or otherwise to choose the persons to serve on the body, or
(b) discrimination in any arrangements concerning membership of the organisation itself.

COMMENCEMENT
    See s. 83 (2), *post*, and the note "orders under this section" thereto.

POWER TO AMEND
    By s. 80 (1) the Secretary of State has power to amend this section by order and also to repeal it.

DISCRIMINATION
    S. 82 (1) to be construed in accordance with s. 5 (1).

PART
    S. 82 (7) (a): reference to a Part is a reference to the Part of the Act so numbered.

PARTS II TO IV
    I.e. ss. 6–42.

WHOLLY OR MAINLY
    See the note to s. 10, *ante*.

ACT
  This includes a deliberate omission: s. 82 (1).

COMMENTARY
  See paras. [32] and [33], *ante.*

---

50. Indirect Access to benefits etc.

(1) References in this Act to the affording by any person of access to benefits, facilities or services are not limited to benefits, facilities or services provided by that person himself, but include any means by which it is in that person's power to facilitate access to benefits, facilities or services provided by any other person (the "actual provider").

(2) Where by any provision of this Act the affording by any person of access to benefits, facilities or services in a discriminatory way is in certain circumstances prevented from being unlawful, the effect of the provision shall extend also to the liability under this Act of any actual provider.

COMMENCEMENT
  See s. 83 (2), *post*, and the note "orders under this section" thereto.

BENEFITS, FACILITIES AND SERVICES
  Examples given in s. 29 (2).

ACCESS
  Defined in s. 82 (1). See also references to access in ss. 48, 29, 22 and 30.

DISCRIMINATORY
  Discrimination defined in s. 82 (1) with reference to s. 5 (1).

PERSON
  S. 19, Interpretation Act 1889, includes a body corporate or unincorporate.

---

51. Acts done under statutory authority

(1) Nothing in Parts II to IV shall render unlawful any act done by a person if it was necessary for him to do it in order to comply with a requirement—

  (*a*) of an Act passed before this Act; or
  (*b*) of an instrument made or approved (whether before or after the passing of this Act) by or under an Act passed before this Act.

(2) Where an Act passed after this Act re-enacts (with or without modification) a provision of an Act passed before this Act, subsection (1) shall apply to that provision as re-enacted as if it continued to be contained in an Act passed before this Act.

COMMENCEMENT
  See s. 83 (2), *post*, and the note "orders under this section" thereto.

PART
  S. 82 (7) (*a*): reference to a Part is a reference to the Part of the Act so numbered.

PARTS II TO IV
  I.e. ss. 6–42.

ACT
  S. 82 (1) includes a deliberate omission.

PERSON
S. 19, Interpretation Act 1889: includes a body corporate or unincorporate.

DISCRIMINATORY STATUTES
Power of the EOC to review discriminatory statutes: s. 55.

PASSED BEFORE/AFTER THIS ACT
This Act received Royal Assent on 12th November, 1975.

COMMENTARY
See para. [28], *ante.*

52. Acts safeguarding national security

(1) Nothing in Parts II to IV shall render unlawful an act done for the purpose of safeguarding national security.

(2) A certificate purporting to be signed by or on behalf of a Minister of the Crown and certifying that an act specified in the certificate was done for the purpose of safeguarding national security shall be conclusive evidence that it was done for that purpose.

(3) A document purporting to be a certificate such as is mentioned in subsection (2) shall be received in evidence and, unless the contrary is proved, shall be deemed to be such a certificate.

COMMENCEMENT
See s. 83 (2), *post*, and the note "orders under this section" thereto.

PART
S. 82 (7) (*a*): reference to a Part is a reference to the Part of the Act so numbered.

PARTS II TO IV
I.e. ss. 6–42 of the Act.

ACT
Includes a deliberate omission: s. 82 (1).

CONCLUSIVE EVIDENCE
Accordingly, no evidence to the contrary is admissible (*Kerr* v. *John Mottram, Ltd.*, [1940] Ch. 657; [1940] 2 All E.R. 629) but other evidence is not made inadmissible (*A.G.* v. *Bournemouth Corporation*), [1902] 2 Ch. 714, C.A.).

COMMENTARY
See para. [29], *ante.*

PART VI

EQUAL OPPORTUNITIES COMMISSION

53. Establishment and duties of Commission

(1) There shall be a body of Commissioners named the Equal Opportunities Commission, consisting of at least eight but not more than fifteen individuals each appointed by the Secretary of State on a full-time or part-time basis, which shall have the following duties—

(*a*) to work towards the elimination of discrimination,
(*b*) to promote equality of opportunity between men and women generally, and

(*c*) to keep under review the working of this Act and the Equal Pay Act 1970 and, when they are so required by the Secretary of State or otherwise think it necessary, draw up and submit to the Secretary of State proposals for amending them.

(2) The Secretary of State shall appoint—

(*a*) one of the Commissioners to be chairman of the Commission, and

(*b*) either one or two of the Commissioners (as the Secretary of State thinks fit) to be deputy chairman or deputy chairmen of the Commission.

(3) The Secretary of State may by order amend subsection (1) so far a it regulates the number of Commissioners.

(4) Schedule 3 shall have effect with respect to the Commission.

COMMENCEMENT
See s. 83 (2), *post*, and the note "orders under this section" thereto.

COMMISSIONER
S. 82 (1) means a member of the EOC

COMMISSION
Constitution of the EOC set out in Sch. 3. Duties of the EOC set out in greater detail in ss. 54, 55 *et seq.*

DISCRIMINATION
S. 82 (1), defined in relation to s. 5 (1).

MEN
S. 82 (1) and s. 5 (2).

WOMEN
S. 82 (1) and s. 5 (2).

EQUAL PAY ACT 1970
Set out in Schedule 1, *post.*

SECRETARY OF STATE
S. 12, Interpretation Act 1889: one of Her Majesty's principal Secretaries of State for the time being.

INDIVIDUALS
See the note to s. 7, *ante.*

ORDERS UNDER THIS SECTION
At the time of going to press no order had been made under sub-s. (3).

ORDERS
For general provisions as to orders, see s. 81 (1), (2), (4) and (5), *post.*

COMMENTARY
See paras. [**127**] and [**128**], *ante.*

---

54. Research and education

(1) The Commission may undertake or assist (financially or otherwise) the undertaking by other persons of any research, and any educational activities, which appear to the Commission necessary or expedient for the purposes of section 53 (1).

(2) The Commission may make charges for educational or other facilities or services made available by them.

COMMENCEMENT
See s. 83 (2), *post*, and the note "orders under this section" thereto.

EDUCATION
S. 82 (1): includes any form of training or instruction.

COMMISSION
S. 53 and Sch. 3.

EOC
S. 82 (1).

PERSONS
S. 19, Interpretation Act 1889: includes a body corporate or unincorporate.

COMMENTARY
See para. [128], *ante*.

55. Review of discriminatory provisions in health and safety legislation

(1) Without prejudice to the generality of section 53 (1), the Commission, in pursuance of the duties imposed by paragraphs (*a*) and (*b*) of that subsection—

    (*a*) shall keep under review the relevant statutory provisions in so far as they require men and women to be treated differently, and

    (*b*) if so required by the Secretary of State, make to him a report on any matter specified by him which is connected with those duties and concerns the relevant statutory provisions.

Any such report shall be made within the time specified by the Secretary of State, and the Secretary of State shall cause the report to be published.

(2) Whenever the Commission think it necessary, they shall draw up and submit to the Secretary of State proposals for amending the relevant statutory provisions.

(3) The Commission shall carry out their duties in relation to the relevant statutory provisions in consultation with the Health and Safety Commission.

(4) In this section "the relevant statutory provisions" has the meaning given by section 53 of the Health and Safety at Work etc. Act 1974.

COMMENCEMENT
See s. 83 (2), *post*, and the note "orders under this section" thereto.

COMMISSION
See s. 53 and Sch. 3; s. 82 (1): the EOC.

HEALTH AND SAFETY COMMISSION
This body is established under the Health and Safety at Work Act 1974.

HEALTH AND SAFETY AT WORK ACT 1974
44 Halsbury's Statutes (3rd Edn.), pp. 215, 1083.

SECRETARY OF STATE
S. 12, Interpretation Act 1889: one of Her Majesty's principal Secretaries of State for the time being.

COMMENTARY
See para. [128], *ante*.

56. Annual reports

(1) As soon as practicable after the end of each calendar year the Commission shall make to the Secretary of State a report on their activities during the year (an "annual report").

(2) Each annual report shall include a general survey of developments, during the period to which it relates, in respect of matters falling within the scope of the Commission's duties.

(3) The Secretary of State shall lay a copy of every annual report before each House of Parliament, and shall cause the report to be published.

COMMENCEMENT
See s. 83 (2), *post*, and the note "orders under this section" thereto.

DUTIES OF THE COMMISSION
For scope, see s. 53.

COMMISSION
See s. 53 and Sch. 3; s. 82 (1): EOC.

SECRETARY OF STATE
One of Her Majesty's principal Secretaries of State for the time being.

LAY . . . BEFORE . . . PARLIAMENT
For meaning see the Laying Documents before Parliament (Interpretation) Act 1948, s. 1 (1), 32 Halsbury's Statutes (3rd Edn.), p. 677.

COMMENTARY
See para. [**129**], *ante*.

Investigations

57. Power to conduct formal investigations

(1) Without prejudice to their general power to do anything requisite for the performance of their duties under section 53 (1), the Commission may if they think fit, and shall if required by the Secretary of State, conduct a formal investigation for any purpose connected with the carrying out of those duties.

(2) The Commission may, with the approval of the Secretary of State, appoint, on a full-time or part-time basis, one or more individuals as additional Commissioners for the purposes of a formal investigation.

(3) The Commission may nominate one or more Commissioners, with or without one or more additional Commissioners, to conduct a formal investigation on their behalf, and may delegate any of their functions in relation to the investigation to the persons so nominated.

COMMENCEMENT
See s. 83 (2), *post*, and the note "orders under this section" thereto.

COMMISSIONER
S. 82 (1): means a member of the EOC.

COMMISSION
S. 53 and Sch. 3; s. 82 (1): the EOC.

FUNCTIONS OF THE COMMISSION
See s. 53.

ADDITIONAL COMMISSIONERS
Sch. 3, paras. 7, *et seq.*

FORMAL INVESTIGATION
See further ss. 58–61 and 69, *post.*

SECRETARY OF STATE
One of Her Majesty's principal Secretaries of State for the time being.

INDIVIDUALS
See note to s. 7, *ante.*

CONDUCT OF INVESTIGATIONS
Regulations have been made concerning the conduct of formal investigations: the Sex Discrimination (Formal Investigations) Regulations 1975, S.I. 1975 No. 1993.

COMMENTARY
See para. [**131**], *ante.*

---

58. Terms of reference

(1) The Commission shall not embark on a formal investigation unless the requirements of this section have been complied with.

(2) Terms of reference for the investigation shall be drawn up by the Commission or, if the Commission were required by the Secretary of State to conduct the investigation, by the Secretary of State after consulting the Commission.

(3) It shall be the duty of the Commission to give general notice of the holding of the investigation unless the terms of reference confine it to activities of persons named in them, but in such a case the Commission shall in the prescribed manner give those persons notice of the holding of the investigation.

(4) The Commission or, if the Commission were required by the Secretary of State to conduct the investigation, the Secretary of State after consulting the Commission may from time to time revise the terms of reference; and subsections (1) and (3) shall apply to the revised investigation and terms of reference as they applied to the original.

COMMENCEMENT
See s. 83 (2), *post,* and the note "orders under this section" thereto.

COMMISSION
S. 53 and Sch. 3; s. 82 (1): the EOC.

FORMAL INVESTIGATION
S. 82 (1): investigation under s. 57.

NOTICE
S. 82 (1): a notice in writing.

SECRETARY OF STATE
S. 12, Interpretation Act: one of Her Majesty's principal Secretaries of State for the time being.

PERSONS
S. 19, Interpretation Act: includes a body corporate or unincorporate.

PRESCRIBED MANNER
See s. 82 (1) and S.I. 1975 No 1995.

REGULATIONS
  See s. 57.

COMMENTARY
  See para. [132], *ante.*

---

59. Power to obtain information

(1) For the purposes of a formal investigation the Commission, by a notice in the prescribed form served on him in the prescribed manner,—

    (*a*) may require any person to furnish such written information as may be described in the notice, and may specify the time at which, and the manner and form in which, the information is to be furnished;

    (*b*) may require any person to attend at such time and place as is specified in the notice and give oral information about, and produce all documents in his possession or control relating to, any matter specified in the notice.

(2) Except as provided by section 69, a notice shall be served under subsection (1) only where—

    (*a*) service of the notice was authorised by an order made by or on behalf of the Secretary of State, or

    (*b*) the terms of reference of the investigation state that the Commission believe that a person named in them may have done or may be doing acts of all or any of the following descriptions—

        (i) unlawful discriminatory acts,

        (ii) contraventions of section 37,

        (iii) contraventions of sections 38, 39, or 40, and

        (iv) acts in breach of a term modified or included by virtue of an equality clause,

    and confine the investigation to those acts.

(3) A notice under subsection (1) shall not require a person—

    (*a*) to give information, or produce any documents, which he could not be compelled to give in evidence, or produce, in civil proceedings before the High Court or the Court of Session, or

    (*b*) to attend at any place unless the necessary expenses of his journey to and from that place are paid or tendered to him.

(4) If a person fails to comply with a notice served on him under subsection (1) or the Commission has reasonable cause to believe that he intends not to comply with it, the Commission may apply to a county court for an order requiring him to comply with it or with such directions for the like purpose as may be contained in the order; and section 84 (penalty for neglecting witness summons) of the County Courts Act 1959 shall apply to failure without reasonable excuse to comply with any such order as it applies in the cases there provided.

(5) (*Applies to Scotland.*)

(6) A person commits an offence if he—

    (*a*) wilfully alters, suppresses, conceals or destroys a document which he has been required by a notice or order under this section to produce, or

(b) in complying with such a notice or order, knowingly or recklessly makes any statement which is false in a material particular,

and shall be liable on summary conviction to a fine not exceeding £400.

(7) Proceedings for an offence under subsection (6) may (without prejudice to any jurisdiction exercisable apart from this subsection) be instituted—

(a) against any person at any place at which he has an office or other place of business;

(b) against an individual at any place where he resides, or at which he is for the time being.

COMMENCEMENT
See s. 83 (2), *post*, and the note "orders under this section" thereto.

FORMAL INVESTIGATION
S. 82 (1) means investigation under s. 57. For regulations, see s. 57.

COMMISSION
S. 53 and Sch. 3; s. 82 (1): EOC.

NOTICE
S. 82 (1): notice in writing.

PRESCRIBED
S. 82 (1): prescribed by regulations made by the Secretary of State by statutory instrument. See S.I. 1975 No. 1993.

ORDER
S. 81 usual form of order, excluding an order under s. 59 (2).

UNLAWFUL DISCRIMINATORY ACTS
S. 82 (1) construed in accordance with s. 5 (1).

ACTS
S. 82 (1): includes deliberate omissions.

EQUALITY CLAUSE
S. 82 (1): meaning given in s. 1 (2) Equal Pay Act 1970 (as set out in s. 8 (1) of this Act).

NON-DISCLOSURE OF INFORMATION
S. 61.

COUNTY COURTS ACT 1959
7 Halsbury's Statutes (3rd Edn.), p. 302.

PERSON
S. 19, Interpretation Act: includes a body corporate or unincorporate. See s. 2, Interpretation Act in relation to summary convictions. S. 1 (1) (a), Interpretation Act 1889: masculine includes feminine and plural.

INDIVIDUAL
See the note "Individuals" to s. 7, *ante*.

SECRETARY OF STATE
S. 12, Interpretation Act 1889: one of Her Majesty's principal Secretaries of State for the time being.

HIGH COURT
S. 13, Interpretation Act 1889: Her Majesty's High Court of Justice.

COUNTY COURT
S. 6, Interpretation Act 1889: a court under the County Courts Act 1888, now County Courts Act 1959 by virtue of s. 205 (4).

See Interpretation Act 1889, s. 20, 32 Halsbury's Statutes (3rd Edn.), p. 450. Writing is to be construed as including references to printing, lithography, photography and other modes of representing or reproducing words in a visible form.

SUBSECTION (6): WILFULLY
This means deliberately and intentionally, as distinct from accidentally or inadvertently; see *R.* v. *Senior* [1899] 1 Q.B. 283, at pp. 290, 291, *per* Lord Russell of Killowen, C.J.; see also, in particular, *R.* v. *Walker* (1934), 24 Cr. App. Rep. 117; *Eaton* v. *Cobb*, [1950] 1 All E.R. 1016; *Arrowsmith* v. *Jenkins*, [1963] 2 Q.B. 561; [1963] 2 All E.R. 210; *Rice* v. *Connolly*, [1966] 2 Q.B. 414, [1966] 2 All E.R. 649; and *Ingleton* v. *Dibble*, [1972] 1 Q.B. 480; [1972] 1 All E.R. 275.

KNOWINGLY/RECKLESSLY/FALSE/SUMMARY CONVICTION
See notes to s. 15, *ante.*

MATERIAL PARTICULAR
A particular may be material on the mere ground that it renders more credible something else; *R.* v. *Tyson* (1867), L.R. 1 C.C.R. 107.

SUBSECTION (7)
Jurisdiction exercisable apart from this subsection: see in particular, the Magistrates' Courts Act 1952, ss. 1–3, 21 Halsbury's Statutes (3rd Edn.), pp. 185–90.

RESIDES
See note to s. 32, *ante.*

COMMENTARY
See paras. [**133**], [**134**], [**135**], *ante.*

60. Recommendations and reports on formal investigations

(1) If in the light of any of their findings in a formal investigation it appears to the Commission necessary or expedient, whether during the course of the investigation or after its conclusion,—

    (*a*) to make to any persons, with a view to promoting equality of opportunity between men and women who are affected by any of their activities, recommendations for changes in their policies or procedures, or as to any other matters, or

    (*b*) to make to the Secretary of State any recommendations, whether for changes in the law or otherwise,

the Commission shall make those recommendations accordingly.

(2) The Commission shall prepare a report of their findings in any formal investigations conducted by them.

(3) If the formal investigation is one required by the Secretary of State—

    (*a*) the Commission shall deliver the report to the Secretary of State, and
    (*b*) the Secretary of State shall cause the report to be published,

and unless required by the Secretary of State the Commission shall not publish the report.

(4) If the formal investigation is not one required by the Secretary of State, the Commission shall either publish the report, or make it available for inspection in accordance with subsection (5).

(5) Where under subsection (4) a report is to be made available for inspection, any person shall be entitled, on payment of such fee (if any) as may be determined by the Commission—

(a) to inspect the report during ordinary office hours and take copies of all or any part of the report, or

(b) to obtain from the Commission a copy, certified by the Commission to be correct, of the report.

(6) The Commission may if they think fit determine that the right conferred by subsection (5) (a) shall be exercisable in relation to a copy of the report instead of, or in addition to, the original.

(7) The Commission shall give general notice of the place or places where, and the times when, reports may be inspected under subsection (5).

COMMENCEMENT
See s. 83 (2), *post*, and the note "orders under this section" thereto.

COMMISSION
S. 53 and Sch. 3; s. 82 (1): the EOC.

INVESTIGATIONS
S. 82 (1); see s. 57.

MEN
S. 82 (1) and s. 5 (2).

WOMEN
S. 82 (1) and s. 5 (2).

NON-INCLUSION OF PREJUDICIAL MATTERS
See s. 61 (3).

PERSON
S. 19, Interpretation Act 1889: includes a body corporate or unincorporate.

SECRETARY OF STATE
S. 12, Interpretation Act 1889: one of Her Majesty's principal Secretaries of State for the time being.

COMMENTARY
See para. [136], *ante*.

---

61. Restriction on disclosure of information

(1) No information given to the Commission by any person ("the informant") in connection with a formal investigation shall be disclosed by the Commission, or by any person who is or has been a Commissioner, additional Commissioner or employee of the Commission, except—

(a) on the order of any court, or

(b) with the informant's consent, or

(c) in the form of a summary or other general statement published by the Commission which does not identify the informant or any other person to whom the information relates, or

(d) in a report of the investigation published by the Commission or made available for inspection under section 60 (5), or

(e) to the Commissioners, additional Commissioners or employees of the Commission, or, so far as may be necessary for the proper performance of the functions of the Commission, to other persons, or

(f) for the purpose of any civil proceedings under this Act to which the Commission are a party, or any criminal proceedings.

(2) Any person who discloses information in contravention of subsection (1) commits an offence and shall be liable on summary conviction to a fine not exceeding £400.

(3) In preparing any report for publication or for inspection the Commission shall exclude, so far as is consistent with their duties and the object of the report, any matter which relates to the private affairs of any individual or business interests of any person where the publication of that matter might, in the opinion of the Commission, prejudicially affect that individual or person.

COMMENCEMENT
 See s. 83 (2), *post*, and the note "orders under this section" thereto.

COMMISSION
 S. 53 and Sch. 3; s. 82 (1): the EOC.

COMMISSIONER
 S. 82 (1): a member of the commission.

ADDITIONAL COMMISSIONER
 Appointed under s. 57 (2).

EMPLOYEES OF THE COMMISSION
 Sch. 3, para. 8.

FUNCTIONS OF THE COMMISSION
 S. 53.

CIVIL PROCEEDINGS
 Civil proceedings to which the Commission is a party: see ss. 71, 72, 73.

REPORT
 S. 60.

PERSON
 See s. 2, Interpretation Act 1889 in relation to summary offences.

INDIVIDUAL
 See the note, Individuals to s. 7, *ante*.

SUMMARY CONVICTION
 See the note to s. 15, *ante*.

FORMAL INVESTIGATION
 S. 82 (1): an investigation under s. 57.

COMMENTARY
 See para. [137], *ante*.

PART VII

ENFORCEMENT

General

62. No further sanctions for breach of Act

(1) A contravention of this Act shall incur as such no sanction, whether civil or criminal, except to the extent (if any) expressly provided by this Act.

(2) In subsection (1) "sanction" includes the granting of an injunction or declaration, but does not include the making of an order of certiorari, mandamus or prohibition.

(3) Subsection (2) does not affect the remedies available under section 66 (2), notwithstanding that subsection (2) would prevent those remedies being obtainable in the High Court.

(4) (*Applies to Scotland.*)

COMMENCEMENT
See s. 83 (2), *post*, and the note "orders under this section" thereto.

SANCTIONS PROVIDED BY THE ACT
S. 65: on a complaint being presented to the Industrial Tribunal, compensation up to the amount specified in Sch. 1, para. 20 (1) (*b*), TULRA 1974 (this may be increased under s. 65 (3)).
S. 61: misdisclosure of information: a fine not exceeding £40.
S. 65: power of the Industrial Tribunal to make recommendations, which if not complied with result in a fine.
S. 66: civil proceedings for breach of Part III.

INJUNCTION
See generally, as to injunctions, the title Injunction in 17 Halsbury's Statutes (3rd Edn.), pp. 809–811, and 21 Halsbury's Laws (3rd Edn.), pp. 343–439, and 1 Halsbury's Laws (4th Edn.), paras. 168 *et seq.*

CERTIORARI, MANDAMUS AND PROHIBITION
Considered in 1 Halsbury's Laws (4th Edn.), paras. 80 *et seq.*

AMENDMENT
Certain proposals for amending this section are made in Sch. 4, RRB.

COMMENTARY
See para. [95], *ante.*

Enforcement in employment field

63. Jurisdiction of industrial tribunals

(1) A complaint by any person ("the complainant") that another person ("the respondent")—

(*a*) has committed an act of discrimination against the complainant which is unlawful by virtue of Part II, or

(*b*) is by virtue of section 41 or 42 to be treated as having committed such an act of discrimination against the complainant,

may be presented to an industrial tribunal.

(2) Subsection (1) does not apply to a complaint under section 13 (1) of an act in respect of which an appeal, or proceedings in the nature of an appeal, may be brought under any enactment.

COMMENCEMENT
See s. 83 (2), *post*, and the note "orders under this section" thereto.

DISCRIMINATION
S. 82 (1) to be construed in accordance with s. 5 (1).

INDUSTRIAL TRIBUNAL
> Means a tribunal established under s. 12 of the Industrial Training Act: s. 82 (1).

CONCILIATION
> See s. 64.

POWERS OF THE INDUSTRIAL TRIBUNAL
> Where complaint is justified: s. 65.

COMPLAINT
> See generally ss. 64, 65 and 73 (3), *post*.

TIME LIMIT FOR BRINGING COMPLAINTS
> See s. 76.

VALIDITY OF CONTRACTS
> Settling a complaint to which s. 63 (1) applies: s. 77.

PERSON
> S. 19, Interpretation Act 1889: includes a body corporate or unincorporate.

ACT
> S. 82 (1) includes a deliberate omission.

PART II
> I.e. ss. 6–21 of the Act.

PART
> See s. 82 (7).

COMMENTARY
> See Chapter 8, *ante*.

---

64. Conciliation in employment cases

(1) Where a complaint has been presented to an industrial tribunal under section 63, or under section 2 (1) of the Equal Pay Act 1970, and a copy of the complaint has been sent to a conciliation officer, it shall be the duty of the conciliation officer—

(a) if he is requested to do so both by the complainant and the respondent, or

(b) if, in the absence of requests by the complainant and the respondent, he considers that he could act under this subsection with a reasonable prospect of success,

to endeavour to promote a settlement of the complaint without its being determined by an industrial tribunal.

(2) Where, before a complaint such as is mentioned in subsection (1) has been presented to an industrial tribunal, a request is made to a conciliation officer to make his services available in the matter by a person who, if the complaint were so presented, would be the complainant or respondent, subsection (1) shall apply as if the complaint had been so presented and a copy of it had been sent to the conciliation officer.

(3) In proceeding under subsection (1) or (2), a conciliation officer shall where appropriate have regard to the desirability of encouraging the use of other procedures available for the settlement of grievances.

(4) Anything communicated to a conciliation officer in connection with the performance of his functions under this section shall not be admissible in evidence in any proceedings before an industrial tribunal except with the consent of the person who communicated it to that officer.

COMMENCEMENT
See s. 83 (2), *post*, and the note "orders under this section" thereto.

INDUSTRIAL TRIBUNAL
S. 82 (1) means a tribunal established under s. 12 of the Industrial Training Act 1964.

CONCILIATION OFFICER
S. 82 (1): a person appointed under para. 26 (1) of Sch. 1, TULRA 1974.

EQUAL PAY ACT 1970
For amended text, see Sch. 1, *post*. See also 12 Halsbury's Statutes (3rd Edn.), p. 563.
For s. 2 (1), see substitutions made by s. 8 (6), *ante*, and Sch. 1, Part 2, para. 1 (1), *post*.

COMPLAINANT AND RESPONDENT
See s. 63 (1), *ante*.

COMPENSATION
See Employment Protection Act 1975: s. 77 (1), (2).

COMMENTARY
See para. [102], *ante*.

---

65. Remedies on complaint under section 63

(1) Where an industrial tribunal finds that a complaint presented to it under section 63 is well-founded the tribunal shall make such of the following as it considers just and equitable—

    (a) an order declaring the rights of the complainant and the respondent in relation to the act to which the complaint relates;

    (b) an order requiring the respondent to pay to the complainant compensation of an amount corresponding to any damages he could have been ordered by a county court or by a sheriff court to pay to the complainant if the complaint had fallen to be dealt with under section 66;

    (c) a recommendation that the respondent take within a specified period action appearing to the tribunal to be practicable for the purpose of obviating or reducing the adverse effect on the complainant of any act of discrimination to which the complaint relates.

(2) The amount of compensation awarded to a person under subsection (1) (b) shall not exceed the amount for the time being specified in paragraph 20 (1) (b) of Schedule I to the Trade Union and Labour Relations Act 1974.

(3) If without reasonable justification the respondent to a complaint fails to comply with a recommendation made by an industrial tribunal under subsection (1) (c), then, if they think it just and equitable to do so—

    (a) the tribunal may increase the amount of compensation required to be paid to the complainant in respect of the complaint by an order made under subsection (1) (b), or

    (b) if an order under subsection (1) (b) could have been made but was not, the tribunal may make such an order.

COMMENCEMENT
See s. 83 (2), *post*, and the note "orders under this section" thereto.

INDUSTRIAL TRIBUNAL
S. 82 (1): means a tribunal established under s. 12 of the Industrial Training Act 1964.

ACT
S. 82 (1): includes a deliberate omission.

TRADE UNION AND LABOUR RELATIONS ACT 1974
12 Halsbury's Statutes (3rd Edn.), p. 563.

SECTION 73
Power of Industrial Tribunal to make orders referred to in s. 65 (1) (*a*) and (1) (*c*) on a complaint brought by the Commission.

COMPLAINANT AND RESPONDENT
See s. 63 (1), *ante.*

COMMENTARY
See para. [**106**], *ante.* See also Employment Protection Act 1975, s. 77.

Enforcement of Part III

66. Claims under Part III

(1) A claim by any person ("the claimant") that another person ("the respondent")—

    (*a*) has committed an act of discrimination against the claimant which is unlawful by virtue of Part III, or

    (*b*) is by virtue of section 41 or 42 to be treated as having committed such an act of discrimination against the claimant,

may be made the subject of civil proceedings in like manner as any other claim in tort or (in Scotland) in reparation for breach of statutory duty.

(2) Proceedings under subsection (1)—

    (*a*) shall be brought in England and Wales only in a county court, and

    (*b*) (*applies to Scotland*),

but all such remedies shall be obtainable in such proceedings as, apart from this subsection, would be obtainable in the High Court or the Court of Session, as the case may be.

(3) As respects an unlawful act of discrimination falling within section 1 (1) (*b*) (or, where this section is applied by section 65 (1) (*b*) section 3 (1) (*b*)) no award of damages shall be made if the respondent proves that the requirement or condition in question was not applied with the intention of treating the claimant unfavourably on the ground of his sex or marital status as the case may be.

(4) For the avoidance of doubt it is hereby declared that damages in respect of an unlawful act of discrimination may include compensation for injury to feelings whether or not they include compensation under any other head.

(5) Civil proceedings in respect of a claim by any person that he has been discriminated against in contravention of section 22 or 23 by a body to which section 25 (1) applies shall not be instituted unless the claimant has given notice of the claim to the Secretary of State and either the Secretary of State has by notice informed the claimant that the Secretary of State does not require further time to consider the matter, or the period of two months has elapsed since the claimant gave notice to the Secretary of State; but nothing in this subsection applies to a counterclaim.

(6) For the purposes of proceedings under subsection (1)—

(*a*) section 91 (1) (power of judge to appoint assessors) of the County Courts Act 1959 shall apply with the omission of the words "on the application of any party", and

(*b*) the remuneration of assessors appointed under the said section 91 (1) shall be at such rate as may be determined by the Lord Chancellor with the approval of the Minister for the Civil Service.

(7) (*Applies to Scotland.*)

(8) A county court or sheriff court shall have jurisdiction to entertain proceedings under subsection (1) with respect to an act done on a ship, aircraft or hovercraft outside its district, including such an act done outside Great Britain.

COMMENCEMENT
See s. 83 (2), *post*, and the note "orders under this section" thereto.

DISCRIMINATION
S. 82 (1) to be construed in accordance with s. 5 (1).

PART
S. 82 (7) reference to a Part is a reference to the Part of the Act so numbered.

PART III
Ss. 22–36 of this Act.

GROUNDS OF SEX
See ss. 1 and 2.

MARITAL STATUS
See s. 3.

NOTICE
S. 82 (1): notice in writing.

SHIP, AIRCRAFT, HOVERCRAFT
See s. 36.

COUNTY COURTS ACT 1959
17 Halsbury's Statutes (3rd Edn.), p. 302.

SECTION 74
Rules in relation to questions and replies concerning claims under s. 66.

SECTION 84
Financial provision under ss. 66 (6) (*b*), 66 (7).

SECTION 77
Validity of contracts settling a claim to which the section applies.

PERSON
S. 19, Interpretation Act 1889: includes a body corporate or unincorporate.

SECRETARY OF STATE
S. 12, Interpretation Act 1889: one of Her Majesty's principal Secretaries of State for the time being.

GREAT BRITAIN
S. 82 (1): includes such of the territorial waters of the UK as are adjacent to Great Britain. See further, s. 30, *ante*.

CLAIMS
Time limit for presenting claims, see s. 76 (2), (5), (6), *post.*

COUNTY COURTS ACT 1959, S. 91 (1)
See 7 Halsbury's Statutes (3rd Edn.), p. 358.

MONTHS
I.e. calendar months: Interpretation Act 1889, s. 3.

HOVERCRAFT
See Hovercraft Act 1968, s. 4 (1), 31 Halsbury's Statutes (3rd Edn.), p. 729.

AMENDMENT
Certain proposals for amending s. 66 (2) have been made in RRB, Sch. 4.

COMMENTARY
See Chapter 9, *ante.*

Non-discrimination notices

67. Issue of non-discrimination notice

(1) This section applies to—

    (*a*) an unlawful discriminatory act, and

    (*b*) a contravention of section 37, and

    (*c*) a contravention of section 38, 39 or 40, and

    (*d*) an act in breach of a term modified or included by virtue of an equality clause,

and so applies whether or not proceedings have been brought in respect of the act.

(2) If in the course of a formal investigation the Commission become satisfied that a person is committing, or has committed, any such acts, the Commission may in the prescribed manner serve on him a notice in the prescribed form ("a non-discrimination notice") requiring him—

    (*a*) not to commit any such acts, and

    (*b*) where compliance with paragraph (*a*) involves changes in any of his practices or other arrangements—

        (i) to inform the Commission that he has effected those changes and what those changes are, and

        (ii) to take such steps as may be reasonably required by the notice for the purpose of affording that information to other persons concerned.

(3) A non-discrimination notice may also require the person on whom it is served to furnish the Commission with such other information as may be reasonably required by the notice in order to verify that the notice has been complied with.

(4) The notice may specify the time at which, and the manner and form in which, any information is to be furnished to the Commission, but the time at which any information is to be furnished in compliance with the notice shall not be later than five years after the notice has become final.

(5) The Commission shall not serve a non-discrimination notice in respect of any person unless they have first—

    (*a*) given him notice that they are minded to issue a non-discrimination notice in his case, specifying the grounds on which they contemplate doing so, and

(b) offered him an opportunity of making oral or written representations in the matter (or both oral and written representations if he thinks fit) within a period of not less than 28 days specified in the notice, and

(c) taken account of any representations so made by him.

(6) Subsection (2) does not apply to any acts in respect of which the Secretary of State could exercise the powers conferred on him by section 25 (2) and (3); but if the Commission become aware of any such acts they shall give notice of them to the Secretary of State.

(7) Section 59 (4) shall apply to requirements under subsection (2) (b), (3) and (4) contained in a non-discrimination notice which has become final as it applies to requirements in a notice served under section 59 (1).

COMMENCEMENT
See s. 83 (2), *post*, and the note "orders under this section" thereto.

DISCRIMINATION
S. 82 (1) to be construed in accordance with s. 5 (1).

EQUALITY CLAUSE
S. 82 (1): has the meaning given in s. 1 (2) of the Equal Pay Act 1970 (see s. 8 (1) and Sch. 1).

PROCEEDINGS
Either in the county court (s. 66) or in the Industrial Tribunal (s. 63). See also s. 72.

FORMAL INVESTIGATION
See ss. 82 (1) and 57.

COMMISSION
S. 53 and Sch. 3; s. 82 (1): the EOC.

NOTICE
S. 82 (1): notice in writing.

INFORMATION
See s. 59.

FINAL
S. 82 (4) for the time when notice becomes final.

PERSON
S. 19, Interpretation Act 1889: includes a body corporate or unincorporate. S. 1 (1) (a) and (b), Interpretation Act: masculine includes feminine and plural.

SECRETARY OF STATE
S. 12, Interpretation Act 1889: one of Her Majesty's principal Secretaries of State for the time being.

PRESCRIBED MANNER/PRESCRIBED FORM
I.e. in the manner and form prescribed by regulations. See s. 82 (1), *post*, and the Sex Discrimination (Formal Investigations) Regulations 1975, S.I. 1975 No. 1993.

NON-DISCRIMINATION NOTICE
See further, ss. 68–70.

WRITTEN
See note to s. 59, *ante*.

FIVE YEARS AFTER
See note "Six weeks after etc." to s. 68, below.

COMMENTARY
See paras. [138] and [139], *ante*.

68. Appeal against non-discrimination notice

(1) Not later than six weeks after a non-discrimination notice is served on any person he may appeal against any requirement of the notice—

    (*a*) to an industrial tribunal, so far as the requirement relates to acts which are within the jurisdiction of the tribunal;

    (*b*) to a county court or to a sheriff court so far as the requirement relates to acts which are within the jurisdiction of the court and are not within the jurisdiction of an industrial tribunal.

(2) Where the court or tribunal considers a requirement in respect of which an appeal is brought under subsection (1) to be unreasonable because it is based on an incorrect finding of fact or for any other reason, the court or tribunal shall quash the requirement.

(3) On quashing a requirement under subsection (2) the court or tribunal may direct that the non-discrimination notice shall be treated as if, in place of the requirement quashed, it had contained a requirement in terms specified in the direction.

(4) Subsection (1) does not apply to a requirement treated as included in a non-discrimination notice by virtue of a direction under subsection (3).

COMMENCEMENT
    See s. 83 (2), *post.*

NON-DISCRIMINATION NOTICE
    A notice under s. 67.

INDUSTRIAL TRIBUNAL
    S. 82 (1) means a tribunal established under s. 12 of the Industrial Training Act 1964. Jurisdiction of tribunal: see s. 63, and EPA 1970, s. 2 (1), as substituted by s. 8 (6), *ante*, and Sch. 1, Part 1, para. 2 (1), *post.*

ACTS
    S. 82 (1): includes a deliberate omission.

COUNTY COURT JURISDICTION
    See s. 66.

REQUIREMENTS
    See s. 67.

COUNTY COURT
    S. 6, Interpretation Act 1889: court under the County Courts Act 1888, now County Courts Act 1959 by virtue of s. 205 (4).

SIX WEEKS AFTER ETC.
    In calculating the period the *dies a quo* is not to be reckoned: see, in particular *Goldsmiths Co.* v. *West Metropolitan Ry. Co.*, [1904] 1 K.B. 1; [1900–3] All E.R. Rep. 677, and *Stewart* v. *Chapman*, [1951] 2 K.B. 792; [1951] 1 All E.R. 613.

ACT
    Includes a deliberate omission: s. 82 (1).

APPEAL
    See S.I. 1975 Nos. 2098 (England and Wales), 2099 (Scotland) for procedure.

COMMENTARY
    See para. [**140**], *ante.*

69. Investigation as to compliance with non-discrimination notice

(1) If—

(a) the terms of reference of a formal investigation state that its purpose is to determine whether any requirements of a non-discrimination notice are being or have been carried out, but section 59 (2) (b) does not apply, and

(b) section 58 (3) is complied with in relation to the investigation on a date ("the commencement date") not later than the expiration of the period of five years beginning when the non-discrimination notice became final,

the Commission may within the period referred to in subsection (2) serve notices under section 59 (1) for the purposes of the investigation without needing to obtain the consent of the Secretary of State.

(2) The said period begins on the commencement date and ends on the later of the following dates—

(a) the date on which the period of five years mentioned in subsection (1)
    (b) expires;

(b) the date two years after the commencement date.

COMMENCEMENT
See s. 83 (2), *post*, and the note "orders under this section" thereto.

FORMAL INVESTIGATION
S. 82 (1); see s. 57.

NON-DISCRIMINATION NOTICE
S. 82 (1); see s. 67.   As to when a non-discrimination notice becomes final: see s. 82 (4), *post*.

REQUIREMENTS
See s. 67.

COMMISSION
S. 53 and Sch. 3; s. 82 (1): the EOC.

SECRETARY OF STATE
S. 12, Interpretation Act 1889: one of Her Majesty's principal Secretaries of State for the time being.

FIVE YEARS BEGINNING
In calculating this period the *dies a quo* is to be included; see *Hare* v. *Gocher*, [1962] 2 Q.B. 641; [1962] 2 All E.R. 763, and *Trow* v. *Ind Coope (West Midlands), Ltd.*, [1967] 2 Q.B. at 909; [1967] 2 All E.R. 900, C.A.

COMMENTARY
See para. [141], *ante*.

---

70. Register of non-discrimination notices

(1) The Commission shall establish and maintain a register ("the register") of non-discrimination notices which have become final.

(2) Any person shall be entitled, on payment of such fee (if any) as may be determined by the Commission,—

(a) to inspect the register during ordinary office hours and take copies of any entry, or (*b*) to obtain from the Commission a copy, certified by the Commission to be correct, of any entry in the register.

(3) The Commission may, if they think fit, determine that the right conferred by subsection (2) (*a*) shall be exercisable in relation to a copy of the register instead of, or in addition to, the original.

(4) The Commission shall give general notice of the place or places where, and the times when, the register or a copy of it may be inspected.

COMMENCEMENT
See s. 83 (2), *post*, and the note "orders under this section" thereto.

COMMISSION
S. 53 and Sch. 3; s. 82 (1) the EOC.

NON-DISCRIMINATION NOTICES
See s. 67.

FINAL
S. 82 (4) for rules to ascertain when a notice has become final.

NOTICE
S. 82 (1): notice in writing.

COMMENTARY
See para. [**142**], *ante*.

Other enforcement by Commission

71. Persistent discrimination

(1) If, during the period of five years beginning on the date on which either of the following became final in the case of any person, namely,—

(*a*) a non-discrimination notice served on him,

(*b*) a finding by a court or tribunal under section 63 or 66, or section 2 of the Equal Pay Act 1970, that he has done an unlawful discriminatory act or an act in breach of a term modified or included by virtue of an equality clause,

it appears to the Commission that unless restrained he is likely to do one or more acts falling within paragraph (*b*), or contravening section 37, the Commission may apply to a county court for an injunction, or to the sheriff court for an order, restraining him from doing so; and the court, if satisfied that the application is well-founded, may grant the injunction or order in the terms applied for or in more limited terms.

(2) In proceedings under this section the Commission shall not allege that the person to whom the proceedings relate has done an act which is within the jurisdiction of an industrial tribunal unless a finding by an industrial tribunal that he did that act has become final.

COMMENCEMENT
See s. 83 (2), *post*, and the note "orders under this section" thereto.

FINAL
S. 82 (4) for rules to ascertain when a notice has become final and when a tribunal decision becomes final.

NON-DISCRIMINATION NOTICE
See s. 67.

EQUAL PAY ACT 1970
See Sch. 1. S. 2 of the Act is amended by s. 8 (6), *ante*, and Sch. 1, Part I, para. 2, *post.*

UNLAWFUL DISCRIMINATORY ACT
S. 82 (1) to be construed in accordance with s. 5 (1).

ACT
S. 82 (1): includes a deliberate omission.

EQUALITY CLAUSE
S. 82 (1) meaning given in s. 1 (2) of the Equal Pay Act 1970.

COMMISSION
S. 53 and Sch. 3; s. 82 (1): the EOC.

COUNTY COURT
S. 6, Interpretation Act 1889: county court under the County Courts Act 1888, now County Courts Act 1959 by virtue of s. 205 (4).

PRELIMINARY ACTION IN EMPLOYMENT CASES
See s. 73, below.

FIVE YEARS BEGINNING
See note to s. 69, *ante.*

WITHIN THE JURISDICTION OF THE INDUSTRIAL TRIBUNAL
See s. 73 (4), *post.*

COMMENTARY
See para. [**144**], *ante.*

---

72. Enforcement of ss. 38 to 40

(1) Proceedings in respect of a contravention of section 38, 39, or 40 shall be brought only by the Commission in accordance with the following provisions of this section.

(2) The proceedings shall be—

    (*a*) an application for a decision whether the alleged contravention occurred, or

    (*b*) an application under subsection (4) below,

or both.

(3) An application under subsection (2) (*a*) shall be made—

    (*a*) in a case based on any provision of Part II, to an industrial tribunal, and

    (*b*) in any other case to a county court or sheriff court.

(4) If it appears to the Commission—

    (*a*) that a person has done an act which by virtue of section 38, 39 or 40 was unlawful, and

    (*b*) that unless restrained he is likely to do further acts which by virtue of that section are unlawful,

the Commission may apply to a county court for an injunction, or to a sheriff court for an order, restraining him from doing such acts; and the court, if satisfied that the application is well-founded, may grant the injunction or an order in the terms applied for or more limited terms.

(5) In proceedings under subsection (4) the Commission shall not allege that the person to whom the proceedings relate has done an act which is unlawful under this Act and within the jurisdiction of an industrial tribunal unless a finding by an industrial tribunal that he did that act has become final.

COMMENCEMENT
See s. 83 (2), *post*, and the note "orders under this section" thereto.

COMMISSION
S. 53 and Sch. 3; s. 82 (1): the EOC.

PART
S. 82 (7): reference to Part is a reference to the Part of the Act so numbered.

PART II
I.e. ss. 6–21.

INDUSTRIAL TRIBUNAL
S. 82 (1): means a tribunal established under s. 12 of the Industrial Training Act 1964.

WITHIN THE JURISDICTION OF THE INDUSTRIAL TRIBUNAL
See s. 73 (4), *post*.

ACT
S. 82 (1): includes a deliberate omission.

FINAL
S. 82 (4) for assessment of when a finding becomes final.

TIME LIMIT
The time limit for bringing proceedings under this section set out in s. 76.

SUBSECTION (4)
For applications under sub-s. (4) see s. 73, below. Certain proposals for amending this subsection are made in RRB, Sch. 4.

INJUNCTION
See note to s. 62, *ante*.

COMMENTARY
See para. [**147**], *ante*.

---

73. Preliminary action in employment cases

(1) With a view to making an application under section 71 (1) or 72 (4) in relation to a person the Commission may present to an industrial tribunal a complaint that he has done an act within the jurisdiction of an industrial tribunal, and if the tribunal considers that the complaint is well-founded they shall make a finding to that effect and, if they think it just and equitable to do so in the case of an act contravening any provision of Part II may also (as if the complaint had been presented by the person discriminated against) make an order such as is referred to in section 65 (1) (*a*), or a recommendation such as is referred to in section 65 (1) (*c*), or both.

(2) Subsection (1) is without prejudice to the jurisdiction conferred by section 72 (2).

(3) Any finding of an industrial tribunal under—

(*a*) this Act, or
(*b*) the Equal Pay Act 1970,

in respect of any act shall, if it has become final, be treated as conclusive—

(i) by the county court or sheriff court on an application under section 71 (1) or 72 (4) or in proceedings on an equality clause,
(ii) by an industrial tribunal on a complaint made by the person affected by the act under section 63 or in relation to an equality clause.

(4) In sections 71 and 72 and this section, the acts "within the jurisdiction of an industrial tribunal" are those in respect of which such jurisdiction is conferred by sections 63 and 72 and by section 2 of the Equal Pay Act 1970.

COMMENCEMENT
See s. 83 (2), *post*, and the note "orders under this section" thereto.

COMMISSION
S. 53 and Sch. 3; s. 82 (1): the EOC.

INDUSTRIAL TRIBUNAL
S. 82 (1): means a tribunal established under s. 12 of the Industrial Training Act 1964.

ACT
S. 82 (1): includes a deliberate omission.

JURISDICTION OF THE INDUSTRIAL TRIBUNAL
Ss. 63, 72 and s. 2 EPA.

EQUAL PAY ACT 1970
See Sch. 1; 40 Halsbury's Statutes (3rd Edn.), p. 561. This act is now amended by s. 8, *ante*, and Sch. 1, Part I, *post*. The amended text of the Act is set out in Sch. 1, Part II, *post*.

FINAL
S. 82 (4) for assessment of date on which the finding became final.

EQUALITY CLAUSE
S. 82 (1): meaning given in s. 1 (2) of the Equal Pay Act 1970.

PART
S. 82 (7): reference to a Part is a reference to the Part of the Act so numbered.

PART II
I.e. ss. 6–21.

COMPLAINT
Time limit for presenting a complaint: see s. 76, *post*.

COMMENTARY
See para. [145], *ante*.

Help for persons suffering discrimination

74. Help for aggrieved persons in obtaining information etc.

(1) With a view to helping a person ("the person aggrieved") who considers he may have been discriminated against in contravention of this Act to decide

whether to institute proceedings and, if he does so, to formulate and present his case in the most effective manner, the Secretary of State shall by order prescribe—

    (*a*) forms by which the person aggrieved may question the respondent on his reasons for doing any relevant act, or on any other matter which is or may be relevant;

    (*b*) forms by which the respondent may if he so wishes reply to any questions.

    (2) Where the person aggrieved questions the respondent (whether in accordance with an order under subsection (1) or not)—

    (*a*) the question, and any reply by the respondent (whether in accordance with such an order or not) shall, subject to the following provisions of this section, be admissible as evidence in the proceedings;

    (*b*) if it appears to the court or tribunal that the respondent deliberately, and without reasonable excuse omitted to reply within a reasonable period or that his reply is evasive or equivocal, the court or tribunal may draw any inference from that fact that it considers it just and equitable to draw, including an inference that he committed an unlawful act.

    (3) The Secretary of State may by order—

    (*a*) prescribe the period within which questions must be duly served in order to be admissible under subsection (2) (*a*), and

    (*b*) prescribe the manner in which a question, and any reply by the respondent, may be duly served.

    (4) Rules may enable the court entertaining a claim under section 66 to determine, before the date fixed for the hearing of the claim, whether a question or reply is admissible under this section or not.

    (5) This section is without prejudice to any other enactment or rule of law regulating interlocutory and preliminary matters in proceedings before a county court, sheriff court or industrial tribunal, and has effect subject to any enactment or rule of law regulating the admissibility of evidence in such proceedings.

    (6) In this section "respondent" includes a prospective respondent and "rules"—

    (*a*) in relation to county court proceedings, means county court rules;

    (*b*) (*applies to Scotland*).

COMMENCEMENT
    See s. 83 (2), *post*, and the note "orders under this section" thereto.

DISCRIMINATION
    S. 82 (1): defined with reference to s. 5 (1).

PROCEEDINGS
    In the Industrial Tribunal or county court, see ss. 62–76 and in particular, s. 63 and s. 66.

ORDER
    S. 81: power of Secretary of State to make orders, exercisable by statutory instrument.

FORMS
    See the Sex Discrimination (Questions and Replies) Order 1975, S.I. 1975 No. 2048. See also 126 *New Law Journal* 139, 140.

ACT
    S. 82 (1): includes a deliberate omission.

TRIBUNAL
    The Industrial Tribunal; s. 82 (1): a tribunal established under s. 12 of the Industrial Training Act 1964.

SECRETARY OF STATE
    S. 12, Interpretation Act 1889: one of Her Majesty's principal Secretaries of State for the time being.

COUNTY COURT RULES
    Rules made under the County Courts Act 1959, s. 102.

COMMENTARY
    See para. [135], *ante*.

75. Assistance by Commission

(1) Where, in relation to proceedings or prospective proceedings either under this Act or in respect of an equality clause, an individual who is an actual or prospective complainant or claimant applies to the Commission for assistance under this section, the Commission shall consider the application and may grant it if they think fit to do so on the ground that—

(a) the case raises a question of principle, or

(b) it is unreasonable, having regard to the complexity of the case or the applicant's position in relation to the respondent or another person involved or any other matter, to expect the applicant to deal with the case unaided,

or by reason of any other special consideration.

(2) Assistance by the Commission under this section may include—

(a) giving advice;

(b) procuring or attempting to procure the settlement of any matter in dispute;

(c) arranging for the giving of advice or assistance by a solicitor or counsel;

(d) arranging for representation by any person including all such assistance as is usually given by a solicitor or counsel in the steps preliminary or incidental to any proceedings, or in arriving at or giving effect to a compromise to avoid or bring to an end any proceedings,

but paragraph (d) shall not affect the law and practice regulating the descriptions of persons who may appear in, conduct, defend and address the court in, any proceedings.

(3) In so far as expenses are incurred by the Commission in providing the applicant with assistance under this section the recovery of those expenses (as taxed or assessed in such manner as may be prescribed by rules or regulations) shall constitute a first charge for the benefit of the Commission—

(a) on any costs or expenses which (whether by virtue of a judgment or order of a court or tribunal or an agreement or otherwise) are payable to the applicant by any other person in respect of the matter in connection with which the assistance is given, and

(b) so far as relates to any costs or expenses, on his rights under any compromise or settlement arrived at in connection with that matter to avoid or bring to an end any proceedings.

(4) The charge conferred by subsection (3) is subject to any charge under the Legal Aid Act 1974, or any charge or obligation for payment in priority to other debts under the Legal Aid and Advice (Scotland) Acts 1967 and 1972, and is subject to any provision in any of those Acts for payment of any sum into the legal aid fund.

(5) In this section "respondent" includes a prospective respondent and "rules or regulations"—

    (*a*) in relation to county court proceedings, means county court rules;

    (*b*) (*applies to Scotland*);

    (*c*) in relation to industrial tribunal proceedings, means regulations made under paragraph 21 of Schedule 1 to the Trade Union and Labour Relations Act 1974.

COMMENCEMENT
    See s. 83 (2), *post*, and the note "orders under this section" thereto.

INDIVIDUAL
    See note to s. 7, *ante*.

EQUALITY CLAUSE
    S. 82 (1): has the meaning given in s. 1 (2) of the Equal Pay Act 1970; see Sch. 1.

COMPLAINANT
    Proceedings brought before the Industrial Tribunal: see s. 63.

CLAIMANT
    Proceedings brought before the county court: see s. 66.

COMMISSION
    S. 53 and Sch. 3; s. 82 (1): the EOC.

PROCEEDINGS
    In the Industrial Tribunal or county court, see ss. 62–76 and in particular, s. 63 and s. 66.

TRIBUNAL
    The Industrial Tribunal: s. 82 (1): a tribunal established under s. 12 of the Industrial Training Act 1964.

TRADE UNION AND LABOUR RELATIONS ACT 1974
    44 Halsbury's Statutes (3rd Edn.), p. 1766.

LEGAL AID ACT 1974
    44 Halsbury's Statutes (3rd Edn.), p. 1035.

PERSON
    S. 19, Interpretation Act 1889: includes a body corporate or unincorporate.

COMMENTARY
    See para. [**145**], *ante*.

Period within which proceedings to be brought

76. Period within which proceedings to be brought

(1) An industrial tribunal shall not consider a complaint under section 63 unless it is presented to the tribunal before the end of the period of three months beginning when the act complained of was done.

(2) A county court or a sheriff court shall not consider a claim under section 66 unless proceedings in respect of the claim are instituted before the end of the period of six months beginning—

(*a*) when the act complained of was done, or

(*b*) in a case to which section 66 (5) applies, when the restriction on the institution of proceedings imposed by that provision ceased to operate.

(3) A county court or sheriff court shall not consider an application under section 72 unless it is made before the end of the period of six months beginning when the act to which it relates was done.

(4) An industrial tribunal shall not consider a complaint under section 73 (1) unless it is presented to the tribunal before the end of the period of six months beginning when the act complained of was done.

(5) A court or tribunal may nevertheless consider any such complaint, claim or application which is out of time if, in all the circumstances of the case, it considers that it is just and equitable to do so.

(6) For the purposes of this section—

(*a*) where the inclusion of any term in a contract renders the making of the contract an unlawful act that act shall be treated as extending throughout the duration of the contract, and

(*b*) any act extending over a period shall be treated as done at the end of that period, and

(*c*) a deliberate omission shall be treated as done when the person in question decided upon it,

and in the absence of evidence establishing the contrary a person shall be taken for the purposes of this section to decide upon an omission when he does an act inconsistent with doing the omitted act or, if he has done no such inconsistent act, when the period expires within which he might reasonably have been expected to do the omitted act if it was to be done.

COMMENCEMENT
See s. 83 (2), *post*, and the note "orders under this section" thereto.

INDUSTRIAL TRIBUNAL
S. 82 (1): a tribunal established under s. 12 of the Industrial Training Act 1964.

ACT
S. 82 (1): includes a deliberate omission.

COUNTY COURT
S. 6, Interpretation Act 1889: court under the County Courts Act 1959, by virtue of s. 205 (4).

MONTH
S. 3, Interpretation Act 1889: a calendar month.

THREE (SIX) MONTHS BEGINNING ETC.
See note "five years beginning etc." to s. 69, *ante*.

PERSON
S. 19, Interpretation Act 1889: includes body corporate or unincorporate.

AMENDMENT
Proposals have been made in RRB, Sch. 4, to amend sub-ss. (2) and (3).

COMMENTARY
See paras. [100], [109] and [119], *ante*.

PART VIII

SUPPLEMENTAL

77. Validity and revision of contracts

(1) A term of a contract is void where—

- (*a*) its inclusion renders the making of the contract unlawful by virtue of this Act, or
- (*b*) it is included in furtherance of an act rendered unlawful by this Act, or
- (*c*) it provides for the doing of an act which would be rendered unlawful by this Act.

(2) Subsection (1) does not apply to a term the inclusion of which constitutes, or is in furtherance of, or provides for, unlawful discrimination against a party to the contract, but the term shall be unenforceable against that party.

(3) A term in a contract which purports to exclude or limit any provision of this Act or the Equal Pay Act 1970 is unenforceable by any person in whose favour the term would operate apart from this subsection.

(4) Subsection (3) does not apply—

- (*a*) to a contract settling a complaint to which section 63 (1) of this Act or section 2 of the Equal Pay Act 1970 applies where the contract is made with the assistance of a conciliation officer;
- (*b*) to a contract settling a claim to which section 66 applies.

(5) On the application of any person interested in a contract to which subsection (2) applies, a county court or sheriff court may make such order as it thinks just for removing or modifying any term made unenforceable by that subsection; but such an order shall not be made unless all persons affected have been given notice of the application (except where under rules of court notice may be dispensed with) and have been afforded an opportunity to make representations to the court.

(6) An order under subsection (5) may include provision as respects any period before the making of the order.

ACT
   Includes a deliberate omission: s. 82 (1).

DISCRIMINATION
   S. 82 (1) to be construed in accordance with s. 5 (1).

EQUAL PAY ACT 1970
   See Sch. 1. The Act, unamended, is set out at 40 Halsbury's Statutes (3rd Edn.), p. 561.

CONCILIATION OFFICER
   S. 82 (1): a person appointed under para. 26 (1) of Sch. 1 of the Trade Union and Labour Relations Act 1974.

NOTICE
   S. 82 (1): notice in writing.

PERSON
   S. 19, Interpretation Act 1889: includes a body corporate or unincorporate.

COMMENTARY
   See para. **[18]**, *ante.*

78. Educational Charities in England and Wales

(1) This section applies to any trust deed or other instrument—

    (*a*) which concerns property applicable for or in connection with the provision of education in any establishment in paragraphs 1 to 5 of the Table in section 22, and

    (*b*) which in any way restricts the benefits available under the instrument to persons of one sex.

(2) If on the application of the trustees, or of the responsible body (as defined in section 22), the Secretary of State is satisfied that the removal or modification of the restriction would conduce to the advancement of education without sex discrimination, he may by order make such modifications of the instrument as appear to him expedient for removing or modifying the restriction, and for any supplemental or incidental purposes.

(3) If the trust was created by gift or bequest, no order shall be made until 25 years after the date on which the gift or bequest took effect, unless the donor or his personal representatives, or the personal representatives of the testator, have consented in writing to the making of the application for the order.

(4) The Secretary of State shall require the applicant to publish notice—

    (*a*) containing particulars of the proposed order, and

    (*b*) stating that representations may be made to the Secretary of State within a period specified in the notice.

(5) The period specified in the notice shall not be less than one month from the date of the notice.

(6) The applicants shall publish the notice in such manner as may be specified by the Secretary of State, and the cost of any publication of the notice may be defrayed out of the property of the trust.

(7) Before making the order the Secretary of State shall take into account any representations duly made in accordance with the notice.

(8) This section does not apply in Scotland.

EDUCATION
    S. 82 (1): includes any form of training or instruction.

DISCRIMINATION
    S. 82 (1) to be construed in accordance with s. 5 (1).

NOTICE
    S. 82 (1): notice in writing.

ORDER
    For making of orders see s. 81.

SECRETARY OF STATE
    S. 12, Interpretation Act 1889: one of Her Majesty's principal Secretaries of State for the time being.

MONTH
    S. 3, Interpretation Act 1889: a calendar month.

WRITING
    See s. 20, Interpretation Act 1889, 32 Halsbury's Statutes (3rd Edn.), p. 450.

COMMENTARY
    See para. [20], *ante*.

79. (*Applies to Scotland.*)

EDUCATION
   S. 82 (1) includes any form of instruction or training.

DISCRIMINATION
   S. 82 (1) to be construed in accordance with s. 5 (1).

ORDER
   For making of order see s. 81.

NOTICE
   S. 82 (1): notice in writing.

SECRETARY OF STATE
   S. 12, Interpretation Act 1889: one of Her Majesty's principal Secretaries of State for the time being.

COMMENTARY
   See para. [20], *ante.*

---

80. Power to amend certain provisions of Act

(1) The Secretary of State may by an order the draft of which has been approved by each House of Parliament—

> (*a*) amend any of the following provisions, namely, sections 6 (3), 7, 19, 20 (1), (2) and (3), 31 (2), 32, 34, 35 and 43 to 48 (including any such provision as amended by a previous order under this subsection);
>
> (*b*) amend or repeal any of the following provisions namely, sections 11 (4), 12 (4), 33 and 49 (including any such provision as amended by a previous order under this subsection);
>
> (*c*) amend Part II, III or IV so as to render lawful an act which, apart from the amendment, would be unlawful by reason of section 6 (1) or (2), 29 (1), 30 or 31;
>
> (*d*) amend section 11 (1) so as to alter the number of partners specified in that provision.

(2) The Secretary of State shall not lay before Parliament the draft of an order under subsection (1) unless he has consulted the Commission about the contents of the draft.

(3) An order under subsection (1) (*c*) may make such amendments to the list of provisions given in subsection (1) (*a*) as in the opinion of the Secretary of State are expedient having regard to the contents of the order.

PART II
   Ss. 6–21.

PART III
   Ss. 22–36.

PART IV
   Ss. 37–42.

ORDERS
   S. 81

PART
    S. 82 (7): reference to the Part of the Act so numbered.

COMMISSION
    S. 53 and Sch. 3; s. 82 (1): the EOC.

SECRETARY OF STATE
    S. 12, Interpretation Act 1889: one of Her Majesty's principal Secretaries of State for the time being.

LAY BEFORE PARLIAMENT
    See Laying of Documents before Parliament (Interpretation) Act 1948, s. 1 (1), 32 Halsbury's Statutes (3rd Edn.), p. 677.

---

81. Orders

(1) Any power of the Secretary of State to make orders under the provisions of this Act (except sections 14 (2) (*d*), 27, 47 (4) (*b*) and 59 (2)) shall be exercisable by statutory instrument.

(2) An order made by the Secretary of State under the preceding provisions of this Act (except sections 14 (2) (*d*), 27, 47 (4) (*b*), 59 (2) and 80 (1)) shall be subject to annulment in pursuance of a resolution of either House of Parliament.

(3) Subsections (1) and (2) do not apply to an order under section 78 or 79, but—

    (*a*) an order under section 78 which modifies an enactment, and
    (*b*) (*applies to Scotland*),

shall be made by statutory instrument subject to annulment in pursuance of a resolution of either House of Parliament.

(4) An order under this Act may make different provision in relation to different cases or classes of case, may exclude certain cases or classes of case, and may contain transitional provisions and savings.

(5) Any power conferred by this Act to make orders includes power (exercisable in the like manner and subject to the like conditions) to vary or revoke any order so made.

SECRETARY OF STATE
    S. 12, Interpretation Act 1889: one of Her Majesty's principal Secretaries of State for the time being.

STATUTORY INSTRUMENT
    See generally the Statutory Instruments Act 1946, 32 Halsbury's Statutes (3rd Edn.), p. 668.

SUBJECT TO ANNULMENT
    Ibid., ss. 5 (1) and 7 (1).

---

82. General interpretation provisions

(1) In this Act, unless the context otherwise requires—

    "access" shall be construed in accordance with section 50;
    "act" includes a deliberate omission;
    "advertisement" includes every form of advertisement, whether to the public or not, and whether in a newspaper or other publication, by

television or radio, by display of notices, signs, labels, showcards or goods, by distribution of samples, circulars, catalogues, price lists or other material, by exhibition of pictures, models or films, or in any other way, and references to the publishing of advertisements shall be construed accordingly;

"associated employer" shall be construed in accordance with subsection (2);

"the Commission" means the Equal Opportunities Commission;

"Commissioner" means a member of the Commission;

"conciliation officer" means a person appointed under paragraph 26 (1) of Schedule 1 to the Trade Union and Labour Relations Act 1974;

"designate" shall be construed in accordance with subsection (3);

"discrimination" and related terms shall be construed in accordance with section 5 (1);

"dispose", in relation to premises, includes granting a right to occupy the premises, and any reference to acquiring premises shall be construed accordingly;

"education" includes any form of training or instruction;

. . . . .

"employment" means employment under a contract of service or of apprenticeship or a contract personally to execute any work or labour, and related expressions shall be construed accordingly;

"employment agency" means a person who, for profit or not, provides services for the purpose of finding employment for workers or supplying employers with workers;

"equality clause" has the meaning given in section 1 (2) of the Equal Pay Act 1970 (as set out in section 8 (1) of this Act);

"estate agent" means a person who, by way of profession or trade, provides services for the purpose of finding premises for persons seeking to acquire them or assisting in the disposal of premises;

"final" shall be construed in accordance with subsection (4);

"firm" has the meaning given by section 4 of the Partnership Act 1890;

"formal investigation" means an investigation under section 57;

"further education" has the meaning given by section 41 (a) of the Education Act 1944 and in Scotland has the meaning given by section 145 (21) of the Education (Scotland) Act 1962;

"general notice", in relation to any person, means a notice published by him at a time and in a manner appearing to him suitable for securing that the notice is seen within a reasonable time by persons likely to be affected by it;

"genuine occupational qualification" shall be construed in accordance with section 7 (2);

"Great Britain" includes such of the territorial waters of the United Kingdom as are adjacent to Great Britain;

"independent school" has the meaning given by section 114 (1) of the Education Act 1944 and in Scotland has the meaning given by section 145 (23) of the Education (Scotland) Act 1962;

"industrial tribunal" means a tribunal established under section 12 of the Industrial Training Act 1964;

"man" includes a male of any age;

. . . . .

"near relative" shall be construed in accordance with subsection (5);

"non-discrimination notice" means a notice under section 67;

"notice" means a notice in writing;

"prescribed" means prescribed by regulations made by the Secretary of State by statutory instrument;

"profession" includes any vocation or occupation;

"proprietor", in relation to any school, has the meaning given by section 114 (1) of the Education Act 1944 and in Scotland has the meaning given by section 145 (37) of the Education (Scotland) Act 1962;

．　　．　　．　　．　　．

"retirement" includes retirement (whether voluntary or not) on grounds of age, length of service or incapacity;

"school" has the meaning given by section 114 (1) of the Education Act 1944, and in Scotland has the meaning given by section 145 (42) of the Education (Scotland) Act 1962;

．　　．　　．　　．　　．

"trade" includes any business;

"training" includes any form of education or instruction;

"university" includes a university college and the college, school or hall of a university;

"upper limit of compulsory school age" means, subject to section 9 of the Education Act 1962, the age that is that limit by virtue of section 35 of the Education Act 1944 and the Order in Council made under that section;

"woman" includes a female of any age.

(2) For the purposes of this Act two employers are to be treated as associated if one is a company of which the other (directly or indirectly) has control or if both are companies of which a third person (directly or indirectly) has control.

(3) Any power conferred by this Act to designate establishments or persons may be exercised either by naming them or by identifying them by reference to a class or other description.

(4) For the purposes of this Act a non-discrimination notice or a finding by a court or tribunal becomes final when an appeal against the notice or finding is dismissed, withdrawn or abandoned or when the time for appealing expires without an appeal having been brought; and for this purpose an appeal against a non-discrimination notice shall be taken to be dismissed if, notwithstanding that a requirement of the notice is quashed on appeal, a direction is given in respect of it under section 68 (3).

(5) For the purposes of this Act a person is a near relative of another if that person is the wife or husband, a parent or child, a grandparent or grandchild, or a brother or sister of the other (whether of full blood or half-blood or by affinity), and "child" includes an illegitimate child and the wife or husband of an illegitimate child.

(6) Except so far as the context otherwise requires, any reference in this Act to an enactment shall be construed as a reference to that enactment as amended by or under any other enactment including this Act.

(7) In this Act, except where otherwise indicated—

(*a*) a reference to a numbered Part, section or Schedule is a reference to the Part or section of, or the Schedule to, this Act so numbered, and

(*b*) a reference in a section to a numbered subsection is a reference to the subsection of that section so numbered, and (*c*) a reference in a section, subsection or Schedule to a numbered paragraph is a reference to the paragraph of that section, subsection or Schedule so numbered, and

(*d*) a reference to any provision of an Act (including this Act) includes a Schedule incorporated in the Act by that provision.

SUBSECTION (1)
The definitions omitted where indicated by dots apply to Scotland.

ESTABLISHMENTS
See ss. 22 and 24.

NON-DISCRIMINATION NOTICE
See s. 67.

NEAR-RELATIVE
See s. 32.

TRADE UNION AND LABOUR RELATIONS ACT 1974
44 Halsbury's Statutes (3rd Edn.), p. 1766.

PARTNERSHIP ACT 1890
24 Halsbury's Statutes (3rd Edn.), p. 500.

EDUCATION ACT 1944
11 Halsbury's Statutes (3rd Edn.), p. 153.

INDUSTRIAL TRAINING ACT 1964
12 Halsbury's Statutes (3rd Edn.), p. 219.

EDUCATION ACT 1962
11 Halsbury's Statutes (3rd Edn.), p. 314.

WRITING
S. 20, Interpretation Act 1889: construed as including references to printing, lithography, photography and other modes of representing or reproducing words in a visible form.

EQUAL OPPORTUNITIES COMMISSION
Body established by s. 52, *ante*.

GREAT BRITAIN
See note to s. 30, *ante*.

STATUTORY INSTRUMENT
See Statutory Instruments Act 1946, 32 Halsbury's Statutes (3rd Edn.), p. 668.

CONTROL
Not defined in this Act, but for a definition which applies for the purposes of certain provisions of the Tax Acts, see the Income and Corporation Taxes Act 1970, s. 534, 33 Halsbury's Statutes (3rd Edn.), p. 695.

EMPLOYMENT
As this definition includes both employment under a contract of service or apprenticeship and employment under a contract personally to execute any work or labour, it appears that the distinction between a contract of service and a contract for services (as to which, see, e.g., the note "Contract of service" to the Trade Union and Labour Relations Act 1974, s. 30 (1), 44 Halsbury's Statutes (3rd Edn.), p. 1784) is not of importance here.
As to service of the Crown, see s. 85, *post*.

TERRITORIAL WATERS OF THE UNITED KINGDOM
The question of the extent of territorial waters is a much disputed question of international law and practice. There is, however, general agreement that the territorial waters of a country extend to at least three nautical miles (one marine league) from

the shore, measured from low-water mark, and this is the rule to which the United Kingdom, in common with many other countries, adhered until recently for all purposes. In fact this limit measured from low-water mark has found its way into the definition of "the territorial waters of Her Majesty's dominions" in the Territorial Waters Jurisdiction Act 1878, s. 7. Its recognition also found expression in the Customs Consolidation Act 1876, s. 179 (repealed), and is now implicit in the provisions of the Customs and Excise Act 1952, ss. 75, 76 and 173 (3), and s. 107 (4) of that Act. Some countries now claim greater limits, and in some cases there is the claim that the limit should be measured not from low-water mark, but from arbitrary base lines joining points on the coast (see *Anglo-Norwegian Fisheries Case*, [1951] International Courts of Justice Reports 116, and note also the provisions of the Territorial Waters Order in Council 1964, dated 25th September 1964; 23 Halsbury's Statutory Instruments, title Waters and Watercourses (baselines)). It may be that for the purposes of the law relating to sea fishing, at any rate, the territorial waters of the United Kingdom now extend at least to the exclusive fishery limits laid down in the Fishery Limits Act 1964, s. 1, and possibly even cover the outer belt described in that section. However, the Continental Shelf Act 1964, s. 1 (1), expressly recognises that the "continental shelf" of the United Kingdom lies outside its territorial waters, and there is recent authority for saying that the three-mile limit still generally applies; see *R.* v. *Kent Justices, Ex parte Lye*, [1967] 2 Q.B. 153; [1967] 1 All E.R. 560; *Post Office* v. *Estuary Radio, Ltd.*, [1968] 2 Q.B. 740; [1967] 3 All E.R. 663, C.A. It seems, therefore, that the reference in this section to the territorial waters of the United Kingdom must be construed in the light of the three-mile limit; cf. *Direct United States Cable Co.* v. *Anglo-American Telegraph Co.* (1877), 2 App. Cas. 394. See also *The Fagernes*, [1927] P. 311, C.A. (statement of appropriate officer of the Crown as to extent of territorial waters conclusive).

---

83. Transitional and commencement provisions, amendments and repeals

(1) The provisions of Schedule 4 shall have effect for making transitional provision for the purposes of this Act.

(2) Parts II to VII shall come into operation on such day as the Secretary of State may by order appoint, and different days may be so appointed for different provisions and for different purposes.

(3) Subject to subsection (4)—

(*a*) the enactments specified in Schedule 5 shall have effect subject to the amendments specified in that Schedule (being minor amendments or amendments consequential on the preceding provisions of this Act), and

(*b*) the enactments specified in Schedule 6 are hereby repealed to the extent shown in column 3 of that Schedule.

(4) The Secretary of State shall by order provide for the coming into operation of the amendments contained in Schedule 5 and the repeals contained in Schedule 6, and those amendments and repeals shall have effect only as provided by an order so made.

(5) An order under this section may make such transitional provision as appears to the Secretary of State to be necessary or expedient in connection with the provisions thereby brought into operation, including such adaptations of those provisions, or of any provisions of this Act then in operation, as appear to the Secretary of State necessary or expedient in consequence of the partial operation of this Act.

ORDER
    See s. 81.

SECRETARY OF STATE
S. 12, Interpretation Act 1889: one of Her Majesty's principal Secretaries of State for the time being.

PART
S. 82 (7) a reference to the Part of the Act so numbered.

PARTS II TO VII
Ss. 6–76.

ORDER UNDER THIS SECTION
The Sex Discrimination (Commencement) Order 1975, S.I. 1975 No. 1845, specifying 29th December for the coming into force of Parts II–VII and the amendments and repeals in Schs. 5 and 6, with the following exceptions:
(i) S. 8 (6), so far as it (a) amends the Equal Pay Act 1970, s. 6, to provide that an equality clause and the provisions of s. 3 (4) of the Act of 1970 shall operate in relation to terms relating to membership of an occupational pension scheme so far as those terms relate to any matter in respect of which the scheme has to conform with the equal access of Part IV of the Act of 1975; (b) provides that the Act of 1970 shall have effect as set out in Part II of Sch. 1 of the 1975 Act, comes into force on 6th April, 1978, with transitional provisions as set out in art. 4 (2) of S.I. 1975 No. 1845;
(ii) Ss. 22 and 25, so far as they relate to the admission of pupils to educational establishments, do not apply before 1st September 1976;
(iii) Ss. 53 and 56 come into force on 12th November, 1975 and 1st January, 1976 respectively.
The Sex Discrimination (Commencement) (Amendment) Order 1975, S.I. 1975 No. 2112, created a further exception. It shall not be unlawful to publish or cause to be published an advertisement (otherwise unlawful under s. 38) before 1st April, 1976 if the advertisement was prepared for printing before 15th December, 1975.
For general provisions as to orders, see s. 81 (1), (2), (4), (5), *ante*.

---

84. Financial provisions
There shall be defrayed out of money provided by Parliament—
(*a*) sums required by the Secretary of State for making payments under paragraph 5 or 14 of Schedule 3, and for defraying any other expenditure falling to be made by him under or by virtue of this Act;
(*b*) payments falling to be made under section 66 (6) (*b*) or (7) in respect of the remuneration of assessors; and
(*c*) any increase attributable to the provisions of this Act in the sums payable out of money provided by Parliament under any other Act.

SECRETARY OF STATE
One of Her Majesty's principal Secretaries of State for the time being: s. 12, Interpretation Act 1889.

---

85. Application to Crown
(1) This Act applies—
(*a*) to an act done by or for purposes of a Minister of the Crown or government department, or
(*b*) to an act done on behalf of the Crown by a statutory body, or a person holding a statutory office,
as it applies to an act done by a private person.

(2) Parts II and IV apply to—

    (*a*) service for purposes of a Minister of the Crown or government department, other than service of a person holding a statutory office, or

    (*b*) service on behalf of the Crown for purposes of a person holding a statutory office or purposes of a statutory body,

as they apply to employment by a private person, and shall so apply as if references to a contract of employment included references to the terms of service.

(3) Subsections (1) and (2) have effect subject to section 17.

(4) Subsections (1) and (2) do not apply in relation to service in—

    (*a*) the naval, military or air forces of the Crown, or

    (*b*) any women's service administered by the Defence Council.

(5) Nothing in this Act shall render unlawful discrimination in admission to the Army Cadet Force, Air Training Corps, Sea Cadet Corps or Combined Cadet Force, or any other cadet training corps for the time being administered by the Ministry of Defence.

(6) This Act (except section 8 (1) and (6)) does not apply to employment in the case of which the employee may be required to serve in support of a force or service mentioned in subsection (4) (*a*) or (*b*).

(7) Subsection (2) of section 10 shall have effect in relation to any ship, aircraft or hovercraft belonging to or possessed by Her Majesty in right of the Government of the United Kingdom as it has effect in relation to a ship, aircraft or hovercraft mentioned in paragraph (*a*) or (*b*) of that subsection, and section 10 (5) shall apply accordingly.

(8) The provisions of Parts II to IV of the Crown Proceedings Act 1947 shall apply to proceedings against the Crown under this Act as they apply to proceedings in England and Wales which by virtue of section 23 of that Act are treated for the purposes of Part II of that Act as civil proceedings by or against the Crown, except that in their application to proceedings under this Act section 20 of that Act (removal of proceedings from county court to High Court) shall not apply.

(9) The provisions of Part V of the Crown Proceedings Act 1947 shall apply to proceedings against the Crown under this Act as they apply to proceedings in Scotland which by virtue of the said Part are treated as civil proceedings by or against the Crown, except that in their application to proceedings under this Act the proviso to section 44 of that Act (removal of proceedings from the sheriff court to the Court of Session) shall not apply.

(10) In this section "statutory body" means a body set up by or in pursuance of an enactment, and "statutory office" means an office so set up; and service "for purposes of" a Minister of the Crown or government department does not include service in any office in Schedule 2 (Ministerial offices) to the House of Commons Disqualification Act 1975 as for the time being in force.

ACT
    S. 82 (1): includes a deliberate omission.

PART
    S. 82 (7): a reference to the Part of the Act so numbered.

PARTS II AND IV
    I.e. ss. 6–21 and 37–42 of the Act.

CROWN PROCEEDINGS ACT 1947
    8 Halsbury's Statutes (3rd Edn.), p. 844.

HOUSE OF COMMONS DISQUALIFICATION ACT 1975
    45 Halsbury's Statutes (3rd Edn.), p. 1594.

CROWN
    S. 30, Interpretation Act 1889: shall be construed as a reference to the Sovereign for
    the time being.

DEFENCE COUNCIL
    As to the establishment of this body, see the Defence (Transfer of Functions) Act 1964,
    s. 1, 6 Halsbury's Statutes (3rd Edn.), p. 795.

COMMENTARY
    See paras. [60] and [94].

86. Government appointments outside section 6

(1) This section applies to any appointment by a Minister of the Crown or government department to an office or post where section 6 does not apply in relation to the appointment.

(2) In making the appointment, and in making the arrangements for determining who should be offered the office or post, the Minister of the Crown or government department shall not do an act which would be unlawful under section 6 if the Crown were the employer for the purposes of this Act.

CROWN
    S. 30, Interpretation Act 1889: construed as a reference to the Sovereign for the time
    being.

ACT
    S. 82 (1) includes a deliberate omission.

EMPLOYER
    See s. 82 (1).

COMMENTARY
    See para. [61], *ante*.

87. Short title and extent

(1) This Act may be cited as the Sex Discrimination Act 1975.

(2) This Act (except paragraph 16 of Schedule 3) does not extend to Northern Ireland.

COMMENTARY
    See para. [149], *ante*.

SCHEDULES

SCHEDULE 1

Section 8

EQUAL PAY ACT 1970

PART I

AMENDMENTS OF ACT

1.—(1) In section 1 (6), paragraph (b) is repealed and the following is inserted after paragraph (c): "and men shall be treated as in the same employment with a woman if they are men employed by her employer or any associated employer at the same establishment or at establishments in Great Britain which include that one and at which common terms and conditions of employment are observed either generally or for employees of the relevant classes".

(2) Section 1 (7) is repealed.

(3) The following is substituted for section 1 (8)—

"(8) This section shall apply to—

(a) service for purposes of a Minister of the Crown or government department, other than service of a person holding a statutory office, or

(b) service on behalf of the Crown for purposes of a person holding a statutory office or purposes of a statutory body,

as it applies to employment by a private person, and shall so apply as if references to a contract of employment included references to the terms of service.

(9) Subsection (8) does not apply in relation to service in—

(a) the naval, military or air forces of the Crown, or

(b) any women's service administered by the Defence Council.

(10) In this section "statutory body" means a body set up by or in pursuance of an enactment, and "statutory office" means an office so set up; and service "for purposes of" a Minister of the Crown or government department does not include service in any office in Schedule 2 (Ministerial offices) to the House of Commons Disqualification Act 1975 as for the time being in force."

(4) The following subsections are inserted at the end of section 1—

"(11) For the purposes of this Act it is immaterial whether the law which (apart from this subsection) is the proper law of a contract is the law of any part of the United Kingdom or not.

(12) In this Act "Great Britain" includes such of the territorial waters of the United Kingdom as are adjacent to Great Britain.

(13) Provisions of this section and section 2 below framed with reference to women and their treatment relative to men are to be read as applying equally in a converse case to men and their treatment relative to women".

2.—(1) The following is substituted for section 2 (1)—

"(1) Any claim in respect of the contravention of a term modified or included by virtue of an equality clause, including a claim for arrears of remuneration or damages in respect of the contravention, may be presented by way of a complaint to an industrial tribunal."

(2) After section 2 (1) there is inserted—

"(1A) Where a dispute arises in relation to the effect of an equality clause the employer may apply to an industrial tribunal for an order declaring the rights of the employer and the employee in relation to the matter in question."

(3) In section 2 (2)—

(a) for "failing to comply with their equal pay clauses" there is substituted "contravening a term modified or included by virtue of their equality clauses", and

(b) after "the question may be referred by him" there is inserted "as respects all or any of them", and

(c) after "claim by the women" there is inserted "or woman".

(4) Section 2 (6) is repealed.

(5) In section 2 (7), the words "and there shall be paid" onwards are repealed.

3. In section 6 the following is substituted for subsection (1)—

"(1) Neither an equality clause nor the provisions of section 3 (4) above shall operate in relation to terms—

(a) affected by compliance with the laws regulating the employment of women, or (*b*) affording special treatment to women in connection with pregnancy or childbirth.

(1A) An equality clause and those provisions—

(*a*) shall operate in relation to terms relating to membership of an occupational pension scheme (within the meaning of the Social Security Pensions Act 1975) so far as those terms relate to any matter in respect of which the scheme has to conform with the equal access requirements of Part IV of that Act; but

(*b*) subject to this, shall not operate in relation to terms related to death or retirement, or to any provision made in connection with death or retirement."

4. Section 8 is repealed.

5. In section 9 (1), the words "Except as provided by subsection (2) below", and sections 9 (2) to (5) and 10 (4) are repealed.

6.—(1) For references to an equal pay clause in each place where they occur there are substituted references to an equality clause.

(2) For the words "the Industrial Court", in each place where they occur, there are substituted the words "the Industrial Arbitration Board"; in sections 4 and 10 for the words "Court" and "Court's" in each place where they occur there are substituted respectively "Board" and "Board's", and in section 5 for the word "Board" in each place where it occurs there is substituted "Agricultural Wages Board" and for the word "Court" in each place where it occurs there is substituted "Industrial Arbitration Board".

COMMENCEMENT
    See s. 83 (2), *ante*, and the note "Orders under this section" thereto.

PARA. I: EMPLOYED . . . AT THE SAME ESTABLISHMENT . . . IN GREAT BRITAIN
    See the note "Employment . . . at an establishment in Great Britain" to s. 8, *ante*.

DEFENCE COUNCIL
    See the note to s. 85, *ante*.

UNITED KINGDOM
    See the note to s. 7, *ante*.

GREAT BRITAIN
    See the note to s. 30, *ante*.

PARA. 6: INDUSTRIAL ARBITRATION BOARD
    The Industrial Court established by the Industrial Courts Act 1919, Part I, is now known as the Industrial Arbitration Board; see the Trade Union and Labour Relations Act 1974, s. 25 (1), Sch. 3, para. 3, 44 Halsbury's Statutes (3rd Edn.), pp. 1778, 1812.

DEFINITIONS
    For "equality clause", see the Equal Pay Act 1970, s. 1 (2), as set out in Part II of this Schedule, *post*; for "employment", "employer" and "employee", see s. 1 (6) (*a*) of that Act; as to associated employers, see s. 1 (6) (*c*) of that Act; for "industrial tribunal", see s. 2 (7) of that Act. Note as to "statutory body", "statutory office" and "for purposes of", the sub-s. (10) set out in para. 1 (3) above, and as to "Great Britain", the sub-s. (12) set out in para. 1 (4) above.

EQUAL PAY ACT 1970
    For the amended text of the Act, see Part II of this Schedule, *post*.

TRANSITIONAL PROVISION
    See s. 83 (1), *ante*, and Sch. 4, para. 5, *post*.

Part II

Act as amended

1970 CHAPTER 41

An Act to prevent discrimination, as regards terms and conditions of employment, between men and women.

[29th May 1970]

1.—(1) If the terms of a contract under which a woman is employed at an establishment in Great Britain do not include (directly or by reference to a collective agreement or otherwise) an equality clause they shall be deemed to include one.

(2) An equality clause is a provision which relates to terms (whether concerned with pay or not) of a contract under which a woman is employed (the "woman's contract"), and has the effect that—

(a) where the woman is employed on like work with a man in the same employment—

(i) if (apart from the equality clause) any term of the woman's contract is or becomes less favourable to the woman than a term of a similar kind in the contract under which that man is employed, that term of the woman's contract shall be treated as so modified as not to be less favourable, and

(ii) if (apart from the equality clause) at any time the woman's contract does not include a term corresponding to a term benefiting that man included in the contract under which he is employed, the woman's contract shall be treated as including such a term;

(b) where the woman is employed on work rated as equivalent with that of a man in the same employment—

(i) if (apart from the equality clause) any term of the woman's contract determined by the rating of the work is or becomes less favourable to the woman than a term of a similar kind in the contract under which that man is employed, that term of the woman's contract shall be treated as so modified as not to be less favourable, and

(ii) if (apart from the equality clause) at any time the woman's contract does not include a term corresponding to a term benefiting that man included in the contract under which he is employed and determined by the rating of the work, the woman's contract shall be treated as including such a term.

(3) An equality clause shall not operate in relation to a variation between the woman's contract and the man's contract if the employer proves that the variation is genuinely due to a material difference (other than the difference of sex) between her case and his.

(4) A woman is to be regarded as employed on like work with men if, but only if, her work and theirs is of the same or a broadly similar nature, and the differences (if any) between the things she does and the things they do are not of practical importance in relation to terms and condition of employment; and accordingly in comparing her work with theirs regard shall be had to the frequency or otherwise with which any such differences occur in practice as well as to the nature and extent of the differences.

(5) A woman is to be regarded as employed on work rated as equivalent with that of any men if, but only if, her job and their job have been given an equal value, in terms of the demand made on a worker under various headings (for instance effort, skill, decision), on a study undertaken with a view to evaluating in those terms the jobs to be done by all or any of the employees in an undertaking or group of undertakings, or would have been given an equal value but for the evaluation being made on a system setting different values for men and women on the same demand under any heading.

(6) Subject to the following subsections, for purposes of this section—

    (a) "employed" means employed under a contract of service or of apprentice-ship or a contract personally to execute any work or labour, and related expressions shall be construed accordingly;

    (c) two employers are to be treated as associated if one is a company of which the other (directly or indirectly) has control or if both are companies of which a third person (directly or indirectly) has control,

and men shall be treated as in the same employment with a woman if they are men employed by her employer or any associated employer at the same establishment or at establishments in Great Britain which include that one and at which common terms and conditions of employment are observed either generally or for employees of the relevant classes.

(8) This section shall apply to—

    (a) service for purposes of a Minister of the Crown or government department, other than service of a person holding a statutory office, or

    (b) sevice on behalf of the Crown for purposes of a person holding a statutory office or purposes of a statutory body,"

as it applies to employment by a private person, and shall so apply as if references to a contract of employment included references to the terms of service.

(9) Subsection (8) does not apply in relation to service in—

    (a) the naval, military or air forces of the Crown, or

    (b) any women's service administered by the Defence Council.

(10) In this section "statutory body" means a body set up by or in pursuance of an enactment, and "statutory office" means an office so set up; and service "for purposes of" a Minister of the Crown or government department does not include service in any office in Schedule 2 (Ministerial offices) to the House of Commons Disqualification Act 1975 as for the time being in force.

(11) For the purposes of this Act it is immaterial whether the law which (apart from this subsection) is the proper law of a contract is the law of any part of the United Kingdom or not.

(12) In this Act "Great Britain" includes such of the territorial waters of the United Kingdom as are adjacent to Great Britain.

(13) Provisions of this section and section 2 below framed with reference to women and their treatment relative to men are to be read as applying equally in a converse case to men and their treatment relative to women.

2. Disputes as to, and enforcement of, requirement of equal treatment

(1) Any claim in respect of the contravention of a term modified or included by virtue of an equality clause, including a claim for arrears of remuneration or damages in respect of the contravention, may be presented by way of a complaint to an industrial tribunal.

(1A) Where a dispute arises in relation to the effect of an equality clause the employer may apply to an industrial tribunal for an order declaring the rights of the employer and the employee in relation to the matter in question.

(2) Where it appears to the Secretary of State that there may be a question whether the employer of any women is or has been contravening a term modified or included by virtue of their equality clauses, but that it is not reasonable to expect them to take steps to have the question determined, the question may be referred by him as respects all or any of them to an industrial tribunal and shall be dealt with as if the reference were of a claim by the women or woman against the employer.

(3) Where it appears to the court in which any proceedings are pending that a claim or counter-claim in respect of the operation of an equality clause could more conveniently be disposed of separately by an industrial tribunal, the court may

direct that the claim or counter-claim shall be struck out; and (without prejudice to the foregoing) where in proceedings before any court a question arises as to the operation of an equality clause, the court may on the application of any party to the proceedings or otherwise refer that question, or direct it to be referred by a party to the proceedings, to an industrial tribunal for determination by the tribunal, and may stay or sist the proceedings in the meantime.

(4) No claim in respect of the operation of an equality clause relating to a woman's employment shall be referred to an industrial tribunal otherwise than by virtue of subsection (3) above, if she has not been employed in the employment within the six months preceding the date of the reference.

(5) A woman shall not be entitled, in proceedings brought in respect of a failure to comply with an equality clause (including proceedings before an industrial tribunal), to be awarded any payment by way of arrears of remuneration or damages in respect of a time earlier than two years before the date on which the proceedings were instituted.

(7) In this section "industrial tribunal" means a tribunal established under section 12 of the Industrial Training Act 1964.

3. Collective agreements and pay structures

(1) Where a collective agreement made before or after the commencement of this Act contains any provision applying specifically to men only or to women only, the agreement may be referred by any party to it or by the Secretary of State, to the Industrial Arbitration Board constituted under Part I of the Industrial Courts Act 1919 to declare what amendments need to be made in the agreement, in accordance with subsection (4) below, so as to remove that discrimination between men and women.

(2) Where on a reference under subsection (1) above the Industrial Arbitration Board have declared the amendments needing to be made in a collective agreement in accordance with that subsection, then—

    (*a*) in so far as the terms and conditions of a person's employment are dependent on that agreement, they shall be ascertained by reference to the agreement as so amended, and any contract regulating those terms and conditions shall have effect accordingly; and

    (*b*) if the Industrial Arbitration Board make or have made, under section 8 of the Terms and Conditions of Employment Act 1959 or any other enactment, an award or determination requiring an employer to observe the collective agreement, the award or determination shall have effect by reference to the agreement as so amended.

(3) On a reference under subsection (1) above the Industrial Arbitration Board may direct that all or any of the amendments needing to be made in the collective agreement shall be treated as not becoming effective until a date after their decision, or as having been effective from a date before their decision but not before the reference to them, and may specify different dates for different purposes; and subsection (2) above and any such contract, award or determination as is there mentioned shall have or be deemed to have had effect accordingly.

(4) Subject to section 6 below, the amendments to be made in a collective agreement under this section shall be such as are needed—

    (*a*) to extend to both men and women any provision applying specifically to men only or to women only; and

    (*b*) to eliminate any resulting duplication in the provisions of the agreement in such a way as not to make the terms and conditions agreed for men, or those agreed for women, less favourable in any respect than they would have been without the amendments;

but the amendments shall not extend the operation of the collective agreement to men or to women not previously falling within it, and where accordingly a provision applying specifically to men only or to women only continues to be required for a category of men or of women (there being no provision in the agreement for women or, as the case may be, for men of that category), then the provision shall be limited to men or women of that category but there shall be made to it such amendments, if any, as are needed to secure that the terms and conditions of the men or women of that category are not in any respect less favourable than those of all persons of the other sex to whom the agreement applies.

(5) For purposes of this section "collective agreement" means any agreement as to terms and conditions of employment, being an agreement between—

(a) parties who are or represent employers or organisations of employers or associations of such organisations; and

(b) parties who are or represent organisations of employees or associations of such organisations;

but includes also any award modifying or supplementing such an agreement.

(6) Subsections (1) to (4) above (except subsection (2) (b) and subsection (3) in so far as it relates to subsection (2) (b)) shall have effect in relation to an employer's pay structure as they have effect in relation to a collective agreement, with the adaptation that a reference to the Industrial Arbitration Board may be made by the employer or by the Secretary of State; and for this purpose "pay structure" means any arrangements adopted by an employer (with or without any associated employer) which fix common terms and conditions of employment for his employees or any class of his employees, and of which the provisions are generally known or open to be known by the employees concerned.

(7) In this section the expression "employment" and related expressions, and the reference to an associated employer, shall be construed in the same way as in section 1 above, and section 1 (8) shall have effect in relation to this section as well as in relation to that section.

4. Wages regulation orders

(1) Where a wages regulation order made before or after the commencement of this Act contains any provision applying specifically to men only or to women only, the order may be referred by the Secretary of State to the Industrial Arbitration Board to declare what amendments need to be made in the order, in accordance with the like rules as apply under section 3 (4) above to the amendment under that section of a collective agreement, so as to remove that discrimination between men and women; and when the Board have declared the amendments needing to be so made, the Secretary of State may by order made by statutory instrument coming into operation not later than five months after the date of the Board's decision direct that (subject to any further wages regulation order) the order referred to the Board shall have effect subject to those amendments.

(2) A wages regulation order shall be referred to the Industrial Arbitration Board under this section if the Secretary of State is requested so to refer it either—

(a) by a member or members of the wages council concerned with the order who was or who were appointed as representing employers; or

(b) by a member or members of that wages council who was or who were appointed as representing workers;

or if in any case it appears to the Secretary of State that the order may be amendable under this section.

(3) Where by virtue of section 12 (1) of the Wages Councils Act 1959 a contract between a worker and an employer is to have effect with modifications specified in section 12 (1), then (without prejudice to the general saving in section 11 (7) of that Act for rights conferred by or under other Acts) the contract as so modified shall have effect subject to any further term implied by virtue of section 1 above.

(4) In this section "wages regulation order" means an order made or having effect as if made under section 11 of the Wages Councils Act 1959.

5. Agricultural wages orders

(1) Where an agricultural wages order made before or after the commencement of this Act contains any provision applying specifically to men only or to women only, the order may be referred by the Secretary of State to the Industrial Arbitration Board to declare what amendments need to be made in the order, in accordance with the like rules as apply under section 3 (4) above to the amendment under that section of a collective agreement, so as to remove that discrimination between men and women; and when the Industrial Arbitration Board have declared the amendments needing to be so made, it shall be the duty of the Agricultural Wages Board, by a further agricultural wages order coming into operation not later than five months after the date of the Industrial Arbitration Board's decision, either to make those amendments in the order referred to the Industrial Arbitration Board or otherwise to replace or amend that order so as to remove the discrimination.

(2) Where the Agricultural Wages Board certify that the effect of an agricultural wages order is only to make such amendments of a previous order as have under this section been declared by the Industrial Arbitration Board to be needed, or to make such amendments as aforesaid with minor modifications or modifications of limited application, or is only to revoke and reproduce with such amendments a previous order, then the Agricultural Wages Board may instead of complying with paragraphs 1 and 2 of Schedule 4, or in the case of Scotland paragraphs 1 and 2 of Schedule 3, to the Agricultural Wages Act give notice of the proposed order in such manner as appears to the Agricultural Wages Board expedient in the circumstances, and may make the order at any time after the expiration of seven days from the giving of the notice.

(3) An agricultural wages order shall be referred to the Industrial Arbitration Board under this section if the Secretary of State is requested so to refer it either—

(a) by a body for the time being entitled to nominate for membership of the Agricultural Wages Board persons representing employers (or, if provision is made for any of the persons representing employers to be elected instead of nominated, then by a member or members representing employers); or

(b) by a body for the time being entitled to nominate for membership of the Agricultural Wages Board persons representing workers (or, if provision is made for any of the persons representing workers to be elected instead of nominated, then by a member or members representing workers);

or if in any case it appears to the Secretary of State that the order may be amendable under this section.

(4) In this section "the Agricultural Wages Board" means the Agricultural Wages Board for England and Wales or the Scottish Agricultural Wages Board, "the Agricultural Wages Act" means the Agricultural Wages Act 1948 or the Agricultural Wages (Scotland) Act 1949 and "agricultural wages order" means an order of the Agricultural Wages Board under the Agricultural Wages Act.

6. Exclusion from ss. 1 to 5 of pensions etc.

(1) Neither an equality clause nor the provisions of section 3 (4) above shall operate in relation to terms—

(a) affected by compliance with the laws regulating the employment of women, or

(b) affording special treatment to women in connection with pregnancy or childbirth.

(1A) An equality clause and those provisions—

(a) shall operate in relation to terms relating to membership of an occupational pension scheme (within the meaning of the Social Security Pensions Act 1975) so far as those terms relate to any matter in respect of which the scheme has to conform with the equal access requirements of Part IV of that Act; but

(b) subject to this, shall not operate in relation to terms related to death or retirement, or to any provision made in connection with death or retirement.

(2) Any reference in this section to retirement includes retirement, whether voluntary or not, on grounds of age, length of service or incapacity.

7. Service pay

(1) The Secretary of State or Defence Council shall not make, or recommend to Her Majesty the making of, any instrument relating to the terms and conditions of service of members of the naval, military or air forces of the Crown or of any women's service administered by the Defence Council, if the instrument has the effect of making a distinction, as regards pay, allowances or leave, between men and women who are members of those forces or of any such service, not being a distinction fairly attributable to differences between the obligations undertaken by men and those undertaken by women as such members as aforesaid.

(2) The Secretary of State or Defence Council may refer to the Industrial Arbitration Board for their advice any question whether a provision made or proposed to be made by any such instrument as is referred to in subsection (1) above ought to be regarded for purposes of this section as making a distinction not permitted by that subsection.

9. Commencement

(1) The foregoing provisions of this Act shall come into force on the 29th December 1975 and references in this Act to its commencement shall be construed as referring to the coming into force of those provisions on that date.

10. Preliminary references to Industrial Arbitration Board

(1) A collective agreement, pay structure or order which after the commencement of this Act could under section 3, 4 or 5 of this Act be referred to the Industrial Arbitration Board to declare what amendments need to be made as mentioned in that section may at any time not earlier than one year before that commencement be referred to the Board under this section for their advice as to the amendments needing to be so made.

(2) A reference under this section may be made by any person authorised by section 3, 4 or 5, as the case may be, to make a corresponding reference under that section, but the Secretary of State shall not under this section refer an order to the Industrial Arbitration Board unless requested so to do as mentioned in section 4 (2) or 5 (3), as the case may be, nor be required to refer an order if so requested.

(3) A collective agreement, pay structure or order referred to the Industrial Arbitration Board under this section may after the commencement of this Act be again referred to the Board under section 3, 4, or 5; but at that commencement any reference under this section (if still pending) shall lapse.

11. Short title, interpretation and extent

(1) This Act may be cited as the Equal Pay Act 1970.

(2) In this Act the expressions "man" and "woman" shall be read as applying to persons of whatever age.

(3) This Act shall not extend to Northern Ireland.

EQUAL PAY ACT 1970
> This Part of this Schedule contains the text of the Equal Pay Act 1970 as amended by s. 8 and Part 2 of the Schedule, *ante*; see s. 8 (6), *ante*.

COMMENCEMENT
> See s. 83 (2), *ante*, and the note "Orders under this section" thereto.

SCHEDULE 2

Section 27

TRANSITIONAL EXEMPTION ORDERS FOR EDUCATIONAL ADMISSIONS

Public sector (England and Wales)

1. Where under section 13 of the Education Act 1944 (as set out in Schedule 3 to the Education Act 1968) a responsible body submits to the Secretary of State, in accordance with subsection (1) or (2) of that section, proposals for an alteration in its admissions arrangements such as is mentioned in section 27 (1) of this Act the submission of those proposals shall be treated as an application for the making by the Secretary of State of a transitional exemption order, and if he thinks fit the Secretary of State may make the order accordingly.

2. Regulations under section 33 of the Education Act 1944 may provide for the submission to the Secretary of State of an application for the making by him of a transitional exemption order in relation to a special school, and for the making by him of the order.

3. Regulations under section 100 of the Education Act 1944 may provide for the submission to the Secretary of State of an application for the making by him of a transitional exemption order in relation to an establishment—

 (*a*) which is designated under section 24 (1), and
 (*b*) in respect of which grants are payable under subsection (1) (*b*) of the said section 100,

and for the making by him of the order.

4. Regulations under section 5 (2) of the Local Government Act 1974 may provide for the submission to the Secretary of State of an application for the making by him of a transitional exemption order in relation to any educational establishment maintained by a local education authority and not falling within paragraphs 1 to 3, and for the making by him of the order.

Private sector (England and Wales)

5.—(1) In the case of an establishment in England or Wales not falling within paragraphs 1 to 4 the responsible body may submit to the Equal Opportunities Commission set up under Part VI an application for the making by the Commission of a transitional exemption order in relation to the establishment, and if they think fit the Commission may make the order accordingly.

(2) An application under this paragraph shall specify the transitional period proposed by the responsible body to be provided for in the order, the stages by which within that period the body proposes to move to the position where section 22 (*b*) is complied with, and any other matters relevant to the terms and operation of the order applied for.

(3) The Commission shall not make an order on an application under this paragraph unless they are satisfied that the terms of the application are reasonable having regard to the nature of the premises at which the establishment is carried on, the accommodation, equipment and facilities available, and the financial resources of the responsible body.

6–9. (*Apply to Scotland.*)

COMMENCEMENT
 See s. 83 (2), *ante*, and the note "Orders under this section" thereto.

PARA. 1: TRANSITIONAL EXEMPTION ORDER
 See the note to s. 27, *ante*.

PARA. 2: SPECIAL SCHOOL
 See the note to s. 22, *ante*.

PARA. 4: LOCAL EDUCATION AUTHORITY
See the note to s. 15, *ante.*

PARA. 5: PART VI
I.e., Part VI (ss. 53–61) of this Act; see s. 82 (7), *ante.*

DEFINITIONS
For "responsible body", see s. 22, *ante;* for "transitional exemption order", see s. 27 (1), *ante.*

REGULATIONS
At the time of going to press no regulations containing provisions made by virtue of para. 2, 3 or 4 above had been made.

SCHEDULE 3

Section 53

EQUAL OPPORTUNITIES COMMISSION

Incorporation and status

1. On the appointment by the Secretary of State of the first Commissioners, the Commission shall come into existence as a body corporate with perpetual succession and a common seal.

2.—(1) The Commission is not an emanation of the Crown, and shall not act or be treated as the servant or agent of the Crown.

(2) Accordingly—

   (a) neither the Commission nor a Commissioner or member of its staff as such is entitled to any status, immunity, privilege or exemption enjoyed by the Crown;

   (b) the Commissioners and members of the staff of the Commission as such are not civil servants; and

   (c) the Commission's property is not property of, or held on behalf of, the Crown.

Tenure of office of Commissioners

3.—(1) A Commissioner shall hold and vacate his office in accordance with the terms of his appointment.

(2) A person shall not be appointed a Commissioner for more than five years.

(3) With the consent of the Commissioner concerned, the Secretary of State may alter the terms of an appointment so as to make a full-time Commissioner into a part-time Commissioner or vice versa, or for any other purpose.

(4) A Commissioner may resign by notice to the Secretary of State.

(5) The Secretary of State may terminate the appointment of a Commissioner if satisfied that—

   (a) without the consent of the Commission, he failed to attend the meetings of the Commission during a continuous period of six months beginning not earlier than nine months before the termination; or

   (b) he is an undischarged bankrupt, or has made an arrangement with his creditors, or is insolvent within the meaning of paragraph 9 (2) of Schedule 3 to the Conveyancing and Feudal Reform (Scotland) Act 1970; or

   (c) he is by reason of physical or mental illness, or for any other reason, incapable of carrying out his duties.

(6) Past service as a Commissioner is no bar to re-appointment.

Tenure of office of chairman and deputy chairmen

4.—(1) The chairman and each deputy chairman shall hold and vacate his office in accordance with the terms of his appointment, and may resign by notice to the Secretary of State.

(2) The office of the chairman or a deputy chairman is vacated if he ceases to be a Commissioner.

(3) Past service as chairman or a deputy chairman is no bar to re-appointment.

Remuneration of Commissioners

5. The Secretary of State may pay, or make such payments towards the provision of, such remuneration, pensions, allowances or gratuities to or in respect of the Commissioners or any of them as, with the consent of the Minister for the Civil Service, he may determine.

6. Where a person ceases to be a Commissioner otherwise than on the expiry of his term of office, and it appears to the Secretary of State that there are special circumstances which make it right for that person to receive compensation, the Secretary of State may with the consent of the Minister for the Civil Service direct the Commission to make to that person a payment of such amount as, with the consent of that Minister, the Secretary of State may determine.

Additional Commissioners

7.—(1) Paragraphs 2 (2), 3 (1) and (6), and 6 shall apply to additional Commissioners appointed under section 57 (2) as they apply to Commissioners.

(2) The Commission may pay, or make such payments towards the provision of, such remuneration, pensions, allowances or gratuities to or in respect of an additional Commissioner as the Secretary of State, with the consent of the Minister for the Civil Service, may determine.

(3) With the approval of the Secretary of State and the consent of the additional Commissioner concerned, the Commission may alter the terms of an appointment of an additional Commissioner so as to make a full-time additional Commissioner into a part-time additional Commissioner or vice versa, or for any other purpose.

(4) An additional Commissioner may resign by notice to the Commission.

(5) The Secretary of State, or the Commission acting with the approval of the Secretary of State, may terminate the appointment of an additional Commissioner if satisfied that—

(a) without reasonable excuse he failed to carry out the duties for which he was appointed during a continuous period of three months beginning not earlier than six months before the termination; or
(b) he is a person such as is mentioned in paragraph 3 (5) (b); or
(c) he is by reason of physical or mental illness, or for any other reason, incapable of carrying out his duties.

(6) The appointment of an additional Commissioner shall terminate at the conclusion of the investigation for which he was appointed, if not sooner.

Staff

8. The Commission may, after consultation with the Secretary of State, appoint such officers and servants as they think fit, subject to the approval of the Minister for the Civil Service as to numbers and as to remuneration and other terms and conditions of service.

9.—(1) Employment with the Commission shall be included among the kinds of employment to which a superannuation scheme under section 1 of the Superannuation

Act 1972 can apply, and accordingly in Schedule 1 to that Act (in which those kinds of employment are listed) the words "Equal Opportunities Commission" shall be inserted at the appropriate place in alphabetical order.

(2) Where a person who is employed by the Commission and is by reference to that employment a participant in a scheme under section 1 of the Superannuation Act 1972 becomes a Commissioner or an additional Commissioner, the Minister for the Civil Service may determine that his service as a Commissioner or additional Commissioner shall be treated for the purposes of the scheme as service as an employee of the Commission; and his rights under the scheme shall not be affected by paragraph 5 or 7 (2).

10. The Employers' Liability (Compulsory Insurance) Act 1969 shall not require insurance to be effected by the Commission.

Proceedings and business

11.—(1) Subject to the provisions of this Act, the Commission may make arrangements for the regulation of their proceedings and business, and may vary or revoke those arrangements.

(2) The arrangements may, with the approval of the Secretary of State, provide for the discharge under the general direction of the Commission of any of the Commission's functions by a committee of the Commission, or by two or more Commissioners.

(3) Anything done by or in relation to a committee, or Commissioners, in the discharge of the Commission's functions shall have the same effect as if done by or in relation to the Commission.

12. The validity of any proceedings of the Commission shall not be affected by any vacancy among the members of the Commission or by any defect in the appointment of any Commissioner or additional Commissioner.

13. The quorum for meetings of the Commission shall in the first instance be determined by a meeting of the Commission attended by not less than five Commissioners.

Finance

14. The Secretary of State shall pay to the Commission expenses incurred or to be incurred by it under paragraphs 6, 7 and 8, and, with the consent of the Minister for the Civil Service and the Treasury, shall pay to the Commission such sums as the Secretary of State thinks fit for enabling the Commission to meet other expenses.

15.—(1) The Commission shall keep proper accounts of their income and expenditure, and shall prepare and send to the Secretary of State statements of account in relation to each financial year of the Commission.

(2) The financial year of the Commission shall be the twelve months ending on 31st March.

Disqualification Acts

16.—(1) In Part II of Schedule 1 to the House of Commons Disqualification Act 1975 and Part II of Schedule 1 to the Northern Ireland Assembly Disqualification Act 1975 (bodies of which all members are disqualified under those Acts) there shall (at the appropriate place in alphabetical order) be inserted the following entry:—

"The Equal Opportunities Commission".

(2) In Part III of Schedule 1 to each of those Acts of 1975 (other disqualifying offices) there shall (at the appropriate place in alphabetical order) be inserted the following entry:—

"Additional Commissioner of the Equal Opportunities Commission".

Schedule 3

COMMENCEMENT
See s. 83 (2), *ante,* and the note "Orders under this section" thereto.

SIX (THREE) MONTHS BEGINNING, ETC.
See the note "Five years beginning, etc" to s. 69, *ante.*

DEFINITIONS
For "the Commission" and "Commissioner", see s. 77 (1), *ante.*

SCHEDULE 4

TRANSITIONAL PROVISIONS

Section 83

1. Section 12 does not apply, as respects any organisation,—

   (a) to contributions or other payments falling to be made to the organisation by its members or by persons seeking membership, or

   (b) to financial benefits accruing to members of the organisation by reason of their membership,

where the payment falls to be made, or the benefit accrues, before 1st January 1978 under rules of the organisation made before the passing of this Act.

2. Until 1st January 1978, section 12 (2) does not apply to any organisation of members of the teaching profession where at the passing of this Act—

   (a) the organisation is an incorporated company with articles of association, and

   (b) the articles of association restrict membership to persons of one sex (disregarding any minor exceptions), and

   (c) there exists another organisation within paragraphs (a) and (b) which is for persons of the opposite sex and has objects, as set out in the memorandum of association, which are substantially the same as those of the first mentioned organisation, subject only to differences consequential on the difference of sex.

3.—(1) Until a date specified by order made by the Secretary of State the courses of training to be undergone by men as a condition of the issue of certificates to them under the Midwives Act 1951 or the Midwives (Scotland) Act 1951 (as amended by section 20) must be courses approved in writing by or on behalf of the Secretary of State for the purposes of this paragraph.

(2) Until the date specified under sub-paragraph (1), section 9 of the Midwives Act 1951 and section 10 of the Midwives (Scotland) Act 1951 (regulation of persons other than certified midwives attending women in childbirth) shall have effect as if for the words from the beginning to (but not including) "attends a woman in childbirth" where they first occur there were substituted the words—

"If a person other than—

   (a) a woman who is a certified midwife, or

   (b) in a place approved in writing by or on behalf of the Secretary of State a man who is a certified midwife."

The amendment made by this sub-paragraph shall be read without regard to the sections 35A and 37A inserted in the said Acts of 1951 by section 20 (4) and (5).

(3) On and after the said date the words to be substituted for those, in the said sections 9 and 10, mentioned in sub-paragraph (2) are—

"If a person who is not a certified midwife".

(4) An order under this paragraph shall be laid in draft before each House of Parliament, and section 6 (1) of the Statutory Instruments Act 1946 (Parliamentary control by negative resolution of draft instruments) shall apply accordingly.

4.—(1) If the responsible body for any educational establishment which (apart from this sub-paragraph) would be required to comply with the provisions of section 22 (*b*), and of section 25 so far as they apply to acts to which section 22 (*b*) relates, from the commencement of those provisions, is of the opinion that it would be impracticable for it to do so, it may before that commencement apply for an order authorising discriminatory admissions during the transitional period specified in the order.

(2) Section 27 (2) to (5) and Schedule 2 shall apply for the purposes of sub-paragraph (1) as they apply in relation to transitional exemption orders.

5.(1) Section 6 of the Equal Pay Act 1970 (as amended by paragraph 3 of Schedule 1 to this Act) shall apply as if the references to death or retirement in subsection (1A) (*b*) of the said section 6 included references to sums payable on marriage in pursuance of a contract of employment made before the passing of this Act, or the commutation, at any time, of the right to such sums.

(2) In relation to service within section 1 (8) of the said Act of 1970 (service of the Crown) for the reference in this paragraph to a contract of employment made before the passing of this Act there shall be substituted a reference to terms of service entered into before the passing of this Act.

PARA. I: PASSING OF THIS ACT
This Act was passed, i.e., received the Royal Assent, on 12th November, 1975.

PARA. 3: CERTIFIED MIDWIFE
For definition, see the Midwives Act 1951, s. 32.

LAID . . . BEFORE . . . PARLIAMENT
For meaning, see the Laying of Documents before Parliament (Interpretation) Act 1948, s. 1 (1).

PARA. 4: COMMENCEMENT OF THOSE PROVISIONS
As to the commencement of ss. 22 and 25, *ante*, see s. 83 (2), *ante*, and the note "Orders under this section" thereto.

ORDER AUTHORISING DISCRIMINATORY ADMISSIONS
It is submitted that the power to make orders under para. 4 above is not intended to be exercisable by statutory instrument. See, as to the making of orders, s. 81, *ante*.

DEFINITIONS
For "responsible body", see s. 22, *ante*; for "transitional exemption order", see s. 27 (1), *ante*.

EQUAL PAY ACT 1970, SS. 1 (8), 6
S. 1 (8) is substituted by s. 8 (6) and Sch. 1, Part I, para. 1 (3), *ante*, and s. 6 (1A) is inserted by virtue of Sch. 1, Part I, para. 3, *ante*, and the amended text of that Act is set out in Sch. 1, Part II, *ante*.

SCHEDULE 5

Section 83

MINOR AND CONSEQUENTIAL AMENDMENTS

Factories Act 1961 (*c*. 34)

1. In section 15 (2) (unfenced machinery: operations carried out by specified male persons) the word "male" shall be omitted.

2. (*Applies to Scotland.*)

Schedule 5

Health and Safety at Work etc. Act 1974 (*c.* 37)

3. In Schedule 1, after the entry relating to the Emergency Laws (Miscellaneous Provisions) Act 1953, there is inserted the following—

1954 c. 57.	The Baking Industry (Hours of Work) Act 1954.	The whole Act.

Trade Union and Labour Relations Act 1974 (*c.* 52)

4. In Schedule 1, in paragraph 26 (1), after "paragraph" there is inserted "and in section 64 of the Sex Discrimination Act 1975".

COMMENCEMENT
See s. 83 (4), *ante*; and the note "Orders under this section" thereto.

SCHEDULE 6

FURTHER REPEALS

Section 83

Session and Chapter	Short Title	Extent of Repeal
7 & 8 Geo. 6. c. 31.	Education Act 1944.	Section 24 (3).
14 & 15 Geo. 6. c. 53.	Midwives Act 1951.	In section 11 (1), the words "or a male person".
10 & 11 Eliz. 2. c. 47.	Education (Scotland) Act 1962.	Section 82 (2).

COMMENCEMENT
See s. 83 (4), *ante*, and the note "Orders under this section" thereto.

INDEX

207

Printed in Great Britain by William Clowes & Sons, Limited
London, Beccles and Colchester